"In the Ideals of Women is the Strength of a Nation"

A History of the
Polish Women's Alliance of America

by
Angela and Donald Pienkos

EAST EUROPEAN MONOGRAPHS, BOULDER
DISTRIBUTED BY COLUMBIA UNIVERSITY PRESS, NEW YORK

2003

EAST EUROPEAN MONOGRAPHS NO. DCXXXII

Dedicated to

HIS HOLINESS
POPE JOHN PAUL II

SUPREME PONTIFF OF THE UNIVERSAL CHURCH
SON OF POLAND
SHEPHERD, PASTOR, MORAL FORCE

on the Twenty-Fifth Anniversary
of His
Historic Pontificate

1978-2003

CONTENTS

PREFACE

I once read somewhere that "If it is not written down, it never happened."

The activities and happenings of the past 105 years of the Polish Women's Alliance of America have been well documented, have been fully "written down."

That is why this fourth history of the Polish Women's Alliance of America (the first in English) was made possible by the records left for us by our predecessors.

We are deeply grateful to them for being so diligent and for caring so much about our history.

For 105 years the Polish Women's Alliance of Alliance has remained industriously faithful to its mission and goals and everyone will readily admit, with great success.

May we always continue to work, to grow, and to serve in the spirit of our founders as this history so richly illustrates.

Virginia Sikora, National President

For over one-hundred years, the Polish Women's Alliance of America has supported the Polish American community, nurtured the Polish heritage, and encouraged Polish Americans to do great things and give back to their communities. What an amazing century of achievement. I am proud to be a member of the Polish Women's Alliance of America, as was my mother and her mother before her.

When the Polish Women's Alliance of America was formed, women did not have the opportunity to pursue an education or a career. They could not own property or vote, let alone hold public office. Yet the Polish American women of the 1890s refused to be the silent members of their growing immigrant communities.

The founding mothers of the Polish Women's Alliance of America devoted themselves to empowering other Polish American women. They saw that the key to opportunity and success was *economic* empowerment. So they established the PWA of A as a fraternal insurance organization. They gave other women an opportunity for financial stability, as well as a network of friendship and a shared cultural heritage. So many of us, today, owe our success to the vision, dedication, and strength of these amazing women and those that followed them.

The women of the PWA of A also committed themselves to fighting for Poland's liberation from foreign rule. The history of Poland has, at times, been a melancholy one. Every king, kaiser, tsar, or comrade, that warred in Europe, always started by invading Poland. At the same time, Poland has always tried extra hard to be a part of the West in terms of its values and orientation.

I am proud of Poland, and I am proud of the Polish Women's Alliance of America's role in not only fostering a free and prosperous Poland, but in giving Polish Americans a voice and a link to their shared heritage. In five generations over one million individuals have benefited from membership in the Polish Women's Alliance of America. This makes the PWA of A one of the largest and most successful women's movements in our country's history. The women of the PWA of A put our values into action. They have shown that by organizing and cooperating with each other, we can make a real difference.

The Polish Women's Alliance of America has always stood for equality and has remained true to Polish American values. A deep sense of religious faith, a commitment to the well-being and success of the next generation, and a loyalty to the solidarity of the Polish American community are hallmarks of the organization and its members.

They are the humanitarians and the patriots, the protectors, and the nurturers of the Polish-language and culture in this country for our future generations. Most importantly, the women of the PWA of A are our memory – the bond that will hold our community together into the next millennium.

The women of the PWA of A have always been with me, throughout my life. My mother was a proud member of the Polish Women's Alliance of America. She belonged to the St. Bernadette's group. She loved being a member of the Alliance. She was very proud of her Polish heritage and proud to be a member of a Polish heritage organization. She loved the friendship, the insurance, and the economic independence. She admired the charity work and the generous philanthropy of the PWA of A.

I wish the Polish Women's Alliance of America the best of everything in your next chapter – the next century of the PWA of A! I am behind you every step of the way.

Barbara Mikulski
Member of the Senate
Of the United States of America
From the State of Maryland

Honorary Member,
Polish Women's Alliance of America

INTRODUCTION

Duch organizacji żyje w nas!
The spirit of our organization lives in us!

A member of the
Polish Women's Alliance of America

This book is the first completely English language history of the Polish Women's Alliance of America. Its publication comes in connection with several centennial anniversaries of the Alliance, whose name in the Polish language is *Związek Polek w Ameryce.*

The first of these anniversaries on May 16 and 17, 1998, celebrated the founding of the first Polish Women's Alliance of America society (*Towarzystwo Związku Polek w Ameryce*), a group formed in Chicago on May 22, 1898. A second anniversary came on November 22, 1999; exactly one hundred years earlier the leaders of the Polish Women's Alliance of America Society and two other women's groups in Chicago united to create the Polish Women's Alliance of America fraternal insurance benefit society, an association having a national mission and a broad range of activities. A third anniversary recalls the first national convention of the Polish Women's Alliance of America, held on June 12, 1900. At this meeting, twenty-four delegates gathered in Chicago to adopt a constitution and set of by-laws for their Alliance and elected their first national officers.

These actions were significant in themselves; but they also reflected very positively on the courage and idealism of a number of women of Polish origin who wanted to contribute their talents and energies to the advancement and well-being of the immigrant community. Their story deserves to be remembered, together with those of the women who have followed in their footsteps over the succeeding five generations.

One obvious sign of the success of the Polish Women's Alliance of America is its existence more than a century after its conception. In 2003, the PWA of A was the third largest fraternal insurance benefit association organized by persons of Polish origin in the United States and by far the largest organized by women. Among all organizations of its type, the PWA of A was the second largest of all women's "fraternals" (a more appropriate term might be "sorority", although this word has never been used by women's groups of this type) as reflected in the size of its membership. It is also the third largest in terms of financial assets. [1]

A better indicator of the significance of the Polish Women's Alliance of America is the one to be found in the pages of this work. For the history of the PWA of A is a story of the concerted efforts of women to gain an equal standing with men so they might together better serve the interests of the Polish people in America. Over the years, these interests have been many and varied. Nonetheless, they have always had two central objectives: the material and cultural betterment of the people of Polish heritage in this country, and the freedom and well-being of Poland. Over the past one hundred years, much has been achieved by the members of the PWA of A in each of these areas of endeavor.

Yet the PWA of A story has not received the recognition it deserves, either in America or in Poland. This is unfortunate, given both the attainments of the Alliance and the growing attention being paid to the ideas, objectives, and activities of the feminist movement in the United States and elsewhere. Over the past three decades, a variety of "women's issues" has been raised and

---

[1] The source of data and descriptive information about the American fraternal movement is an annual publication, *Statistics of Fraternal Benefit Societies* (Indianapolis: National Fraternal Congress of America). This work covers the fraternal benefit societies belonging to the National Fraternal Congress of America. As of 1999 there were 91 such organizations affiliated with the NFCA. This book also includes information about sixty fraternal societies headquartered in the United States that do not belong to the NFCA and twenty others that are members of the Canadian Fraternal Congress.

The two fraternals organized by Americans of Polish origin that are larger than the Polish Women's Alliance of America are the Polish National Alliance of the United States of North America, founded in 1880, and the Polish Roman Catholic Union of America, formed in 1873. The largest fraternal societies in terms of membership organized by women are the First Catholic Slovak Ladies Association of the United States of America, followed by the Polish Women's Alliance of America. The PWA of A ranks third among all fraternals formed by women in terms of assets, after the First Catholic Slovak Ladies Association and the National Catholic Society of Foresters.

debated. But almost no attention has been given to the PWA of A, an organization created by women, which over the past century has included in its ranks more than seven hundred thousand persons.[2]

One ready explanation for this lies in the absence of information in the English language about the Polish Women's Alliance of America. Ironically, however, the PWA of A story has been missed in Poland too, despite the substantial amount of Polish language published material about its activities over the years. But even if more people in America and in Poland were better informed about the PWA of A and organizations like it, would they better appreciate its story? This is a matter of some doubt.

The problem facing the PWA of A, and all fraternal insurance benefit societies, whether they include women only or have men and women as members, is that very few people nowadays have a grasp of what these kinds of organizations are about. Putting the matter bluntly, the very idea of fraternalism has precious little meaning today.

In America, the terms "fraternal" and "fraternalism" seldom appear in print and the idea of fraternalism is rarely discussed. Fraternals and the work they do are not mentioned in schools, in the history and social studies textbooks used by students, or in the mass media. One might even wonder whether a kind of blackout exists about the fraternal idea. As a result, a general ignorance prevails about the work and mission of the fraternal movement.

The idea of fraternalism in fact has its roots in the "enlightenment era" of eighteenth century Europe. In America, this was a time when our colonial forebears were struggling for freedom from English rule. In Europe, political reformers in France in the West and in Poland in the East were pressing for responsible and representative government, for greater personal and political

---

[2] Thaddeus Radziałowski, in his article "Let Us Join Hands: The Polish Women's Alliance" in *Immigrant Women,* 2nd rev. ed., Editor Maxine Schwartz Seller (Albany: State University of New York Press, 1994), pp. 190 – 196, is one of the few students of the Polish American experience to draw attention to the Polish Women's Alliance of America as a major, if little recognized, women's organization.

rights, and for a more serious commitment to social justice for their fellow citizens. In 1789, the French advocates of change framed their ideas into a memorable and momentous slogan: *liberte, egalite, fraternite,* that is, freedom, equality, fraternity.

Everyone understands the basic meanings of the first two of these words. But with *fraternite* things are quite different. In fact, while this term has a straightforward literal translation, its actual meaning is one that has been largely lost among Americans.

Simply put, *fraternite* (which can be rendered in English as both fraternity and fraternalism) refers to the idea that the truly good society should provide its members with more than personal freedom and equality of rights. What is also needed is the formation of a community whose members can work together to offer their assistance to those who are in need of help.

Today, the motto of the National Fraternal Congress of America, the umbrella organization to which the Polish Women's Alliance of America belongs, puts this principle nicely in its motto: "Joining hands to touch lives." However, because of the events of the past seventy years, millions of Americans have come to believe that only government can provide for the well-being of those in need. Their reliance on government to solve (or at least manage) a variety of social problems has resulted in their concluding that voluntary organizations like the fraternals are at best of only marginal importance as institutions working to achieve the common good.

Not surprisingly, when President George H. W. Bush in 1988 called on Americans to emulate the fraternal ideal in doing more on behalf of their fellow citizens instead of relying on government, his "thousand points of light" metaphor was roundly ridiculed. A not dissimilar response greeted General Colin Powell when he organized a national summit to promote volunteerism on behalf of the less advantaged across the land.

In the past, things were different. The fraternal idea was recognized as a central component in the successful working of American life. The insightful, early nineteenth century French observer of American society, Alexis de Tocqueville, was one of the first to notice its importance when he wrote of our citizens' enthusiasm for voluntary service, civic involvement, and participation in the life of the community. He declared that such activities were at the core of American democracy and concluded that the patriotic feelings that Americans of the 1830's felt for their country "grew by the exercise of these civil rights." [3]

How does it happen that in the United States, where the inhabitants have only recently immigrated to the land which they now occupy . . . where, in short, the instinctive love of country can scarcely exist; how does it happen that everyone takes as zealous an interest in the affairs of his community? . . . It is because everyone, in his sphere, takes an active part in the government of society.

On Tocqueville's words: Lawrence H. Fuchs, an eminent modern scholar of the American immigration and ethnic experience commented:

Tocqueville maintained that Americans combined in political and civic associations to effect remedies to problems that in aristocratic or monarchical societies they would have to endure. In lobbying for remedies, they learned the arts of working with others... and extended their connections and knowledge beyond the small circle of relatives and friends with whom they ordinarily dealt.

The capacity of Americans to form associations in order to achieve some public good constantly amazed him. Given political freedom, Americans saw the possibility of changing their own lives for the better by altering some public condition. Self-interest and patriotism went hand in hand.

---

[3] On the thought of Alexis de Tocqueville, author of *Democracy in America*, note the work of Lawrence H. Fuchs, *The American Kaleidoscope: Race, Ethnicity, and the Civic Culture* (Hanover, N. H.: Wesleyan University Press, 1990). Tocqueville's book continues to be seen as significant. For example, historian Arthur Schlesinger Jr. included it in his essay "The Thirteen Books You Must Read to Understand America," *American Heritage*, February and March 1998. The extensive quotations that follow are from Fuchs.

How significant has been the freedom to associate and to form organizations, among them fraternal organizations, in order to better the condition of society and thereby enhance people's sense of satisfaction with their life in this country? Professor Fuchs here agrees with Tocqueville when he argues that this freedom is, and has been, at the very core of the American idea:

Immigrant settlers from Europe and their progeny were free to maintain affection for and loyalty to their ancestral religions and cultures while at the same time claiming an American identity by embracing the founding myths and participating in the political life of the republic. It was a system of pluralism that began, principally in colonial Pennsylvania, where immigrants of various nationalities and religious backgrounds moved with relative ease into political life. This new invention of Americans – "voluntary pluralism" – in which individuals were free to express their ancestral affections and sensibilities, to choose to be ethnic, however and whenever they wished or not at all by moving across group boundaries easily, was sanctioned and protected by the unifying civic culture . . . of America.

The values that Fuchs and Tocqueville write about seem very much like the principles animating the founders of the Polish Women's Alliance of America, and indeed most fraternalists through the years.

While it is disappointing that contemporary popular recognition of the thinking of historic figures like Tocqueville is weak, what is more discouraging is the seeming lack of interest in his ideas among contemporary scholars of American and Polish American history. According to a recent compilation made by the National Fraternal Congress of America, nearly ten million men and women belonged to United States based fraternal benefit societies. These organizations not only provided their members with life insurance protection valued at more than one quarter of one trillion dollars, on an annual basis they were engaged in distributing more than two hundred and eighty-five million dollars in valuable fraternal benefits to their members and to nonmembers having some particular need. Yet such facts have gone largely unreported and unexamined. [4]

Similarly, scholars of the Polish American immigrant and ethnic experience have tended to play down the place of fraternalism within the Polish community. Amazingly, they have given relatively little attention to the fact that the Polish American fraternals have constituted the most significant, enduring, and explicitly ethnic mass membership associations in this population's experience during the past century. [5]

True, the hundreds of parishes Polish Catholics established in America have, taken together, claimed a much larger number of adherents than have all the Polish American fraternals combined. But here it needs to be recalled that these parishes have never constituted a "Polish" Roman Catholic Church in America. All were from the start neighborhood community institutions operating under the juridical authority of their local Catholic bishops. Moreover, many have gradually lost their original ethnic character as newer non-Polish Catholics have settled in the old Polish

---

[4] A glance at some of the most significant histories of the American people shows that none even mentions the fraternal movement in books running to one thousand pages in length. For example, Charles A. and Mary R. Beard, *The Rise of the American Civilization,* 2 vol.; (New York: Macmillan, 1927), Samuel Eliot Morison, Henry Steele Commager, and William E. Leuchtenburg, *The Growth of the American Republic,* seventh edition, 2 volumes; (New York: Oxford University Press, 1980), and James MacGregor Burns, *The American Experiment* 2 vol. (New York: Knopf, 1982 – 1985).

[5] Several overviews of the Polish American experience have appeared in the English language over the past three decades. These include works by Helena Znaniecka Lopata, James S. Pula, John Bukowczyk, and one by the Polish scholar Andrzej Brożek. All give some mention to the fraternal movement. Yet none except for Brożek, in his *Polish Americans, 1854 to 1939*, gives special attention to its singular importance in defining the character of the community, including its relations with Poland. A recent American scholar who appreciated the fraternals' important place was Frank Renkiewicz. Unfortunately, he did not write a general history of the Polish experience in America. For an example of his work, see his "An Economy of Self-Help: Fraternal Capitalism and the Evolution of Polish America," in *Studies in Ethnicity: The East European Experience in America*, Philip Shashko, Donald E. Pienkos, and Charles A. Ward, editors (Boulder: East European Monographs, 1980).

neighborhoods of America. Many one-time "Polish" parishes have closed for a variety of reasons, and more are likely to meet this fate in the decades to come. Besides, the parishes founded by Polish Catholics and other immigrant peoples in America were created to provide opportunities for religious worship, not to advance an ethnic agenda. In short, the parishes, no matter how significant and successful they may have been in meeting their adherents' many and important spiritual and social needs, were not in essence "Polish," "Italian," "Slovak," "Irish," or "German" institutions.

Such was not the case with the Polish American fraternals. Practically all have continued to proudly proclaim themselves to be Polish organizations and have underscored this commitment in the names they have chosen for themselves. Many of them have succeeded in extending their bases of operation far beyond the neighborhood and have maintained their viability by continually recruiting new members.

That the Polish American fraternal movement has included as many as twenty-four different organizations over the past one hundred and thirty years is yet another sign of the importance its many activists have traditionally attached to the fraternal idea. A look at their evolving histories shows that each fraternal grew out of its founders' distinctive ideology and particular definition of their organization's ethnic mission. Some have emphasized their Catholic identity in defining their members' ethnicity and objectives. Others have stressed the cause of united work on behalf of patriotic beliefs. Some have focused on working with young people. Some, of which the Polish Women's Alliance of America has always been by far the most successful example, identified themselves with the advancement of women's aspirations in playing genuine leadership roles in the community. Yet, whatever their diversity in terms of their specific agendas, what Polish American fraternalists have shared with one another has had a far greater weight.

No discussion of the Polish American fraternal movement can be complete without noting its ethnic solidarity. From the start, a commitment to Poland's independence and well-being was the hallmark of the Polish fraternals in the patriotic wing of the immigrant community, a community that came to be known as Polonia. The largest fraternals were the Polish National Alliance, the Polish Women's Alliance of America, and the Polish Falcons Alliance, followed by a number of smaller regional or local associations. By the outbreak of the First World War, in 1914, all of the fraternals, including those stressing their religious heritage (most prominent of which was the Polish Roman Catholic Union of America) had come to identify with the work of restoring unity and independence to partitioned Poland.

This commitment led to the formation and maintenance of several highly productive "all" Polonia federations acting on behalf of the Polish cause, first in World War I, then again in World War II, and then once more during the Cold War. In each era, this solidarity among the fraternals provided the necessary leadership as well as the organizational muscle enabling thousands of Polish Americans to work effectively in support of Poland's freedom and its people's well-being.

Thanks largely to the fraternals, joined by the Polish Roman Catholic and Polish National Catholic parishes, the organizations of Polish and Polish American veterans, the Polish ethnic press and the cultural and intellectual groupings that together have intertwined with one another to make up Polonia, a vigorous sense of Polishness has been gradually institutionalized over several generations. Without the fraternals' participation, this continuing effort might not have been possible. Undoubtedly it would not have been as successful.

But the activism of the fraternals on Poland's behalf was not rooted in some inchoate set of nationalistic feelings or emotional sentiments directed toward the "old country." Rather, it grew out of their understanding of the fundamental principles defining the fraternal movement. [6]

According to the National Fraternal Congress of America, the fraternal organization operates "solely for the mutual benefit of its

---

[6] For a succinct presentation of the place of the fraternals in helping to shape American Polonia's focus on the Polish cause, see Donald E. Pienkos, "Polish Americans and Poland: A Review of the Record," *Fiedorczyk Lecture in Polish American Studies,* Central Connecticut State University, April 25, 1993.

members and their beneficiaries and not for profit, [it possesses] a lodge system with . . . a representative form of government, and . . . [it] makes provision for the payment of death, sickness, or disability benefits, or both." This defines the bare-bones structure and agenda of the fraternal organization. But the NFCA statement goes further in discussing "the spirit of fraternalism that touches millions of lives":

Life styles may change, but basic human social and economic needs continue to be served by fraternalism's far-reaching efforts . . . . The financial security provided by fraternal insurance is a key component of all fraternal societies; however, non-material benefits are just as important . . . as fraternals seek to respond to the needs of their members and the community at large.

For its part, in 1999 the Polish Women's Alliance of America reported its fraternal benefits included aid to needy members enabling them to maintain their insurance protection, college scholarship awards to eligible members of the organization, and Polish language classes to members of all age groups. Among its many charitable activities, the PWA of A donated funds to more than a dozen humanitarian agencies, including the American Cancer Society; Kiwanis; the Polish American Immigration and Relief Committee; Habitat for Humanity; the National Shrine in Doylestown, Pennsylvania; the Orchard Lake Schools in Michigan; and a number of homes for the aged. It also sponsors youth conferences and a variety of other programs for its members. But this work, worthy as it has been, extends still further to service on behalf of the needs of the people of Poland. Moreover, that fraternal work goes to the very beginnings of the PWA of A more than one hundred years ago.

This book is not first published history of the Alliance. Three times in the past the leaders of the Alliance have commissioned one of their members to write a history of the fraternal. Each appeared in the Polish language and served the readers of its day very well.

The first of these books, published in 1938, is entitled *Historia Związku Polek w Ameryce: Przycinki do poznania duszy wychodźstwa Polskiego w Stanach Zjednoczonych Ameryki Północnej* (A history of the Polish Women's Alliance of America: Contributions to becoming acquainted with the spirit of the Polish emigration in the United States of North America). This work appeared at the time of the Alliance's fortieth anniversary. It was written by Jadwiga Karłowicz, a poet, essayist, and devoted member of the fraternal. Not long after its appearance, Karłowicz was appointed editor-in-chief of the PWA of A fraternal publication, *Głos Polek*. She went on to serve in this capacity for most of the next quarter century. Karłowicz chronicled the rise and development of the Alliance, and emphasized the events and decisions that occurred at the fraternal's national conventions. Her work provided readers with a sense of the ideals that motivated the women who founded the fraternal and defined its mission and program. The book gave a detailed list of the local groups in existence at the time of the Alliance's fortieth anniversary. This material remains very helpful in giving readers an appreciation of the movement at the grass roots level.

A second, well illustrated, history was authored by Maria Loryś, Karłowicz's successor as editor of *Głos Polek*. It appeared in 1980 and was also titled *Historia Związku Polek w Ameryce*. In its format the work followed the model offered by Karłowicz and again offered a chronological, convention-centered account of the fraternal's development from 1939 to 1959. New to this work were a number of biographies of leading PWA of A members.

In 1981, a third volume of the history of the Alliance was published, this one written by Helen Zielinski, then president of the PWA of A. This work, titled *Historia Związku Polek w Ameryce: Sprawy organizacyjne* (A history of the Polish Women's Alliance of America: Organizational matters), departed from the preceding volumes by focusing on the fraternal's structure, with special attention to its local and regional units. The book thus filled a void left by the two earlier works.

All three books make for rewarding reading. But their publication in the Polish language has meant that they have become increasingly inaccessible to the growing number of PWA of A members who are not conversant in Polish.

Helen Wojcik, president of the Polish Women's Alliance of America between 1987 and 1995, and her colleagues in the general administration of the Alliance, decided to authorize the publication of an English language history of the fraternal on the occasion of its centennial. This work is the result of that decision.

Perhaps there will also be other beneficiaries of this work, among them the members of other Polish American organizations interested in learning more about the Polish heritage in this country. Students of American, Polish, and Polish American history may also gain insights into their own fields of interest from this work.

This book is the latest in a series of six works dealing with Polish American fraternals that the authors have published over the past twenty-seven years. It also represents the authors' first major formal collaboration. In 1976 Angela Pienkos authored a brief but comprehensive study of the Federation Life Insurance of America society based in Milwaukee. In 1984 Donald Pienkos wrote a history of the Polish National Alliance of the United States of North America centered in Chicago on the occasion of its centennial, which was observed in 1980; in 2000 he wrote an update to this work. In 1987 Donald completed his centennial history of the Polish Falcons of America, headquartered in Pittsburgh, Pennsylvania. And in 1991 he published a comprehensive study describing the efforts of the organized Polish American community on behalf of the political independence of Poland and the humanitarian needs of its people. That work, though not primarily focused on the fraternals, included a great deal of information about their pivotal role in realizing Polonia's aims on behalf of the Polish people. In 1995 Angela and Donald also wrote a brief history of the PWA of A timed for presentation at its thirty-second national convention. This twenty-four page work was titled, *The Polish Women's Alliance of America: Our Future is as Bright as Our Past is Inspiring*.

We have learned many lessons from these earlier efforts and we hope we have applied them in this work. But let us repeat ourselves if only to make a point we trust future students of the Polish American experience will consider seriously. It is that the Polish American fraternal societies have been and remain important and deserve to be treated as the significant engines they have been in powering the Polish American community. Put simply, their stories need to be told and studied.

We have many people to thank for their kind and generous assistance in this project. Among these are Virginia Sikora, president of the Polish Women's Alliance of America, her predecessors Helen Zielinski, Helen Wojcik, and Delphine Lytell, vice president Sharon Zago, past vice president Elizabeth Kubacki, and treasurer Olga Kaszewicz. Others to whom we are grateful for the information and insights they have shared are Maria Loryś, the former editor of *Głos Polek,* the official publication of the PWA of A; and Mary Piergies, former editor of the paper's English section; past directors Albina Świerzbińska and Łucyna Migała, past secretaries general Julia Stroup and Maria Kubiak; past Indiana district president Joanna Zotkiewicz (a delightful, informative lady who joined the PWA of A in 1918), and Eleanore Tomkalski, past Ohio and West Virginia district president. Past president Wojcik and past director Świerzbińska were very generous in reading the manuscript and making comments, additions, and corrections to the text. Our appreciation also goes to three individuals who helped greatly in editing and typing this work: Leslie Keros, Rosa Stong, and Michelle Falcon.

Sincere thanks are also in order to the women with whom we spoke at various PWA of A events we attended. What they had to say added to our store of knowledge about the organization. Moreover, their infectious enthusiasm about the Polish Women's Alliance of America says much about their pride in the organization and their hopes for it to continue its work far into the future.

THE POLISH WOMEN'S ALLIANCE OF AMERICA STORY:
THE BEGINNINGS

> We need to give much more attention to the place of women in the Polish American community. Women have played an important, in many cases, a dominant role in Polonia. Yet, theirs is a story about which we know precious little.
>
> Thomas Napierkowski, President of the Polish American Historical Association (1995)[1]

One of the significant yet little-known stories of the Polish community in the United States involves an organization named the Polish Women's Alliance of America, or *Związek Polek w Ameryce*.

The Polish Women's Alliance of America story is about a movement of and led by women. The Alliance was formed at a time when women were neither expected nor usually allowed to play publicly recognized decision-making roles in their communities. Established in 1898 and 1899 in Chicago by women who were unhappy they could be little more than followers in the patriotic and church-based associations then serving the needs of the Polish immigrants in this country, the Alliance aimed at remedying things – and in dramatic fashion. Their action was a bold one. At the time only a few women's organizations existed.

The Polish Women's Alliance of America quickly became and has since remained a mass movement, including in its ranks more than seven hundred thousand members over the past century. From the start the PWA of A has played a respected leadership role in the organized Polish immigrant and ethnic community in America. Its members have supported the causes of Poland and

---

[1]Napierkowski's words are from his presidential address at the annual convention of the Polish American Historical Association, January 7, 1995, Chicago.

the advancement of the aspirations of people of Polish origin and ancestry in sharing in the promise of American life. Today, with financial assets exceeding 44 million dollars, the Alliance continues to be a substantial fraternal insurance and benefit association serving both its own members and the general public in a variety of ways.[2]

During two different eras in America's history, women's concerns have won considerable attention. The first was in the sixty years after the Civil War. It was an era in which women activists increasingly demanded to be taken seriously as participants in this country's affairs. This era culminated in 1920 with the passage of the Nineteenth Amendment to the Constitution, wherein women were granted the right to vote in all elections and to hold elective office. This historic decision underscored the right of women to find places for themselves in society beyond the home, if they chose to do so.[3]

A second era of women's assertion of their rights began in the 1960s with the rise of the feminist movement. While controversial ideological issues remain about this movement, it is clear that over the past thirty years women have made extraordinary advances, thanks, at least in part, to their demands for greater equality. By the end of the 1990s, approximately one-half of the American workforce was composed of women. Of greater note, perhaps, is the dramatic advancement of women into the professions of law, medicine, academia, and business. This was partly the result of the success women have enjoyed in the political arena, where they have joined with like-minded men to win approval of a number of federal, state, and local affirmative action laws and regulations of benefit to them.

---

[2]Again, detailed factual information about the Polish Women's Alliance of America and its fellow fraternal benefit societies in the United States and Canada is in the annual publication of the National Fraternal Congress of America, *Statistics of Fraternal Benefit Societies*. For a useful scholarly analysis and history of the fraternal movement in the United States, see Alvin J. Schmidt, *Fraternal Organizations* (Westport, CT: Greenwood Press, 1980).

[3] For an authoritative study of the history of feminism in the United States, see Nancy F. Cott, *The Grounding of Modern Feminism* (New Haven: Yale University Press, 1987).

The Polish Women's Alliance of America is part of this great, often complex story of women's advancement. This is so even though the Alliance has seldom received the recognition it and its members have merited. Certainly, one reason for this history is to present the record of the Polish Women's Alliance of America to a wider audience, so it can be better known and appreciated.

Here at the outset, and before we review the history of the PWA of A, it seems appropriate to answer a key question – not "what" has the organization sought to achieve and has accomplished, but rather "why" is there a Polish Women's Alliance of America at all?

ROOTS OF THE POLISH WOMEN'S ALLIANCE OF AMERICA IN POLAND AND THE UNITED STATES

The PWA of A story is part of the larger story of the massive migrations of the Polish people from their homeland to the United States that began in earnest after the Civil War and ended with the outbreak of World War I in 1914. This was the time of "open immigration" to America. During this nearly fifty-year-long period more than one million ethnic Poles entered the United States, making them a significant element in the massive wave of more than twenty million Europeans who settled here.[4]

But the PWA of A story also involves the efforts of women in the Polish immigrant community to play responsible leadership roles in the burgeoning American Polonia (then called wychodźstwo, or emigration) from the 1880s on. This effort had roots in Poland, where women were also attempting to assert their right to participate in the intellectual, political, social, cultural, and economic life of their foreign-ruled, partitioned country. These are,

---

[4]Estimates of the size of the Polish emigration vary. Three expert efforts are those by Jerzy Zubrzycki, "Emigration from Poland in the 19th and 20th Centuries," *Population Studies: A Journal of Demography* 6 (1952 – 1953): 248 – 272; Victor R. Greene, "Pre-World War I Emigration to the United States: Motives and Statistics," *The Polish Review,* 6, no. 3 (1961), 45 – 68; and Helena Z. Lopata, "Polish Immigration to the United States of America: Problems of Estimation and Parameters," *The Polish Review* 21, no. 4 (1976): 85 – 108.

in short, the "environmental" forces that helped shape the actions and outlooks of the women who founded the Alliance.

Poland, and more precisely its downfall, and the consequent economic, demographic, and cultural developments in the partitioned country that led millions of its people to seek better life and work opportunities abroad, constitute the first set of environmental factors to note in discussing the origins of the Polish Women's Alliance of America in Poland.

Once a large state in east central Europe including more than 400,000 square miles of territory, the Polish kingdom of the fifteenth, sixteenth, and seventeenth centuries extended eastward from the Oder River and included most of the present day country. But the Poland of that time also took in most of today's newly independent states of Ukraine, Belarus, Lithuania, Latvia, and Estonia. To the north was the Baltic Sea, separating Poland from the Scandinavian lands. To the south were the Carpathian Mountains that shielded the country from Bohemia, Hungary, and the Ottoman Turkish Empire.[5]

However, the constitutionally governed and generally prosperous Polish republic fell into a fatal eclipse in the eighteenth century. This calamity was connected with the decay of Poland's domestic governmental system, the decline in its capacity to defend its vast frontiers militarily, and the weakening of its economic life.

Taking full advantage of these unmistakable trends, the three powerful and expansionist states of tsarist Russia, imperial Austria, and the kingdom of Prussia that surrounded Poland acted in concert to seize the Polish lands. On three separate occasions,

---

[5] The most substantial recent history of Poland in the English language is that by Norman Davies, *God's Playground: A History of Poland,* 2 volumes. (New York: Columbia University Press, 1982). Two excellent general histories are those by Adam Zamoyski, *The Polish Way: A Thousand-Year History of the Poles and Their Culture* (New York: Franklin Watts, 1988) and M. K. Dziewanowski, *Poland in the Twentieth Century* (New York: Columbia University Press, 1977). Poland during the partition period is handled in Piotr Wandycz, *The Lands of Partitioned Poland,* 1795 – 1918 (Seattle: University of Washington Press, 1974).

in 1772, 1793, and 1795, Poland was invaded and stripped of sizeable chunks of territory. With the completion of the third of these seizures, Poland actually disappeared as a state from the European map. Polish independence would not be successfully regained until the very last day of the First World War in 1918, five generations later.

On a series of occasions, in 1794, 1807, 1830, 1848, and 1863, independence fighters did try to regain their homeland's freedom. But each time their effort failed, largely because of the crushing military disadvantages they could not overcome in driving the partitioning powers from the country. Worse still, each failed insurrection was ruthlessly put down. Thousands of freedom fighters were killed, imprisoned, or forced into foreign exile. Most of the refugees made their way to France, Switzerland, and England, with smaller numbers eventually settling in the United States. Often they were successful in establishing contacts with one another and even developed connections with compatriots in the occupied lands of partitioned Poland.

After the failure of the great insurrection of 1863, the Russian and German authorities imposed new repressive policies on their Polish subjects. Their ultimate aim was to destroy the Poles' very national identity. Only in the Austrian-ruled Polish lands of "Galicia" were political and cultural conditions less oppressive. Everywhere, however, with the partial exception of the German-ruled regions, economic development and industrialization were greatly retarded.

As the rural population grew, farm land became increasingly scarce and expensive. This helped to force large numbers of people to choose between ever worsening impoverishment and emigration. Millions took the latter course. Many found seasonal work in Western Europe as agricultural laborers, replacing the native inhabitants who were drawn to the burgeoning, industrializing cities of Germany, France, Scandinavia, and Switzerland. In time, some Poles found more permanent work in the coal mines of Germany's Ruhr valley, in Belgium, and in France. From the 1870s onward, they also began to make the even more momentous journeys across the Atlantic Ocean, mainly to the United States, in search of work.[6]

In America an industrial revolution was already in full swing, and masses of laborers were needed in the coal mines and iron and steel works of Pennsylvania and in the nation's rapidly growing factories. As America expanded further westward, new urban centers mushroomed in Illinois, Indiana, Michigan, Ohio, and Wisconsin. The best example of this trend was the city of Chicago, which grew rapidly into one of the country's largest population centers from 300,000 in 1870 to 1,700,000 in 1900. Throughout the American Middle West, new cohorts of immigrant laborers, many of whom were Poles, were in demand. Substantial numbers of Polish newcomers also settled in the northeastern states of New York, New Jersey, Maryland, and Connecticut.

It is impossible to calculate precisely the total number of Poles who settled in the United States in the years between the Civil War and the outbreak of World War I, when open immigration to this country came to an abrupt end. Official methods used to determine the nationalities of immigrants often changed in this period, with Polish immigrants frequently counted as "Germans," "Russians," or "Austrians" by the U.S. authorities, despite the fact that they were simply the Polish subjects in the empires where they had lived. Many immigrants coming from the partitioned Polish lands were in fact Jews and Ukrainians, further complicating the question of accurately estimating the actual size of Polish ethnic migration into the country.

Most Polish immigrants came from the countryside, where the sense of nationality was usually less defined than the identification with one's local village or religious tradition. Some immigrants returned to Poland after a few years in America, having succeeded or failed in saving enough money to improve their living conditions back home. Still, perhaps one million Polish immigrants had settled permanently in the United States on the eve of World War I in 1914. By then a substantial four-million-member

---

[6] For conditions in the countryside leading to the mass emigrations after 1865, see Stefan Kieniewicz, *The Emancipation of the Polish Peasantry* (Chicago: University of Chicago Press, 1969).

community, made up of the foreign born and their offspring were living here. To American observers of the time, the Poles, their language, culture, and folkways were a source of mystery. But in their sheer numbers they already comprised more than three percent of this country's population; in states like Illinois, Wisconsin, Michigan, New York, and Pennsylvania this proportion was far higher.

The members of this largely economically motivated migration gradually established a significant number of neighborhood and community organizations to help meet their many social, informational, economic, and political needs. Most significant were the eight hundred and more Roman Catholic parishes they created and the hundreds of parochial schools that sprouted around them – not to forget the scores of hospitals, orphanages, convents, and even a seminary – that were built under the lead of hundreds of energetic priests, sisters, and brothers who came to America with a missionary zeal to both serve and direct the immigrants' spiritual lives.[7]

Almost as significant as the immigrants' parish institutions were the scores of fraternal benefit societies they founded. The aims of these organizations were to provide assistance, comfort, and fellowship to their members. Their work in fact served to complement the social and community activities already provided

---

[7] On the formation and dynamics of the Polish immigrant and ethnic community in America, see William Thomas and Florian Znaniecki, *The Polish Peasant in Europe and America,* 2 volumes. (New York: Dover Publications, 1958); John J. Bukowczyk, *And My Children Did Not Know Me: A History of the Polish Americans* (Bloomington: Indiana University Press, 1987); Helena Z. Lopata, *Polish Americans,* second revised edition (New Brunswick, NJ: Transaction Publishers, 1994); James S. Pula, *Polish Americans: An Ethnic Community* (New York: Twayne Publishers, 1995).

On aspects of the political experience of the Polonia in Chicago, Detroit, Buffalo, and Milwaukee, see Angela T. Pienkos, editor, *The Ethnic Factor in American Politics: The Polish Experience in Four Cities* (Chicago: Polish American Historical Association, 1978). An unpublished study of the Polish communities around the country is that of William Galush, *Forming* Polonia*: A Study of Four Polish American Communities, 1890 – 1940* (Ph.D. diss., University of Minnesota, 1975).

by the parishes. By World War I, several thousand local fraternal lodges or groups were in existence in Polonia. Nationally, more than twenty Polish fraternal federations were operating and several of these extended too many states of the Union. Polonia also possessed scores of daily newspapers, weeklies, and periodicals, nearly all of them published in Polish. In addition, a wide variety of other local groups were busy serving the cultural, athletic, economic, and political interests of their members.

The two earliest and largest Polish American fraternal societies were the Polish Roman Catholic Union of America (PRCUA), established in 1873 under the leadership of priests and Catholic laymen, and the Polish National Alliance of the United States of North America (PNA), founded in 1880 by patriotic and independence-minded activists and open to all men of Polish origin but without a pronounced concern for their religious ties. Despite their other differences, both fraternals worked to maintain a spirit of ethnic consciousness among the ever expanding immigration.

Early on, the PNA complemented its patriotic appeals with its offer of financial protection to new members through a modestly priced burial insurance program, something that could materially benefit their families. This idea was soon adopted by the PRCUA, and, it eventually became essential to the programs of every other Polish American fraternal, including the Polish Women's Alliance of America.

The early rivalry between the two fraternal movements was sometimes fierce, but it largely subsided by the 1890s, as each organization came to accept the reality of its rival's likely continuation. By the end of the nineteenth century, the PNA included more than twenty-five thousand members and reported financial assets of nearly one hundred thousand dollars. For its part, the PRCUA claimed some ten thousand members and assets of nearly thirty thousand dollars.

By the 1890s, the Polish community in America included as many as 1.5 million people. Thriving, highly institutionalized, immigrant Polonia settlements were to be found in Chicago, Detroit, Buffalo, Milwaukee, Cleveland, Pittsburgh, and many smaller towns as well. In time, the women of Polonia were making increasingly important contributions to the well-being of the community, not only as wives and mothers but also in their ability to find work outside the home to supplement their husbands and parents' incomes. Through such labor they could add substantially to the economic well-being of the family unit. However, in Polonia's early decades women were not much involved in the immigrant community's organizational affairs.[8]

Several scholars of the Polish experience in the United States have focused upon the situation of women in Polonia's formative years. Their findings present an interesting picture of the place of women in the immigrant community. What follows is drawn from the excellent scholarly works by the sociologist Helena Znaniecka Lopata, and historians John Bukowczyk and James Pula, works that have been previously cited. Their work is very much worth summarizing here.

From these scholars, we learn that Polonia's women, as wives, parents, and homemakers, did more than the cooking, shopping, keeping house, and providing for their family's needs. They also were the makers and menders of the family's clothing and of many of the home's furnishings. They kept vegetable gardens and often preserved the produce of their agricultural labors.

Very often, the wife in the Polish immigrant household was responsible for the family budget, the one who kept her husband's and working children's weekly earnings and did what she could to save something for their future needs. Given the very low incomes of the largely unskilled Polish immigrant labor force, what savings she could achieve had a significance that might be hard to appreciate in our time. In addition, the immigrant housewife taught her children and did her best to impart her skills to her daughters, who, like their brothers, were integral members of the family economy.

---

[8] A vivid portrait of the lives of early Polish immigrant women in Chicago is provided in Joseph J. Parot, "The 'Serdeczna Matka' of the Sweatshops: Marital and Family Crises of Immigrant Working Class Women in Late Nineteenth Century Chicago," in *The Polish Presence in Canada and America*, Frank Renkiewicz, ed., (Toronto: The Multicultural History Society of Ontario, 1982), pp. 155 – 182.

But the family's survival was not the only objective in which the Polish immigrant woman played a role. There were also aims like collecting enough money to buy a small farmstead. Later on, among members of the second generation in America, this involved attaining a more practical goal, that of purchasing a home or a rental property. As one grateful Polish immigrant husband put it, "if your wife is thrifty and hard working and if you didn't drink in bars and saved your money, you could get somewhere and buy a house."

A similar tradition prevailed in Poland with women often wielding a good deal of informal authority in the household, regardless of their particular social standing. But there were also differences. In Poland women were discouraged from working outside the home; in America the finances of many an immigrant family required wives and their daughters to seek paying jobs to supplement the family's income. Another common practice among housewives was to take in boarders, usually young, single "greenhorns just off the boat."

Lopata points out that many women left behind temporarily in Poland with their children by emigrating husbands were required to learn many lessons in managing their land and households until they could make the voyage to America. Once in the new land, such women were more likely to seek employment to bolster the family's fortunes.

Despite their increasingly acknowledged roles in the immigrant community, women in turn-of-the-century Polonia faced real restrictions in becoming full-fledged members of the society of their time. Their situation was greatly affected by the extraordinary demands of child rearing that were placed upon the typical immigrant woman. One 1910 study reported that Polish foreign-born women aged thirty-five to forty-four had given birth to six children each, compared to the average of four children among other white foreign-born women. By way of contrast, in 1960, Polish foreign-born women were having an average of two children, slightly below the average for all European foreign-born women.

The Polish immigrant family's emphasis on solidarity together with the importance placed on the proper moral development of daughters limited both their work and educational opportunities outside the home.   When young women gained employment, it was usually as domestics, good training for their future roles as wives and mothers. With the emphasis on work and family, formal education for young women, and young men, too, was not especially prized.   A study of one Polish immigrant community at the start of the twentieth century found that 80 percent of the children, boys and girls alike, had dropped out of school by the seventh grade.

The patriarchal nature of Polish rural society had always restricted the options for women in the larger community, even though their labors were prized as spouses, mothers, homemakers, and keepers of the family budget.   Women could not ordinarily inherit property.   Moreover, a young wife did not have much standing, even in her own home. Authority would come later, after she had sons whose wives could relieve her of some of her duties.

Historian John Bukowczyk has given us a fictitious, but fact-based life history of a Polish immigrant woman he names Maria Kowalska, (who settled in the United States with her husband Jan after 1900). Bukowczyk's account is interesting in its description of Maria's daily routine, one of seemingly endless toil that defined her experience as wife and later as mother.

> For her the workday began well before dawn, and involved her lighting a fire in the wood stove after emptying the ashes from the night before, then cooking breakfast before rousing her husband and the male lodgers. Maria's job also involved tending to her children (she might expect to have five to ten to raise and care for) who had awakened to the sound of voices in their usually cramped dwelling.[9]

After the men left for work, Maria turned to her daily and weekly rounds of household chores.   These included hauling in

[9]The life history of Maria Kowalska presented in the following pages is derived from Bukowczyk, *And My Children Did Not Know Me*, pp. 22 – 26. See also Helena Z. Lopata, "Polish American Families," in *Ethnic Families in America: Patterns and Variations*, Charles H. Mindel and Robert W. Habenstein, editors (New York: Elsevier, 1981).

water from a well for cooking, keeping the house free of dirt, and doing the laundry – all tasks that had to be performed without the benefit of labor-saving appliances.

Bukowczyk then writes of Maria's other duties: tending the family vegetable garden and preserving produce for the coming winter, making her regular walks to the local market to buy the foods she did not grow in her garden, negotiating credit with the grocer until her husband's next pay envelope, even looking after the ducks and chickens the family kept behind their house.

As the afternoon wore on, Maria might have time to mend or sew – perhaps on a sewing machine if the family had prospered. By then it would be time for her to serve the evening's pot of soup which had simmered all afternoon, and wait on the men as they returned in the twilight, dirty and tired from the twelve-hour-long work day.

In addition to her child-rearing and domestic chores, Maria Kowalska made other financial contributions to the family. While she was unlikely to seek work outside the home after the birth of her first child, "Maria would still have 'made' money for the family by saving it. Moreover, any money collected from boarders and lodgers was in effect her 'wage' since she washed their clothes, cooked their food, and cleaned up after them."

Bukowczyk closes his fictitious biographical account by noting that the contributions of the Maria Kowalskis of the early Polish immigrant community gave them real stature in the family. Their successes gave them self-confidence as major role players in the family household. Indeed, if the world of Maria's husband was the workplace, the corner saloon, or the lodge hall, the home was the domain of his wife.

But Bukowczyk's life history hardly provides us with a comprehensive picture of all the Maria Kowalskis of the early Polonia, as he himself notes. For example, we do not learn about the experiences of women who belonged to the immigration's small but nascent middle class. Still, his well-grounded scholarly synthesis, and the studies of Lopata and Pula, gives us some understanding of the life of Polish immigrant women at the time of the birth of the Polish Women's Alliance of America.   Clearly, women, whatever their station in the Polish community, were a major, if little recognized, force contributing to its well-being.

Polonia's women played important roles in their Catholic parishes. This was a result of their generally high level of religious devotion and their strong interest in participating in the various women's groups that served the church. These included the choirs and altar and rosary societies that offered women welcome outlets for social interaction and breaks away from their household duties. Work involving embroidering religious garments and cleaning and beautifying the church were tasks women readily took on, both out of religious sentiment as well as a desire to perform a valued community service. Such activities also gave them opportunities to meet members of the Polish religious sisterhood. Those individuals were both educated and recognized in the local community for their services as teachers, nurses, and custodians in orphanages.   For many immigrant Poles, men and women alike, the sisters were the only "professional" women they were likely to know.   Jadwiga Karłowicz, in her history of the Polish Women's Alliance of America, makes a point of praising the sisters and their work.

At the same time, relatively few women in the early Polish immigrant community chose the religious life for themselves. What is more, women could not generally become members in the organizations of the immigrant community of the time.   Both the Polish Roman Catholic Union and the Polish National Alliance fraternal societies remained men-only organizations until the turn of the century, and most of the other early Polonia organizations followed their lead. Thus, the traditional male-dominated society of Poland's cities, towns, and villages was transferred to American Polonia.   This could not help but be a source of resentment for women activists of the day.

Behind the formation of the Polish Women's Alliance of America was another element at work: the activities of a small but energetic, idealistic, well-educated cadre of women in the early Polonia, in Chicago and elsewhere. It was these individuals who sought to play a recognized role in the immigrant organizations of the day. Some of these women had spouses or fathers who were active in the community. A few could even claim some earlier involvement in the struggle to liberate partitioned Poland itself.

SEEKING A PLACE IN AMERICA

A seminal influence on Polonia's development in America came from the competition between two local Chicago immigrant groups, the Saint Stanislaus society formed in 1864 and the *Gmina Polska* society (or Polish community) founded in 1866. The Saint Stanislaus group's aim was to set up a parish church for the immigrants in the city. The *Gmina Polska* was composed of individuals who identified with the independence cause.[10]

Though these groups were local, their rivalry eventually caused their leaders to set up federations of a nationwide scope to advance their aims. Out of the Saint Stanislaus society came the Polish Organization in America in 1873. This movement was based on the principle of immigrant unity around the Roman Catholic faith and eventually grew into the Polish Roman Catholic Union in America (PRCUA), a national fraternal society eventually based in Chicago and dominated by priests belonging to the Resurrectionist order and their allies.

Emerging somewhat later, in 1880, out of the *Gmina Polska* was the Polish National Alliance (PNA). This movement had a well-defined patriotic character and was not restricted to Roman Catholics. In principle, at least in its early years, the PNA was even open to Lithuanian, Ukrainian, and Jewish immigrants to America. In the eighteenth century those peoples had belonged to the old pre-partition Polish state, which PNA activists wished to restore to independence and unity.

Both groups aimed to improve the material conditions of Poles in America, initially by offering their members the right to burial insurance. But neither the PRCUA nor the PNA gave much thought to the enrollment of women into its ranks.

---

[10] On the early history of Chicago's Polonia, see Andrzej Brożek, *Polish Americans, 1854 – 1939* (Warsaw: Interpress Publishers, 1985) and Donald E. Pienkos, *PNA*, chapter 2.

One who did was Teofila Samolinska. Samolinska was born in Poland in 1848, took part in the 1863 uprising, and was an early supporter of *Gmina Polska*. She arrived in Chicago around 1865. Ever a Polish independence enthusiast, she wrote poetry and succeeded in publishing her work in the pages of Chicago's first Polonia newspaper, *Gazeta Polska*.[11]

In 1878, Samolinska was one of several persons who wrote to Agaton Giller, a leader of the Polish exiles who had participated in the 1863 uprising and then had taken refuge in Switzerland. Her purpose in writing was to ask Giller's advice on the best way for Polish community groups in America to unite in serving the independence cause. Giller responded indirectly to her and her comrades in writing a piece published in a newspaper in Lwów, in the Austrian zone of partitioned Poland. Giller's essay was titled "*List o organizacji* Polaków *w Ameryce*" (On the organization of the Poles in America); it was soon reprinted in the United States. In his essay Giller called on the leaders of the various local Polish societies to form a nationwide organization and to adopt a moderate, nonsectarian program to aid the immigrants in improving their conditions in America and to work publicly for Polish independence.

Giller's ideas inspired the formation of the Polish National Alliance. They also influenced the activists who later established such immigrant organizations as the Polish Falcons Alliance (founded in 1887 and refashioned as a national federation in 1894), the Polish Singers Alliance (1889), and the Polish Women's Alliance of America (1898 – 1900).

For her part, Teofila Samolinska remained active in Chicago's Polish community and supported the PNA program; however, she never became a member. Nevertheless, Samolinska continued to play a noteworthy part in the evolving Polonia, particularly in her activities in the 1880s and 1890s. Significantly, she repeatedly, though without success, put forward the then

---

[11] On the life of Samolinska, see Arthur L. Waldo, *Teofila Samolinska: Matka Związku Narodowego Polskiego w Ameryce* (Teofila Samolinska: Mother of the Polish National Alliance in America). (Chicago: Edward Rozanski, 1980). Karłowicz's description of Samolinska's work is in *Historia Związku Polek,* pp. 22 – 23.

radical notion that women should be directly engaged in the Polish community's organizational affairs.

Samolinska's activities in Polonia ran parallel to what was happening in America and in Poland. In both societies educated women were seeking to be taken seriously by the men who dominated the community.[12] But there was, of course, a difference between the United States and Poland. America was a sovereign country and a democracy. Here, women dissatisfied with their second-class status could organize and demand full equality with men. Already in the 1840s, an organization had been formed to work for women's emancipation, one initially known simply as "the woman's movement." By the 1870s it had settled on a focused and achievable strategy, one urging that women be given the right to vote and to hold public office.

The environment of late nineteenth century partitioned Poland, a land suffering both the repression of its national spirit and economic impoverishment was decidedly different. In the Polish lands, the winning back of national independence was paramount. "Women's issues", such as the achievement of equal rights ("równouprawnienie") and better treatment in the workplace, were somewhat marginalized. One observer put things bluntly: "The Polish women's movement remained subordinate to the wider struggle for Poland's freedom."[13]

In Poland, women increasingly recognized they could gain support for women's equality by first championing the independence cause. In practice, this idea had several consequences. For instance it led many women to seek an education so they could become teachers. Given the widely shared belief that knowledge of Poland's history was indispensable in the

---

[12] For a comprehensive presentation of the rise of the women's movement in partitioned Poland, see Bianka Pietrow-Ennker, introduction, *Women in Polish Society* editors Rudolf Jaworski and Bianka Pietrow Enker (Boulder: East European Monographs, 1992).   Robert Blobaum discusses the political orientations of women activists in "The 'Woman Question" in *Fin-de-Siecle Poland*," presented at the 58th annual meeting of the Polish Institute of Arts and Sciences of America, Kraków, Poland, June 2000.

[13] Pietrow-Ennker, *Women in Polish Society*, p. 1.

forming of patriotic attitudes and beliefs, women who became teachers could gain respect for themselves both as teaching professionals and as activists on behalf of the independence cause.

Already in the tsarist Russian census in 1897 it was reported that women made up 39 percent of the teachers in the Polish lands under St. Petersburg's control. In Austrian-ruled Galicia, more than 6,000 women were employed at the same time as primary school instructors. And in all three zones of partitioned Poland, women were active in the teachers' organizations that had sprung up in the years before World War I.

In the German-run Polish lands, the suppression of the Polish culture was pursued relentlessly. The effort focused on reshaping the curriculum of the region's schools. After 1871, all subjects but religion were required to be taught in the German language. This requirement was extended to religious instruction in 1901. But this last move went a step too far and provoked thousands of schoolchildren to refuse to answer questions put to them in class in German. Such nonviolent mass disobedience was ended only when the authorities declared that the children's continued silence, often in the face of corporal punishment, would result in the schools' withholding of diplomas of graduation.

But Germany's forced assimilation program extended beyond the suppression of the Polish language in the schools. It included persecuting the Roman Catholic Church as a center of age-old Polish national identity and championing German colonization of its Polish provinces. These policies caused many Poles to immigrate to the United States, especially from 1870 to 1900. A key to the attitudes of many members of this first Polish community in the United States was their deep resentment of Germanization, an emotion that helped heighten their own sense of Polish national consciousness. The early patriotic feeling of the Polish immigrants from the German lands was also rooted in their deep-seated commitment to the Polish language and the Roman Catholic faith. Such feelings eventually shaped the thinking of members of the later migrations from the Russian and Austrian-ruled provinces of partitioned Poland. Interestingly, teaching and learning in American Polonia as well as Poland took on a patriotic character. And with so many women in the teaching profession in the Polish lands, it is likely that some at least were able to express patriotic sentiments on some occasions during the school term.

Interestingly, the idealized role of women as mothers and nurturers of the next generation was another element of Polish feminism in the partitioned homeland. This may seem to run counter to what Americans today generally understand the women's movement to be about. But it made sense in Poland, where there was genuine concern for the future of the nation in the face of foreign repression. Moreover, this aspect of Polish feminism was quite in harmony with the Roman Catholic teachings about women. As one modern Polish scholar, Bianka Piotrow-Ennker, has noted:

> [Polish] society's readiness to revere women is even supposed to have increased during the partitions. . . . It was the mothers who kept Polish culture alive during the years of lost freedom by raising their children in the spirit of Polish national traditions. This readiness to accord recognition and respect to women is held to be expressed most clearly in the image of the Matka Polka, the holy mother of Poland: just as Mary – symbolized in the icon of Częstochowa – had been appointed to watch over the Polish nation, so too women – as Mary's successors on earth – were seen as being entrusted with the task of caring for the smallest unit of the nation, the family, and seeing that it had Christian values instilled into it.

In short, Polish feminism departed in various ways from the assertions of women's rights in America from the late nineteenth century onward. The Polish variant emphasized the role of women in articulating and nurturing the ideal of independence and looked to the church to support their aspirations. Such ideas would in turn influence the activists who founded the Polish Women's Alliance of America and even the symbols they came to use, such as the Częstochowa Madonna, in promoting their cause.

Both Polish and American women's activists advocated equal rights for both sexes and objected to the paternalistic treatment of women.   Furthermore, all early feminists generally favored increased wages and improved working conditions for women. In Poland women were becoming a growing presence in the industrial labor force; by 1897, forty percent of the workers in the textile mills of Łódź were women, and they were badly underpaid. Women faced similar conditions in the United States, and here Polish women were likely to hold opinions identical to those of women of other nationalities with whom they worked.

Politically, the American women's movement, at least until the passage in 1920 of the Nineteenth Amendment to the United States Constitution, directed its attention toward the right to vote and to hold elective office at the national level. In Poland, the emphasis was always on winning back the nation's independence. This dichotomy very much affected the founders of the Polish Women's Alliance of America, although the right to vote was discussed regularly in the PWA of A publication *Głos Polek*.

At the turn of the century, women in increasing numbers were attending the universities of partitioned Poland.   By the outbreak of the World War I in 1914, a majority of the students at the Universities of Warsaw and Kraków were women.   Women comprised almost as large a proportion of the student bodies of the country's other universities, too. Already by the 1890s, perhaps three thousand young women had completed their studies in the famed "flying university" in Warsaw, an educational program that did not involve aeronautics! This clandestine institution operated extra legally, often in private homes, after the Russian authorities' decision in 1882 requiring that all courses at the University of Warsaw be taught in Russian.[14]

---

[14] Claire Marie Anderson provides a good overview of the place of women in the patriotic movement in "A History of the Flying University in Poland, 1977 – 1981," (M.A. thesis, University of Wisconsin, Milwaukee, 1995).   The flying university tradition was revived repeatedly in the twentieth century, most recently in the late 1970s when the communist regime's intellectual critics organized academic lectures and even entire courses on subjects covering Poland's "true history," subjects either ignored or distorted in the country's universities on the rulers' orders.   Perhaps the most renowned female graduate in the first flying university was Maria Skłodowska, who later attained international fame in France as the scientist-researcher of radium, Maria Skłodowska Curie.

Many of the students in partitioned Poland's centers of higher learning, men and women alike, were very likely apolitical in their academic and professional studies. Still, issues like peace and war, Poland's destiny, and those having to do with equal rights for women were part of the atmosphere of the partitioned country and were likely subjects for discussion in the student societies of the day. The words and ideas of women of prominence, like the patriotic poet Maria Konopnicka and the novelist Eliza Orzeszkowa, whose novel, *Marta (1873)*, was the first Polish work to focus on women's concerns, were subjects for conversation and debate. Moreover, their stature as intellectuals could only further legitimize the general opinion that women could play a major role in working on behalf of the independence cause. In America, both Konopnicka and Orzeszkowa would later be named honorary members of the Polish Women's Alliance of America in its formative years.

It was in these conditions that the Polish Women's Alliance of America was born. Excluded from full participation and leadership in the organized immigrant communal life of their day, yet interested in the causes that were central to them as members of the Polish community, the women who founded the PWA of A were affected not only by the activities of the American women's movement but also by their knowledge of events in the homeland. Their desire to contribute their talents and energies on behalf of Polonia's patriotic agenda thus led them to form their own association of Polish women in America.[15]

For the women who would take up the struggle, *równouprawnienie* would be especially significant. The term may be translated literally as "equal rights," but to the founders of the PWA of A it possessed a deeper meaning underscoring their equal interest in the patriotic cause of the homeland along with equal rights for women in America. But the catalyst for the formation of the Alliance in 1898 was, in fact, something quite specific.

This involved the refusal of the men leading Polonia's organizations to allow women to join them as equals. Only when

---

[15] On the activities of women in the early American Polonia, see William Galush, "Purity and Power: Chicago Polonian Feminists, 1880 – 1914," *Polish American Studies,* 47, no. 1 (1990): 5 – 24.

their position had been made crystal clear did the founders of the Polish Women's Alliance of America decide to go "on their own."

ORIGINS OF THE POLISH WOMEN'S ALLIANCE OF AMERICA

There are actually several founding birth dates of the Polish Women's Alliance of America. The first was May 22, 1898, when Stefania Chmielinska, a thirty-three year old seamstress only seven years in America, invited several of her friends to the Near South Side Chicago home of her mother, Anna Sznajder.   There Chmielinska persuaded the others to form a society whose aim was to work for the cause of independent Poland. They named their group the Society of the Polish Women's Alliance in America, *Towarzystwo Związku Polek w Ameryce*, and at the same time elected the group's first officers.   Maria Rokosz, the wife of a Polonia and PNA activist, was elected president, Gabryela Laudon vice president, Katarzyna Nawrocka treasurer, and Chmielinska, whose husband's shop, among other things, produced the dress uniforms worn by the Polish Falcons society, became the group's secretary. Nothing more is known about this first meeting, nor do we have many details about the group's activities in the months immediately after.   (Anna Sznajder would remain an active supporter, although she refused to accept any office.)

But activity, and thoughtful discussion, was going on, as is clear from the text of a proclamation that appeared in October 1898 in *Kuryer Polski,* (Polish courier), a daily newspaper published in Milwaukee. It boldly called on the Polish women in America to join the cause of the new Alliance. Significantly, the proclamation listed four aims of a future Polish women's association in America. First and foremost was the promotion of a patriotic spirit among women, something the proclamation's authors declared was already occurring in other immigrant communities in America. Second was the need for a burial insurance program for Polish women.   Third, was the wish to propagate the spirit of ethnic awareness among the children of the Polish immigration. Last, was the formation of a nationwide Polish women's alliance.[16]

---

[16] "Odezwa do Polek w Ameryce," *Kuryer Polski*, Milwaukee, October 25, 1898, is reprinted in Karlowicz, pp. 26 – 27. Andrzej Brożek attributes authorship of the text to Chmielinska.

PROCLAMATION TO THE POLISH WOMEN IN AMERICA

Kuryer Polski, Milwaukee, October 25, 1898

Not long ago there arose from the bosom of the Polish women of Chicago the idea of establishing a greater women's organization, its task the uniting of the Polish women in America, the payment of death benefits, the maintenance of the national spirit in the ranks of its members, and the preservation and inculcation of this feeling within the Polish youth.

A beginning has been made to realize this idea. An organization named the Polish Women's Alliance of America has been established whose task will be to work in the spirit of these above noted aims. A burial program has been established, whereby the members of the Polish Women's Alliance of America will each pay one dollar to the insured member's family in the event of her death. This benefit, however, may not exceed $500 until membership in the Alliance will exceed five hundred, at which time the rate will be determined relative to the size of the membership.

First and foremost the aims of this organization are national and patriotic. Other nationalities in America have possessed similar organizations for some time. They are growing beautifully and yielding clear rewards to their peoples.

We are making ourselves heard to our respected fellow Polish women and calling upon them to join with us. We are seeking to reach all the existing women's organizations in our various Polish communities, in order to extend our hands to them in the cooperative effort.

Entire societies may join us and individuals too, if there is no group belonging to the Polish Women's Alliance of America in the area. More complete information, as well as a copy of our constitution, can be received by writing to the secretary of the Polish Women's Alliance: Katarzyna Nawrocka, 730 West 17th Street, Chicago, Illinois.

Respected countrywomen: we can accomplish much by joining together in the work on behalf of a good idea, having above all as our aim the nurturing of good values among our young Polish boys and girls. Our nationality will be in the future, depending on how our next generation develops. It is our duty to stand guard on behalf of the training of our young people, and to prepare them to be good Polish sons and daughters.

We are hopeful that our words will not die away without an echo, and that they will resound among our Polish countrywomen, who will support our aims and join with us in ties of harmony, friendship and work for the general good.

We earnestly request that copies of this proclamation be reprinted in all Polish publications.

Respectfully,
Maria Rokosz, President
Gabryela Laudon, Vice President
Katarzyna Nawrocka, Secretary
Maria Kraszewska, Financial Secretary
Stefania Chmielinska, Treasurer

A second founding birthday of the PWA of A came at two other meetings held on November 12 and November 20, 1899, nearly one and one-half years after the creation of the Polish Women's Alliance of America society. There, the leaders of the Polish Women's Alliance society were joined by members of several other recently formed Chicago-based women's groups, the Saint Helen's society, the Queen Wanda society, and the White Eagle Society. This time, Chmielinska was elected the first president of the new Alliance, with Maria Rokosz assuming the treasurer's post. Łucja Wołowska, a new figure in the group, and the organizer of the Queen Wanda Society, was named secretary.

Less than seven months later, on June 12, 1900, Chmielinska and her comrades' early efforts were confirmed at the founding convention (*sejm*) of the Polish Women's Alliance of America. The conclave, a one day long affair, was held in

Chicago's Pulaski Hall.   Present were twenty-four delegates who represented eight women's groups, seven of which were from Chicago with one from Pennsylvania.   In all, the new PWA of A counted 264 members in its ranks.

In the century to come, the organization would grow into the third largest fraternal insurance benefit association in the Polish American community. It would also gradually extend its territorial reach far beyond Chicago to include members coast to coast.

These are the facts about the creation of the Polish Women's Alliance of America. But behind these facts is the reality of the refusal by the male-run organizations in the immigrant community of the day to consider women for equal membership in their ranks. True enough, Polonia's leaders might respect women for their piety and devotion to the Church and welcomed the time and labor they willingly gave to the parishes.   But women were accorded no leadership roles in the burgeoning grass roots community institutions of Polonia. These were dominated by priests and their lay colleagues. This men-only leadership cadre usually included the local funeral director, the banker, the attorney, the physician or druggist, and whatever other entrepreneurs or shopkeepers of substance were to be found. Similarly, while fraternals like the PNA and PRCUA enjoyed support from women, neither felt it necessary to extend full membership rights to them.

Looking back, one can well imagine the frustration women activists must have experienced in their efforts to play active roles in the immigrant community.   One early example of this had occurred back in 1884.   That autumn, the PNA held its national convention in La Crosse, Wisconsin.   The gathering came at an especially bad time for the fraternal. After four years in existence, it could count fewer than three hundred members on its lists and was practically bereft of funds.

A delegation of Polish women led by Samolinska attended the meeting and eloquently voiced its strong support for the PNA cause. Its manifestation drew the delegates' praise, but no action was taken to extend membership rights to women, despite the PNA's woes. Several years later, at the 1891 convention of the Polish Roman Catholic Union, it briefly entertained too a modest motion to grant membership to widows of men who had been in its ranks. But even this proposal was rejected.

In only one organization had women enjoyed some membership rights comparable to men: the Polish Falcons Alliance (*Związek Sokołów*), a youth-oriented society founded in Chicago in 1887 with the blessing of local PNA and PRCUA activists. The Falcons' mission linked the promotion of physical fitness programs to building ethnic pride and patriotism among the younger generation of Chicago's Polonia. The motto of the Falcons underscored its aims – *"W zdrowym ciele zdrowy duch!"* (A healthy spirit in a healthy body).

The first Falcons group, or "nest" as it was imaginatively named, was itself inspired by successes enjoyed by the already significant Falcons movement operating in partitioned Poland and by similar German-American "Turners" societies and Czech-American *"Sokols,"* both of which also had their roots in Europe. (The word "turner" came from the German term for "turning," a nineteenth century way of expressing the idea of calisthenics and exercise. While Polish and Czech groups founded on the same principle called Falcons, they too initially used the word "turner" when describing themselves and their activities to Americans.)

Teofila Samolinska was an early enthusiast of the Falcons idea and immediately joined the society. A number of women, most of them in their teens and early twenties, also joined the Falcons nest. By the early 1890s women accounted for one-third of its membership.

In 1894, a national Polish Falcons Alliance was formed by four Falcons societies; it too welcomed women into its ranks. Stefania Chmielinska was an early member, as was Honorata Wołowska, a later president of the PWA of A. Both actually were appointed to be physical fitness instructors in the organization. Together, they and their friends were soon pushing for full women's equality in the very organization they were convinced would be receptive to them. But in this they were disappointed. The Falcons' official position was that while women could belong to their local nests and take part in their activities, they could not be formally counted as members or hold elective office.

On May 22, 1897, matters came to a head when Chmielinska and Wołowska appeared before the national officers of the Falcons' Alliance.   They called on them to grant women members "full, not half equality" with men and to be granted the right to send their own delegates to the upcoming annual convention of the Alliance. But the board flatly turned them down.

Falcons President Casimir Zychlinski justified the decision by stating that the Falcons were preparing to set up a program of paramilitary training for its young men in the expectation that they might soon fight for Poland's independence. The Falcons' chief physical instructor was far less diplomatic. He declared he could not imagine how any future military commander could ever accept being placed in charge of "an army in skirts." Despite these rebuffs, Zychlinski urged Chmielinska, Wołowska, and their friends to continue to participate in the Falcons' physical exercises so they might better prepare themselves for performing their future duties in the household.   Such exercises, he advised, were helpful in making women "healthy, nimble, and graceful."[17]

This rejection proved to be the last straw.   Exclusion from active membership in the older and more well-established PRCUA and PNA was one thing. Dismissal by the Falcons was something else.   Exactly one year to the day after Zychlinski's decision, Chmielinska and her friends met; together they began the work to create a new movement – of women, by women, and for women. This movement would be dedicated to the same patriotic causes that had inspired organizations of the Polish like the PNA and the Falcons. Clearly after their experience in May 1897, there would be no turning back.

---

[17] On the Falcons' opposition to full women's participation in their movement, see Donald E. Pienkos, *One Hundred Years Young*, chapter 2.   Brożek discusses the issue of women's inclusion into the PNA and the PRCUA, in *Polish Americans*, chapter 4.

HEROIC YEARS:
THE POLISH WOMEN'S ALLIANCE OF AMERICA, 1898 – 1918

> I am certain, my dear compatriots, that your
> Alliance will be a stronghold of our heritage, that it
> will be a stronghold – not only for women of Polish
> descent residing in America, but also a vital link
> between their hearts and the land of their fathers.
> Maria Konopnicka, Łwów, 1902[1]

> Women aren't content to advise; they act.
> Ignacy Paderewski, New York, 1914[2]

The May 22, 1898, founding meeting of the first Polish
Women's Alliance society in Chicago had been productive. Officers
were chosen and work was begun on a constitution. Other women
were contacted by means of a proclamation the group published on
October 25, 1898, in *Kuryer Polski*.

The moderation and good sense that were reflected in these
early efforts were greeted favorably in the immigrant community.
Several local pastors even gave their blessings to the endeavor. In
June 1900, only two years after the founding of the first Polish
Women's Alliance society, the newly created national fraternal held
its first convention.

If May 22, 1898, represented the date of the conception of
the Polish Women's Alliance of America, November 12 and
November 20, 1899, marked its birth. On these two evenings,
meetings were called by the officers of the Polish Women's Alliance
of America society at Chicago's Pulaski Hall on the city's near South

---

[1]The renowned poet and author Maria Konopnicka (1842 – 1910) was the first
well-known supporter of the PWA of A in Poland. At its fourth convention in
1903 the Alliance named her its first honorary member, beginning a tradition
that continues to this day. Her biography is in Helen Zielinski, *Historia
Związku Polek*, pp. 11 – 12. See also Czesław Miłosz, *The History of Polish
Literature* (Toronto: Collier-Macmillan, 1969); and *Wielka Encyklopedia
Powszechna*, vol. 5 (The great general encyclopedia. Warsaw: Państwowe
Wydawnictwo Naukowe, 1965).

[2] Maria Loryś, *Historia Zwiazku Polek w Ameryce*, p. 144.

Side, not far from the great Polish immigrant Church of St. Adalbert. These gatherings proved to be highly significant.

The first meeting brought together representatives of the Polish Women's Alliance society led by Stefania Chmielinska and two other Chicago-based groups, the Saint Helen's society and the Queen Wanda society; the former had been formed through Chmielinska's initiative in June, the latter in September. Both had committed themselves to the aims of the PWA of A society as expressed in its *Kuryer Polski* appeal.

The November 12 meeting was highlighted by remarks from a special guest. Theodore Helinski was the general secretary of the Polish National Alliance fraternal and a respected figure in Chicago's Polonia. But Helinski had more than pleasantries to share with his listeners.

Helinski, a prominent advocate of the patriotic work of the Polish National Alliance, had for years championed its expansion through the inclusion of Lithuanian and Ukrainian immigrants into its ranks. But his efforts to gain admission for women were unsuccessful. In fact, the PNA had ignored his advice at its national convention in September. There the issue had not even come up for a vote.

At the November 12 gathering, Helinski proposed that his listeners establish their own Alliance and make it comparable to the existing men's fraternal societies. He suggested that such an organization include not only the wives of PNA members but their mothers, daughters, and sisters, together with women not previously connected with his organization. After making his recommendation, Helinski added that he had offered his view as a private person, not as an officer of the Polish National Alliance.[3]

But Helinski did not have to do much persuading. The events of the previous eighteen months had convinced Chmielinska

---

[3] Karłowicz, *Historia Związku Polek*, pp. 29 – 30. Helinski (1856 – 1921), one of the early PNA leaders, held national office in that organization from 1889 until 1907. In World War I he chaired the Polish Military Commission in America, which registered nearly forty thousand volunteers to serve in the Polish army for service in France on behalf of the Allied cause.

and her comrades that this course of action was both sensible and necessary.

Eight days later, on November 20, 1899, the future founders of the Polish Women's Alliance of America met again. This time they were joined by representatives from a fourth group, the White Eagle society. Also present was a local attorney, Max Drzemała, who reviewed and approved a constitution the members of the Polish Women's Alliance society had drawn up to charter the proposed federation. According to PWA of A historian Jadwiga Karłowicz, this first statement accurately and comprehensively presented the aims of the organization and described its basic structure as it would remain for years after.

Among these was the goal of maintaining a burial insurance program that provided members with coverage of up to five hundred dollars, once the proposed Alliance included five hundred adult members. To help raise funds for this program, new members were to be assessed an initiation fee of fifty cents. Thereafter they were to be required to pay monthly dues of five cents each.

This idea made a great deal of sense. Chmielinska and her comrades, like the men who had preceded them in establishing the PNA and the PRCUA fraternals, understood that organizations based solely on patriotic, religious, or humanitarian foundations were unlikely to last once the initial enthusiasm behind their creation had waned. Similarly, all social groups, by their very nature, always face internal challenges that are rooted in disagreements over strategies, tactics, and personalities. A good way to avoid such divisiveness and breakdown was to set up a fraternal insurance program for the organization; as insurance holders through the fraternal, members were more likely to stick with the program.

Furthermore, by making insurance ownership an essential element of its fraternalism, the PWA of A was able to add a welcome bit of self-interest to its ideological rationales, patriotism and the call for women's equality. A member's financial investment in the Alliance, even if modest in dollars and cents, was a not inconsequential reason for becoming and remaining involved in the organization. Moreover, by setting up the Alliance as a not-for-profit society, Chmielinska and her allies could always emphasize the benevolent and humanitarian aims of their cause. This mission, together with the Alliance's patriotic concern for Poland, served to further enhance its appeal. All these considerations benefited the PWA of A in the years to come.

At the same November 20 meeting, officers were chosen to serve for the next six months, at which time the new Polish Women's Alliance of America was to hold its first convention, or *sejm*. At that proposed meeting, delegates representing the entire membership were to elect a slate of national leaders.

Stefania Chmielinska was chosen to be the first provisional president of the PWA of A. Anastasia Borecka of the White Eagle society became vice president, and Łucja Wołowska of the Queen Wanda society became secretary. Maria Rokosz, who had been elected president of the Polish Women's Alliance Society in May 1898, was elected treasurer. In addition, five women were named as directors. They were Maria Kraszewska, Pelagia Harnacka, Frances Petkowska, Anna Pelka, and Aniela Tomaszewska.

Of these women, four went on to play important roles in the PWA of A in the years to come. Chmielinska would remain a leader at the national level for the next two decades. Following her initial stint as provisional president, she was elected president at several national conventions between 1901 and 1910. Between 1910 and 1920 she served several times as vice president. In the 1920s, Chmielinska was a delegate to its national conventions. In 1931, at the sixteenth PWA of A convention, she was recognized as its first honorary president, a title that has since been bestowed on later former presidents after leaving office. At the same 1931 conclave, the delegates also proclaimed May 22 to be the Alliance's Founders Day. This annual occasion remains a major event within the fraternal.

Maria Rokosz served as treasurer until 1901 and between 1905 and 1906 was elected to the office of director. Aniela Tomaszewska was elected to two one-year terms as treasurer between 1901 and 1903 and then ran, unsuccessfully, for vice president in 1908 and 1910.

But the woman whose PWA of A career continued for the longest time was Łucja Wołowska. Significantly, she eventually served three terms as secretary and then another four as treasurer. Thus Wołowska continued as an elected national officer into the 1920s, in 1924 was the first elected state president for District 1 (Illinois), and afterward remained a respected force at PWA of A conventions into the 1940s. She was influential in other ways too. It was through her efforts that her husband, Frank, became editor of the first PWA of A official publication in 1902; it was named *Głos Polek* (the voice of Polish women). The paper's initial run was short, about one year, its demise a consequence of heavy operating costs. Still, in the years that followed, the Alliance continued to cooperate with Frank Wołowski in his capacity as an editor of Chicago's *Dziennik Narodowy* (Polish national daily) newspaper. With the support of this publication, the Alliance was able to sponsor a regular weekly PWA of A page for its members. This continued until 1910 when the Alliance again decided to launch, and this time sustain, its own publication.[4]

At its February 6, 1900, meeting the new PWA of A leadership or general administration, approved its constitution and authorized the printing and distribution of 1,000 copies of the document. Unfortunately, none of these remain, although there are references to parts of the constitution from contemporary news accounts of the founding convention.

At the same February meeting, the White Eagle society withdrew from the new PWA of A. This necessitated the replacement of Vice President Borecka, a member of the White Eagle society, by Katarzyna Wleklinska. Two board members from the society, Petkowska and Kraszewska, were also replaced.

Apparently, the defection did no serious damage to the PWA of A. Nor for that matter did a major policy change made by the Polish National Alliance only a month later. In March 1900, the

---

[4] Copies of the first issues of *Głos Polek* are in the library of the Alliance, as are issues of the reestablished newspaper dating back to 1911.

PNA held an extraordinary national convention in Chicago for the sole purpose of admitting women to full insured membership status in the fraternal. A resolution to this effect was in fact approved by a margin of 187 to 10. The statement was interesting in recognizing women to be a "formidable force. . . . able to work even more effectively here in America for Poland's good and to deal with the loss of Polishness among our young people."

The PNA action, which followed a similar decision in 1899 by the Polish Roman Catholic Union in America, was a major step in the direction of granting women equality of rights in the Polish immigrant community. At the same time, both moves were in no small measure responses to Chmielinska and her friends' efforts to assert the rights of women in Polonia.

The first *sejm* of the new Alliance was called for June 12, 1900, in response to a request from Honorata Wołowska, a twenty-five-year-old teacher from Poland residing in the town of Braddock, Pennsylvania. No relation to Łucja, Honorata Wołowska had already been active in the Polish Falcons Alliance. She was also the organizer of the first PWA of A group outside the Chicago area, the Society of Polish Women in a Foreign Land. This group was important in various ways and demonstrated the Alliance's possibilities as a truly nationwide movement. It was also the first of nearly forty groups that Honorata Wołowska organized, making her the undisputed true believer in helping it realize its mission.

THE FIRST *SEJM* OF THE POLISH WOMEN'S ALLIANCE OF AMERICA

On Sunday, June 12, 1900 following Mass at Saint Adalbert's Church, twenty-four delegates representing 8 groups and 264 members of the Alliance gathered at Pułaski Hall, a popular South Side Chicago meeting place.

The first convention went on for only one day. After all, many of the delegates had plenty of work ahead of them on Monday! Nonetheless, a great deal was accomplished that afternoon. Most important was the approval of the first PWA of A constitution. Among its rules was one requiring that groups seeking to join the Alliance have at least five members to qualify, (later this was raised to fifteen). Also approved was a provision that each member group be entitled to representation by at least one delegate at future conventions.

Rules for initiation fees and dues were approved with one addition: that each member contributed twelve cents annually to the national office to support the Polish National Fund centered in Raperswyl, Switzerland. Raperwyl was the home of the Polish Museum, established by Agaton Giller and his fellow exiles after the failure of their insurrection against tsarist Russia in 1864.

The Museum served as a center of *emigre* patriotic activity in Western Europe on behalf of Poland's independence. It also functioned as a point of contact between Polish activists in Europe and representatives of the burgeoning Polonia in America. Only with the outbreak of World War I did the center of political agitation for Polish independence shift decisively, first to France and later the United States. (The museum's artifacts were transferred to Poland in the late 1920s.)

The delegates at the first PWA of A *sejm* asserted their identification with the Polish cause in other ways. For one, they called on all Polish women to speak daily with their children in Polish to help them preserve a mastery of their ancestral language and love of their heritage in the new land. For another, they proclaimed the PWA of A's interest in cooperating whenever possible with the other Chicago-based Polonia organizations. A very pertinent example of this came with their resolution to contribute funds to erect a monument to honor Tadeusz Kościuszko, the American Revolutionary War hero and leader of the ill-fated uprising of 1794 to preserve Poland's independence. A statue of Kościuszko was unveiled in Chicago's Humboldt Park in 1904; over the next seven decades it served as a focal point for the annual ceremonies recalling Poland's constitution of May 3, 1791. This event has continued to be an occasion for the organized Polish ethnic community to rededicate itself to the best interests of the ancient homeland.

To spread the word about the PWA of A and its program, the delegates approved a proposal to publish news about its activities in Chicago's *Dziennik Narodowy* paper. Several leaders in the

Alliance, among them Maria Rokosz and Łucja Wołowska, were married to employees at this paper. The editorial policy of *Dziennik Narodowy* was highly sympathetic to the PWA of A cause. The newspaper identified with the patriotic camp in the immigrant community, one of the three wings in Polonia thinking of the time. The others were Catholic and socialist in tone.

At the first convention, elections to fill the four national executive offices and five directorships of the Alliance brought some surprises. Genevieve Zołkowska was elected president; Stefania Chmielinska, vice president; Łucja Wołowska, secretary; and Maria Rokosz, treasurer. Unfortunately, we have next to no information about the election proceedings and why Zołkowska, who chaired the convention, was chosen president rather than Chmielinska, the Alliance's provisional president and the moving spirit of the movement from its conception two years before.

The new constitution provided for annual conventions. This was a fortuitous decision, because the fledgling fraternal almost immediately faced several problems that called for quick, decisive, and authoritative resolution.

REAFFIRMING THE POLISH WOMEN'S ALLIANCE:
THE SECOND *SEJM*

In autumn 1900, shortly after her election, President Zołkowska sailed for Europe and remained there for several months. In December, a meeting of the PWA of A general administration was called. After noting Zołkowska's failures to pay her membership dues and to keep it informed about the date of her return to Chicago, the board took the extraordinary step of removing her from office. Replacing Zołkowska, a move described by the first PWA of A historian, Jadwiga Karłowicz, as a source of embarrassment and unpleasantness, was Vice President Chmielinska.[5]

---

[5] Karłowicz, *Historia Związku Polek*, p. 36. Information on PWA of A conventions prior to 1916 comes primarily from Karłowicz and the author's review of the Milwaukee daily newspaper, *Kuryer Polski*. This publication gave extensive coverage to Polish fraternal activities.

Things eventually turned out better on this seemingly contentious matter than one might have expected. Zołkowska did return to Chicago and her membership in the Alliance was eventually reinstated at the third PWA of A convention in June 1902. Moreover, she continued to support the PWA of A and was active in her local group for many years afterward. But she did not again seek national office.

An even more serious problem involved a dispute over the fraternal's insurance funds. In this case, several leaders of the Alliance, including Treasurer Rokosz and a director named Krentz, made a formal complaint about the legality of the PWA of A insurance program. This matter was settled in spring 1901 at a judicial hearing at which the charges were dismissed. There it was also learned that the complainants had aimed to establish another rival insurance program of their own.

Given these difficulties, the second PWA of A sejm, on June 15, 1901, came not a moment too soon, offering its leaders a timely opportunity to deal with the Alliance's most pressing issues. The daylong conclave brought together delegates from 16 groups representing 506 women. These figures were noteworthy: in just one year and with no real financial resources to help advance its cause, the PWA of A had doubled the number of members and affiliated local groups.

At the sejm, held again at Pulaski Hall, Anna Neumann, another newcomer to the Alliance, played an important role. The forty-one year old Neumann, a seamstress like Chmielinska, had joined the Alliance the year before and was a founder of PWA of A Group 10, also named the Polish Women in a Foreign Land society. She was a union-minded activist and had gained a reputation as an organizer of a women's clothing-makers cooperative. This cooperative was formed to sell its members' products directly to their customers.

At the convention, Neumann was elected recording secretary, responsible for keeping the minutes of the sessions. When elections for the coming year were held, she was chosen vice president; two other newcomers, Antonina Fabiańska and Aniela

Tomaszewska, were elected secretary and treasurer, respectively. Stefania Chmielinska was elected to her first full term as president.

On the all-important insurance question, the delegates established a permanent fund out of which death benefits would be promptly paid in the event of a member's demise. Initiation fees and monthly membership assessments were to be paid directly into the fund. To make sure the still tiny PWA of A would operate on a solvent basis in the future – at the convention its assets were announced as amounting to only $360.04 – the delegates agreed to limit eligibility for the death benefit to members between the ages of seventeen and forty-five.

This was a prudent decision given the high rates of mortality at the time among immigrants, male and female. (Early on, the PWA of A readily provided information on the names, ages, and causes of death of members. For example, in 1911 the average age of those who died was thirty-three. The most frequent causes of death were tuberculosis, heart disease, blood poisoning, childbirth, and pneumonia. Less frequently noted were deaths from cancer, dropsy, and bowel disorder, cirrhosis of the liver, sunstroke, and apoplexy. One twenty-year-old reportedly died that year of a gunshot wound.)

The decision to limit insurance eligibility by age worked. One year later, at the third annual PWA of A convention in June 1902, the fraternal's assets had risen to $1,746.63. This sizable improvement coincided with the Alliance's payment of its first death benefit. This went to the family of Małgorzata Półchłopek, a forty-four-year-old member of Group 6, Chicago's Queen Jadwiga Society. The speedy, businesslike, yet caring handling of the claim proved to be important in helping to build confidence in the organization.

By the third convention, membership was 876; a year later it had risen to 1,400. In June 1906, at its sixth *sejm*, the Alliance counted 4,302 members in its ranks. Its assets were now $15,084, a nearly fifty-fold improvement since the second *sejm* in 1901, when the crucial decision was made to solidify the fraternal's insurance program.

There were other achievements as well in these early years. By the end of 1901, the work of composing a charter defining the Alliance's insurance program was largely finished. On March 17, 1902, the document was delivered to the Illinois state capital in Springfield and there duly approved. The presentation of this charter is yet another major date in PWA of A history. But this period was filled with real accomplishments in the patriotic field as well. The energetic Chmielinska and Neumann both took leadership roles in representing the Alliance in a variety of Chicago Polonia manifestations protesting the mistreatment of Poles in the German-controlled territories of the partitioned homeland. These actions had followed the Berlin government's imposition of the German language in the Polish schools under its control. Already in December 1901, Neumann called for a Chicago-wide meeting of Polonia leaders on behalf of the persecuted people of Poland's Poznań region. This initiative was a first for the PWA of A and would be repeated frequently in the decades to come.

At the Alliance's third annual convention in June 1902, this time a three-day-long gathering, the delegates once again made a series of decisions that would shape the fraternal's future development. As already noted, one was to initiate a PWA of A official monthly publication to be named *Głos Polek* under the editorship of Frank Wołowski. This idea was both sensible and ambitious. But it proved to be a premature move for the still small Alliance. After less than a year, the publication had to be discontinued and the PWA of A returned to its previous practice of relying upon *Dziennik Narodowy* for publicity.

This time the *Dziennik* agreed to expand its coverage and appointed a staff member, Maria Iwanowska, to be editor of a special *Związek Polek* page in the paper. Iwanowska, a member of the Alliance, performed this work from 1903 until 1909, when a second PWA of A member, Jadwiga Michalska, succeeded her. In 1910, at its eighth *sejm* in Milwaukee, the Alliance reestablished *Głos Polek* as a weekly publication. By this time its membership had grown to include more than 7,600 women in 103 local groups in Illinois, Indiana, Pennsylvania, Connecticut, Michigan, Wisconsin, and Ohio.

More immediately successful was the delegates' authorization of a new and special standing committee on educational and cultural matters (*wydział oświaty*). Chaired by Chmielinska, who relinquished the presidency to Anna Neumann to focus her attention upon its work, the PWA of A committee on educational and cultural matters took on a broad set of objectives. One involved establishing an Alliance-sponsored reading room for the Polish community at large. Another aimed to organize lectures for the benefit of young women in a variety of subjects ranging from Polish history to literature. A third initiative offered information about careers and work skills in the pages of *Głos Polek*. The only obstacle facing the committee was lack of money. The convention did not set aside funds to enable it to achieve its aims. But Chmielinska and her committee members immediately began raising funds on their own to achieve their agenda.

In autumn 1902, Chmielinska, joined by a friend, Stefania Laudyn, who was then living in the city of Lwów in the Austrian-ruled section of partitioned Poland, composed a letter to congratulate the famed poet, Maria Konopnicka, on the occasion of the twenty-fifth anniversary of her first publication. They effusively praised Konopnicka for her achievements and urged that she continue to "feed our spirits with your poetic words which touch the depths of our hearts." The committee followed up on this first contact by sponsoring a public event in Konopnicka's honor at Pułaski Hall. The program was a great success; the high point came with the audience's unexpected response to an eloquent speech by Łucja Wołowska about the poet-patriot. At the conclusion of her address, the crowd remained silent for several minutes out of respect for her remarks.

The Alliance's fourth *sejm* in June 1903 took place at the Holy Trinity parish hall on Chicago's Near North Side. This convention brought together more than ninety delegates representing twenty-eight groups. Neumann was reelected president, with Leokadia Kadów defeating the incumbent treasurer, Aniela Tomaszewska, by a 51 to 40 vote. Kadów went on to serve six terms between 1903 and 1914 and contributed much in strengthening the fraternal's financial standing.

Just before the 1903 *sejm*, President Neumann sent out a proclamation (*orędzie*) in which she officially called the delegates together and set the general agenda for the coming conclave. In this precedent-setting action, she emphasized the patriotic and educational mission of the PWA of A. At the *sejm*, and in keeping with the spirit of her statement, the delegates responded by approving a resolution that named Maria Konopnicka an honorary member of the Alliance. In succeeding years, seven other outstanding women of Polish origin would also be so acclaimed.

The novelist Orzeszkowa became the second honorary member of the PWA of A in 1904, at the suggestion of her friend Konopnicka. The famed actress Helena Modjeska was the third to be so designated in 1908. Her recognition came only a few months before her death. Helena Paderewska, wife of the great patriot and pianist, Ignacy Paderewski and a leader in her own right in the humanitarian work for Polish victims of World War I, was honored in 1915 at the time of a visit she and her husband made to Chicago.

Maria Skłodowska Curie was the fifth recipient of an honorary membership in the Alliance. Her recognition came in June 1921, on the occasion of her first visit to the United States at the invitation of a number of leading American women's organizations. Two PWA of A leaders were present for her arrival in New York, President Emilia Napieralska and Secretary Łucja Wołowska. The famed Madame Curie eventually made her way to Chicago, and it was at this time that the general administration of the Alliance named her an honorary member. At the same time, it approved a donation of one thousand dollars to the two-time Nobel laureate. This money was to be used for the purchase of a gram of radium for her research at the Institute of Radiology, in Paris. In 1929 Skłodowska Curie made a second fundraising tour of the United States. Once again, the PWA of A approved a one thousand dollar gift in support of her research.

In 1927 the Alliance named the novelist and essayist Maria Rodziewicz its sixth honorary member. This came after its leaders had learned of Rodziewicz's appeals for humanitarian aid to the needy in her home region in eastern Poland. One of her country's most popular authors of the day, Rodziewicz also took a lead role in welcoming PWA of A members who made the first Alliance-sponsored pilgrimage to the homeland in 1928.

In 1943, during the dark days of World War II, General Władysław Sikorski, Poland's prime minister, and his daughter were killed in an airplane crash off the coast of Spain. His death dealt a devastating blow to the Polish cause, since he was a universally respected spokesman and enjoyed excellent relations with the Western leaders of the anti-Nazi alliance, Franklin D. Roosevelt and Winston Churchill. At the nineteenth PWA of A convention in September 1943, in a gesture of solidarity with the embattled Polish nation, his widow Helena Sikorska was named an honorary member in the Alliance. The decision was also an expression of appreciation for her work for orphans and refugees since 1939.

The most recent recipient of honorary membership in the Alliance is Senator Barbara Mikulski of Maryland. Throughout her career, as a Baltimore social worker, as a member of the U.S. House of Representatives, and later as senator, Mikulski has won wide recognition for her concern for women's rights. She has been at the same time a constant and powerful voice in Washington in support of the Polish people's aspirations for freedom, both in their own land and as refugees in America. Senator Mikulski's selection in 1987 made her the first American-born woman of Polish heritage to be designated as an honorary member of the Alliance.[6]

From its earliest days, the PWA of A had used the Pulaski Hall on Chicago's South Ashland Avenue as its principle meeting place. But in 1903, the building had burned to the ground, requiring the leaders of the Alliance to find new headquarters large enough to hold the rapidly accumulating information being received each month from new member groups and individuals. Increasingly it was becoming evident the Polish Women's Alliance of America would have to have its very own home office.

The decision to establish a permanent headquarters was made at the Alliance's fifth convention in June 1904. That

---

[6] Biographies of PWA of A honorary members through 1980 are in Zielinski, *Historia Związku Polek*, pp. 11 – 16.

November, a building was purchased at 527 (presently 1237) North Ashland Avenue in Chicago, in the very heart of Polish immigrant organizational life on the windy city's near North Side. The building was dedicated on February 25, 1905, in a ceremony at which the Reverend Casimir Sztuczko, pastor of Holy Trinity parish, presided. Sztuczko's presence was significant, for his church was the acknowledged religious home of Polonia's patriotic wing. This wing was led by the Polish National Alliance and included, among other organizations, the Polish Falcons Alliance and the PWA of A. The main religious center of the competing clerical wing in Polonia was a neighboring church, Saint Stanislas Kostka, the mother parish of the Resurrectionist priests in Chicago and their fraternal ally, the PRCUA. Polonia's third wing, the socialists, was in need of no church.

On the day following the dedication ceremonies, a second gala "opening" was held and featured speeches by PWA of A leaders and their friends, recitations by children, and a musical program by the *Moniuszko* chorus and the *Lira Polska* singers. The well-attended event symbolized the Alliance's rising stature in the community.

The first Polish Women's Alliance of America home, purchased for $3,650, was modest and it was soon found to be far too small to meet the Alliance's rapidly growing space needs. In 1911 the general administration decided to build a new home office down the street at 1309 – 1315 North Ashland Avenue. Completed in 1912 at a cost of $72,000, eighteen times more than the first PWA of A home, the new structure represented an impressive yardstick of the Alliance's progress since 1905.

The new building, greatly remodeled and expanded in the 1930s, served as the administrative center of the Polish Women's Alliance of America for the next seven decades. Perhaps as significant, it also came to be the locus of countless patriotic manifestations, cultural events, and charitable actions – not only of the PWA of A itself but of other Polonia organizations as well.

Meanwhile, the Alliance was making progress in other activities too. At the ninth PWA of A *sejm* in South Bend, Indiana, in 1912, the delegates voted 111 to 89 in favor of a new table of insurance rates based on the ages of new members at the time they joined the fraternal.

Until that time, women who entered the Alliance as insured members between the ages of seventeen and forty had paid an initiation fee of one dollar and fifty cents; women between forty and forty-five years of age paid two dollars. Everyone then paid the same monthly insurance assessment, subject to an annual adjustment depending on the number of member deaths during the year. All policies paid the same death benefit of $500. Only women between the ages of seventeen and forty-five could join as insured members, although older women could be granted noninsured social status in the Alliance.

The new rate system enabled the PWA of A to offer life insurance of varying amounts up to a maximum of one thousand dollars. It also rose the age of eligibility to forty-nine for women who wished to join as insured members. This initiative was controversial, having been rejected by a 69 to 54 vote when it first came up at the 1910 *sejm* in Milwaukee. Then the main objection had been the concern that a variable rate system would make membership less attractive to older individuals who were being solicited to join, since their insurance premiums would be higher than those of younger members. But once the measure passed, the new rate schedule won universal acceptance; not a single member of the organization was known to have dropped out on account of the change.

Three other actions taken during these formative years were especially noteworthy. One was the 1910 convention's reestablishment of the Alliance's own fraternal publication, *Głos Polek*, this time as a weekly newspaper that was free for members and available by subscription to non-members. Stefania Laudyn (later Laudyn Chrzanowska) was named the publication's editor. A longtime friend of Chmielinska, Laudyn came from Lwów where she was active in an organization called *Związek Równouprawnienia Kobiet*, (The Alliance of Equal Rights for Women). With one interruption, Laudyn remained editor of *Głos Polek* until 1918; during her tenure, the publication became a zealous supporter of women's rights and educational advancement. Laudyn also emphasized the Polish independence cause, which grew even more important to the PWA of A and American Polonia after the outbreak of the War in August 1914.

A second action involved the expansion of the PWA of A education committee, which was increasingly referred to as the educational department. Under the committee's auspices, the Alliance set up its first summer camp for children in 1910. A Saturday school program was also created to teach young girls and boys about Poland's language, history, and literature. Literacy development was another aim of these schools and the PWA of A established an adult literacy program in its home office after 1912. Local branches of the education department were established outside of Chicago as well, the first of which was in Milwaukee following the *sejm* held there in 1910.

Pride in the PWA of A and its aims became so infectious that its general administration even commissioned a special march for presentation at its events. This composition, "*Łączmy siostry wciąż, serce dłonie*" (Let us unite, Sisters, in one heart), written by the respected Polonia activist Anthony Mallek, debuted on April 14, 1913, and was regularly performed at Alliance functions over the next twenty years. A popular slogan of the education department summed up its members' enthusiasm for its place in PWA of A life: "*Oświata ludu dokonywa cudu*" (The enlightenment of our people works wonders).

A third action was organizational and involved the election, in 1912, of a new intermediate set of officers, originally called state vice presidents and later renamed state presidents. The women elected to these posts were responsible for coordinating the work of the fraternal outside of Chicago, which, after all, was already well supplied with a number of national officers. The first state vice presidents were Stanisława Petrykowska (Wisconsin), Dr. Frances Konrad-Filipiak (Ohio), Stanisława Wawrzon (Indiana), and Frances Szymańska (Michigan); Albina Budaj became the first state vice president for Connecticut and Massachusetts combined. Over the next five years, a total of nine state vice presidents were installed.

Jadwiga Karłowicz, the first PWA of A historian, offers an eloquent overview of the organization's early years, a time filled with its leaders' achievements in the face of the still widespread reluctance to accept women as equal participants in the affairs of the immigrant community. "Our founders," she writes, "showed the world that women know how to work and operate independently." In so doing, they were making the best case they could on behalf of equal rights with men (*równouprawnienie*) in America.

This dedication and idealism was not restricted to the large Polish community in Chicago. By 1906 a number of the sixty-three local societies affiliated with the Polish Women's Alliance of America were located beyond the windy city and its suburbs. They were to be found in places like Braddock, Pennsylvania; South Bend and Whiting, Indiana; Ironwood, Michigan; Milwaukee; and Cleveland and Steubenville, Ohio. Only six years later, in 1912, the Alliance had expanded to include 149 local groups in eight states: Pennsylvania, Indiana, Michigan, Ohio, Wisconsin, New York, Massachusetts, and Connecticut. In 1918, the year World War I ended, the PWA of A had grown to include 281 groups, a nearly five fold increase since 1906.

Individual membership in the Alliance also rose considerably, from 4,302 in 1906, to 10,930 in 1912, to 21,109 in 1918. The organization's financial position improved even more dramatically, from $15,085 in 1906 to $99,314 in 1912. In 1918, at its twelfth *sejm* in Detroit, the fraternal's assets stood at $374,895.

Here, the success of the Polish Women's Alliance of America paralleled the growth of the male-led Polonia fraternals such as the Polish National Alliance and the Polish Roman Catholic Union. This underscored the increasingly important role played by these organizations in the ethnic community. It should be kept in mind that the expansion of the PNA, the PRCUA, and the other Polish fraternals was largely the result of their decision to admit women in the face of the PWA of A challenge. In short, the Polish Women's Alliance of America, by its very existence and success, was a catalyst in the expansion of Polonia's organizational life.

Within the top leadership of the Alliance, there arose a continuing and robust rivalry between its two highest officers, Anna Neumann and Stefania Chmielinska. Their differences and those of their partisans left the organization almost evenly divided for the next fifteen years. Already by 1904 the lines had been drawn with the rivalry played out at each successive biannual convention until 1918, when Neumann decided not to seek another term as president and Chmielinska opted against seeking that office. (From 1918 until 1927 conventions were held every three years, and since then every four years.)

At the 1906 *sejm* in Chicago, Chmielinska's supporters complained about Neumann's work during her two terms as president. Newmann then declared she would not run for reelection, and Chmielinska was elected without opposition. But Chmielinska received only 81 votes, although 125 delegates were present. In 1908, Chmielinska defeated Neumann at the seventh *sejm* in Cleveland, this time by a 67 to 46 margin. However, at the eighth *sejm* in Milwaukee, Neumann turned the tables, this time winning over Chmielinska by a 71 to 58 margin. Neumann was then reelected at South Bend in 1912, this time by a more pronounced vote of 103 to 79. In South Bend, there were spirited contests for most of the elective offices in the Alliance, with Vice President Maria Wejna losing to Jadwiga Pawelkiewicz by seven votes, 76 to 69, and third-place candidate Maria Rokosz garnering another 36 votes. Treasurer Leokadia Kadów was reelected over Łucja Wołowska, 104 to 81. Only in the election for secretary was there a lopsided result; here the dynamic, thirty-year-old American-born Emilia Napieralska easily won a second term, with 148 votes to the combined 39 votes cast for two challengers.

After her 1912 defeat, Chmielinska gave up her presidential ambitions and focused her efforts on the vice presidency. In 1914, she lost her bid for this office but by a scant two votes, 98 to 96. A third candidate won 42 votes; it was not until much later that the PWA of A changed its by-laws to require run-offs if no candidate won a majority of the votes cast in the first round. But in 1916 and 1918 she did win this office and thus Chmielinska served on the same board with Neumann, who ran unopposed for the presidency in both 1914 and 1916. Neumann's victories testified at least in part to her stature as the Alliance's prime spokesperson during the World War I years and her close collaboration with virtuoso pianist and patriot Ignacy Paderewski.

Neumann's standing with Paderewski had fbeen established by her decisive support of his work at a New York meeting of Polonia fraternal leaders soon after the war's outbreak in 1914. There, she and her colleagues heard Paderewski's appeal for financial support for the Polish cause. While the others responded that they could not act immediately without the approval of their boards and declined to commit their organizations' funds to the appeal, Neumann boldly declared that the Polish Women's Alliance of America was willing, there and then, to commit the substantial sum of three thousand dollars to the cause. It was then that the admiring Paderewski made a statement which is still recalled with pride in the Alliance. "Women aren't content to advise" he declared. "They act" (*Kobiety nie radzą, a czynią*). The Alliance's general administration affirmed Neumann's support upon her return to Chicago.

With Neumann's retirement in 1918 and Chmielinska's in 1921, the heroic era in the history of the Polish Women's Alliance of America came to a close. The torch was passed to a representative of the younger generation, the dynamic and articulate Napieralska. An irresistible force in the organization, she was elected president in Detroit by a 154 to 35 margin. Neumann and Chmielinska, meanwhile, continued to contribute to the work of the Alliance. Perhaps the greatest praise for their service was that PWA of A membership was reported at the 1921 convention to be 24,680, including 1,422 insured children. The fraternal's assets stood at $584,206, with 308 local groups to be counted in its ranks.

Any review of the early years of the PWA of A must recognize the magnitude of the achievements of its founders in establishing the first independent women's mass membership organization in American Polonia. The first generation of PWA of A members – patriotic nationalists, equal rights feminists, believers in the value of education, and women committed to playing genuine leadership roles in their community – would even in ordinary circumstances have merited great recognition.

But the years after 1900 were hardly ordinary times. In the United States, the era was marked by economic change and turmoil, the first flowering of the automobile revolution and with it the assembly line, the country's rapid industrialization, the mushrooming of the cities (and with them the growth of the slums), the rise of Broadway, and the birth of mass culture in music, dance, and movies. On the international level, the United States was emerging as a major power, something that was suddenly obvious following its almost effortless military victory in the Spanish-American War of 1898. Within a few years America had become an imperial republic with far-flung territories such as Hawaii, the Philippine Islands, Puerto Rico, and Alaska, and a prestige built on its success in the construction of the Panama Canal and the actions of its leader, President Theodore Roosevelt, in mediating the settlement of the Russo-Japanese War in 1906.

No less significant a measure of America's new global standing and the attractiveness of its way of life was the explosion of immigration to this country that peaked in the first decade of the twentieth century. Immigration exceeded one million persons almost every year in the decade up to the outbreak of the war in 1914; this figure would not be surpassed until the 1990s, when the country's population was three times greater.

Yet, the poverty of millions of Americans and the venality of the country's politics were increasingly serious problems. Reform-minded "muckrakers" attacked the excesses of the rich and the injustices suffered by the underpaid working class. One of the more famous authors was Upton Sinclair, who in 1906 published *The Jungle,* a hair-raising account of the maltreatment of Polish and other eastern European immigrant workers in Chicago's stockyards.

At the same time, America's political life was altered dramatically when President William McKinley was assassinated in 1901 and succeeded by Vice President Theodore Roosevelt. T. R. was nothing like his predecessor – in temperament or in agenda, despite their common membership in the Republican Party. Roosevelt enthusiastically championed workers' rights, as in his support in 1902 of the strike by Pennsylvania's coal miners, many of them Polish immigrants, for union recognition, a living wage, and better working conditions. He pushed through congressional passage of the Pure Food and Drug Act to protect consumers from being poisoned by what they ate and drank. He opposed the power of the great financial and industrial monopolies and backed government programs to preserve the nation's environment. In short, Theodore Roosevelt and his supporters ushered in a new politics for the country, a progressive politics that strenuously championed the principles of governmental reform and social justice.

Progressive ideas took hold, and by the presidential elections of 1912, no fewer than three significant candidates were actively presenting their competing versions of reform to the electorate. The Democratic Party's nominee was Thomas Woodrow Wilson; Roosevelt campaigned as an insurgent "Bull Moose" Progressive; and the Social Democratic party's standard bearer was trade unionist Eugene Debs. Together they won more than 76 percent of the popular vote, with Wilson gaining the presidency, Roosevelt at his heels, the conservative Republican presidential incumbent William Howard Taft finishing a poor third, and Debs receiving a million votes – 6 percent of the total cast and the largest share his movement would ever win in a presidential election.

The progressive era also witnessed the full flowering of the women's rights movement in America. This movement had taken shape as the National Woman Suffrage Association in 1869 under the leadership of Susan B. Anthony and Elizabeth Cady Stanton. By 1910, after a series of mergers with other women's organizations including the Women's Christian Temperance Union, coupled with the support it had gained from sympathetic labor and political groups, the renamed National American Woman Suffrage Association claimed more than seventy-five thousand members around the country. In the years immediately after, the suffrage movement, now under the leadership of Carrie Chapman Catt, succeeded in linking its aim of winning women's right to vote with patriotic support for America's cause in World War I. In 1919, after decades of effort and disappointment, the suffragettes and their allies at last won congressional approval of a constitutional amendment giving women the right to vote in federal elections and to hold national office. A year later, the nineteenth amendment was ratified. Ironically, the achievement of this goal signaled an end to the Progressive era.

All these issues had their effects upon the Polish immigration to the United States, and among its women members too. Women's rights, unionization, and the struggle for better wages and working conditions could not help but be of concern. These issues, moreover, all found their place in the pages of *Głos Polek*, the organ of the PWA of A. But also dramatic in its impact on Polonia and the Polish Women's Alliance of America was the outbreak of World War I.

The Polish Women's Alliance of America had from its inception been committed to the cause of partitioned Poland's restoration to unity and independence. At the first PWA of A *sejm* in 1900, the convention delegates instituted a kind of monthly tax on the membership for the purpose of raising money for the Polish National Fund based in Switzerland. At its second *sejm*, the delegates approved a resolution placing the Alliance firmly in the camp of the patriotic wing of Polonia: "Just as the Polish National Alliance composed of our brothers renders great services to the patriotic cause," they declared, "so also the Polish Women's Alliance, with all Polish women in its ranks will, perhaps, render similar services to our Motherland on this foreign soil" (of America).

In 1904, during the war between tsarist Russia and the Japanese empire, a conflict many in Polonia dreamed might provide the Polish provinces under Russian control with the chance to win back their independence, the leaders of the PWA of A sent a message to the Japanese ambassador to the United States. In it they expressed their support for his country's victory over Russia. The PWA of A was conspicuous in its involvement in manifestations in Chicago on behalf of the pro-independence rebellion in Russian-ruled Poland that broke out during the Russo-Japanese war, although this issue was a bone of contention within the immigrant community. On one side were those who sympathized with Józef Piłsudski and his followers, people like socialist activist Aleksander Dębski. They favored revolutionary action against the embattled tsarist authorities. On the other side stood the partisans of Roman

Dmowski, leader of the Polish National Democratic movement, who argued against rebellion and in favor of loyalty to Russia – in return for the grant of greater autonomy for Poland after the war.

The debate was a difficult one and it resurfaced in World War I between the two leaders and their backers. For the PWA of A, devotion to the independence cause created an added dilemma. Though they favored Poland's freedom, the Alliance's members could not easily accept the violence of a rebellion that was particularly destructive to the women and children of the homeland.

Another opportunity to manifest solidarity with the independence cause came in May 1910, when a sizable delegation of activists from the Polish Women's Alliance of America attended the three-day-long Polish National Congress in Washington, D.C. This gathering took place immediately after the dedication of the new Kościuszko and Pułaski monuments in the nation's capital. The ceremonies were carried out in the presence of President William Howard Taft. Taking part in the historic congress were no fewer than eleven PWA of A members: President Stefania Chmielinska; Vice President Jadwiga Pawelkiewicz; Treasurer Leokadia Kadów; Directors Stanisława Szeszycka, Teofila Śniegocka, Maria Baranowska, Maria Perłowska, and Julia Gronkiewicz; Medical Examiner Dr. Maria Olgiert-Kaczorowska, past president Anna Neumann, and former treasurer Aniela Tomaszewska.[7]

Soon after the Washington meeting, another patriotic gathering was held, this one in the city of Kraków in the Austrian-ruled zone of partitioned Poland. The occasion was the five hundredth anniversary of the great Polish-Lithuanian victory over the Teutonic knights at the battle of Grunwald in 1410. This event

---

[7] Romuald Piątkowski, compiler and editor, *Pamiętnik wzniesienia i odsłonięcia pomników Tadeusza Kościuszki i Kazimierza Pułaskiego tudzież połączonego z tą uroczystością pierwszego kongresu narodowego Polskiego w Washingtonie, D. C.* (Memorial on the occasion of the unveiling of the monuments to Kościuszko and Pułaski and the first Polish national congress in Washington, D. C. Chicago: Polish National Alliance, 1911). Other PWA of A supported monuments to Kościuszko include those erected before 1910 in Chicago, Milwaukee, Buffalo, and Cleveland.

offered Poles from around the globe the extraordinary opportunity to come together to rekindle a new national resolve for independence in the face of foreign domination. Attending these ceremonies and viewing the unveiling of a new monument to the 1410 victory, one financed by Paderewski, were Honorata Wołowska, Dr. Maria Dowiatt-Sass, and Katarzyna Przykłocka. All came as representatives of the PWA of A and the Polish Falcons Alliance headquartered in Pittsburgh.

A stirring moment in Kraków involved the first performance of a new patriotic anthem, "*Rota*" (The oath), which had been commissioned for the occasion. Its words were written by Maria Konopnicka, the first honorary member of the Polish Women's Alliance of America; Feliks Nowowiejski composed the music. This haunting piece, so unlike Poland's two other anthems, the martial "*Jeszcze Polska Nie Zginęła*" and the religious "*Boże Coś Polskę,*" in both tone and message, testified to the Poles' grim resolve to preserve their nationhood in the face of imperial Germany's ruthless colonization and forced assimilation policies: "We'll hold our land, our fathers' land, we'll hold true to our language. Our children shall not be German, for this is Polish soil. We'll keep our precious, holy sod; do help us now, O God!"

In December 1912 PWA of A leaders were again highly visible participants in the patriotic cause. This time the occasion was the reunification of the Polish Falcons movement in Pittsburgh, an event played out before an audience of Polonia leaders representing some thirty-five organizations. Immediately after the reunification convention, all present set to work to establish a new federation in support of the independence cause.

This daylong conference also ended well, at least initially, and out of it came the first nationwide Polonia political action organization to include practically all wings of the large, disparate, and often contentious community. This organization was the Polish National Defense Committee, *Komitet Obrony Narodowej*, or *KON*. *KON* was not the first such effort at federation, of course. Indeed, the list of earlier but unsuccessful attempts to unite Polonia had included the Organization of Poles in America in 1873, the Polish National Alliance in 1880, the Polish League in 1894, and the Polish

National Congress in 1910, as well as a series of clergy-led efforts from the 1890s on. All had failed to raise a tent big enough to include all the major component groups in a community that had grown to four million people of Polish origin by 1914. Factionalism and ideology divided an ethnic community that included patriotic organizations; Catholic institutions and those that were critical of the Church; those that were avowedly secular; the politically conservative, liberal, and socialist; the widely disparate and contentious Polish press; and, of course, women's organizations.

KON ambitiously aimed at overcoming these rivalries. From the start it supported those political groups inside partitioned Poland that favored direct military action in the near future on behalf of the reunification and independence causes. This allied *KON* with groups identified with Józef Piłsudski, as opposed to his rival and nemesis, Roman Dmowski. But given the popularity of Dmowski's views in Polonia, *KON*'s status as a universally accepted federation would be brief.

In June 1913, at its first plenary meeting in Chicago, the Catholic organizations withdrew from *KON*, ostensibly because of their opposition to its admission of the schismatic Polish National Catholic Church. But this was little more than an excuse for Dmowski's supporters to exit *KON*. Soon after they regrouped to establish the Polish National Council, or *Rada Narodowa*, a federation headed by the Very Rev. Paul Rhode, the first Roman Catholic bishop of Polish origin in America. At the time of his election, Rhode was an auxiliary bishop in Chicago; from 1915 until his death in 1943 he was bishop of the diocese of Green Bay, Wisconsin.

In December 1912 in Pittsburgh, the Polish Women's Alliance of America had been represented by President Anna Neumann, Secretary General Emilia Napieralska, and Treasurer Leokadia Kadów. Neumann was asked to serve on *KON*'s provisional executive committee. Both Neumann and Napieralska were also appointed to the federation's fifteen-member temporary board of directors based in Chicago.

Following the Catholic groups' June 1913 walkout, the fraternal organizations still in *KON* were left in a quandary.

Initially, the PNA, the Polish Falcons, and the Polish Women's Alliance of America did stick with *KON*. But these mainstays of Polonia's patriotic wing were increasingly uncomfortable with controversial activists like Aleksander Dębski, head of the Polish Socialist Alliance, and Bishop Francis Hodur of the Polish National Catholic Church. Over the next few months, all three groups disassociated themselves from *KON* and each set up its own fundraising vehicle to support independence. For its part the PWA of A established a *Fundusz Bojowy* (battle fund) and collected several thousand dollars under its auspices.

Throughout this period the PWA of A, despite the ties its leaders maintained with both the Catholic Church and Polonia's patriotic wing, worried that any military action taken in Poland would lead to violence and suffering, with women and children the main victims. Thus it had little choice but to pull back from *KON*'s agenda. All the same, when war broke out in summer 1914, with the Polish lands the killing ground upon which the armies of the empire of Russia battled those of Germany and Austria-Hungary, the Alliance strongly reaffirmed its devotion to the independence cause. At the same time, its leaders worked to organize Polonia's women on behalf of the war's growing list of victims. Its humanitarian agenda would be very important for the Polish Women's Alliance of America throughout the conflict.

A powerful expression of the PWA of A's patriotic stance came as early as September 1914 in a resolution adopted at a rally held at the time of the Alliance's tenth *sejm* in Chicago. Significantly, however, the resolution also emphasized Polonia's duty to contribute to Poland's relief. At this convention, the Alliance underscored its commitment to these causes in various ways; one was to cancel its main banquet and earmark the funds set aside for that event to the relief cause.

More boldly, delegates took the important step of approving a proclamation pledging their support for a free Poland and urging members to contribute to the cause:

> We Polish Women, meeting as representatives
> of the groups of the Polish Women's Alliance in

America from around this country, together with women of the Polish community of the Chicago area, at this general meeting in the national headquarters of the Polish Women's Alliance, after due reflection about the most vital question before us, that of Poland's freedom, proclaim and assert the following:

We solemnly declare that we have never recognized and do not recognize now the wrongful suppression of the Polish nation, its rights, nor the deprivation of Poland's independence and freedom.

We further state, that never will we cease to aspire through our labors and efforts and our means and capabilities to work for the absolute freedom and sovereignty of Poland.

Further, we solemnly declare that we will never be sympathetic with anyone, nor will we think to support anyone connected with any of the present belligerent powers fighting in Poland, neither Austria, which originated the idea of partitioning Poland, nor Russia, nor the traitorous Germans, who have through the past century done so much harm to the Polish nation, and who sing about *Ausrotten.*"

Further, we resolve and commit ourselves to mobilizing our national energy and using every appropriate occasion to present the Polish issue to the forum of world opinion, and first and foremost to join together in a constant effort to gather goods and moneys on behalf of the Polish people. There is a great need for money, money, and more money in order to combat the starvation and impoverishment that our brothers and sisters are suffering. It is our chief and most urgent obligation at the present time! Thus we call on everyone who is in a position to help, give quickly, give generously, and give now!

May our entire Polish people in America from every economic level take action. Now has come the time for deeds.   Let each do her sacred duty on behalf of her brothers and sisters. . . .

At the 1914 *sejm*, a telegram from Paderewski was read aloud calling on Polonia to raise a force of twenty thousand volunteers for military service in Europe against the Teutonic foe. At the time his idea seemed impractical and premature. No means existed to carry out the recruitment of Polish volunteers, especially given America's neutrality in the conflict.   Nevertheless, Paderewski's words were enthusiastically received. Soon after, an effort was initiated to prepare for such a mobilization. Although it initially came to nothing, a Polish military force from the United States was established in 1917 following America's entry into the war.

The last official act of the 1914 convention involved the approval of a series of resolutions setting forth the fraternal's future aims. These included a call for cooperation among Polonia's organizations in support of Polish independence and an appeal to set aside partisan and personal animosities. The press in particular was urged to avoid paying unwarranted attention to differences that could only undermine Polonia's sought-after solidarity.

With the European conflict only weeks old, the Alliance had defined two major roles for itself. One was to collect relief aid to Poland's war victims. The second was to emphasize the PWA of A's image as the voice of solidarity within Polonia in its service to independence. To achieve this second aim, the Alliance began regularly hosting meetings of Polonia organizational representatives at its home office. Both in World War I and again in World War II, the hospitable home of the Polish Women's Alliance of America became the most frequently selected location for gatherings of an all-Polonia character. This could not help but enhance the reputation of the Alliance as a nonpartisan supporter of solidarity within the sprawling and often contentious immigrant and ethnic community.

On October 2, 1914, soon after the adjournment of the PWA of A *sejm*, representatives of the main Polonia fraternals and the clergy met at the Alliance's headquarters. There they organized an all-Polonia federation they named the Polish Central Relief Committee (*Polski Centralny Komitet Ratunkowy, PCKR*). Its aim was to rally the Polish population in the United States on behalf of Poland's humanitarian needs.

At the same time, the PWA of A's political efforts through its *Fundusz Bojowy* gathered momentum. The delegates at the Alliance convention agreed to impose a monthly tax of five cents on all members in support of the fund. Within a year, nearly $14,000 had been collected.

A number of PWA of A activists from around the country came to assume leadership roles in their communities. In Pennsylvania, Honorata Wołowska led the way; in Ohio, much was accomplished under the inspired direction of Dr. Frances Konrad Filipiak, a longtime activist in the Alliance. In June 1915, Madame Helena Paderewska's appeal for assistance to Poland's children inspired a great response from the Alliance's members. The pages of *Głos Polek* were also used extensively, both to paint a picture of war-devastated Poland for the paper's readers and to mobilize the fraternal's relief activities.

Relief work continued throughout the war and took several forms. One was to organize fundraising campaigns, both at the local group and national levels and in conjunction with other institutions, such as the church and the *PCKR*. A second was to gather and produce goods for shipment to occupied Poland, itself no easy feat given the naval blockade that continued throughout the conflict. PWA of A members and their friends stitched sweaters, scarves, mittens, stockings, and bandages. Everything else of use was accepted and shipped whenever this could be arranged. While the total amount and value of the goods gathered by the PWA of A and by the entire Polonia are not known, they were undoubtedly enormous and involved thousands of hours of voluntary labor.

The Alliance was active on the political front too. An early demonstration of its concerns came in spring 1915 when Secretary General Emilia Napieralska traveled to The Hague, capital of the Netherlands, to attend the Women's International Peace Congress. That organization had been formed by Jane Addams (1860 ! 1935) the internationally respected founder of Hull House in Chicago, one of America's earliest and most influential privately supported immigrant welfare agencies.

Napieralska's voyage was a perilous one. Indeed, only a few days after her arrival in Europe, a German submarine torpedoed and sunk the British steamship *Lusitania*; 1,198 passengers (128 of them Americans) lost their lives in this tragedy. At the peace congress, Napieralska marched to the podium, carrying an American flag in one hand and the Polish colors in the other. In her remarks (full copies of which, unfortunately, are not to be found), she forthrightly took issue with the agenda of the congress' organizers. A surviving fragment of her remarks indicates the tenor of her views:

> There will be no peace on earth, nor can there be peace, whatever its cost, so long as the downtrodden nations that are held in bondage cannot gain their liberty. There can be no peace so long as a dismembered Poland is forced to sacrifice its finest people, individuals who must serve in the armies of our three warring oppressors. There can be no peace so long as Poland is prevented from joining the community of nations in freedom and independence.[8]

Significantly, a resolution recognizing the substance of the concerns Napieralska expressed was approved at the peace congress. Moreover, when a delegation of leaders from the congress later visited the PWA of A home office in Chicago to appeal for its leaders' support for "peace at any price," President Neumann and her fellow officers reiterated to them the same view

---

[8] Emilia Napieralska, "*Historya Związku Polek w Strzeszczeniu,*" in *Związek Polek w Ameryce, 1898 – 1923: Pamiętnik Jubileuszowy* "A history of the Polish Women's Alliance in summary," in The Polish Women's Alliance of America, 1898 – 1923: A silver anniversary album) (Chicago: Polish Women's Alliance of America, 1923), p. 11. Napieralska's words generated a very favorable response from some of the leaders of the congress. See Emily Balch's words in Jane Addams *et al, Women at the Hague: The International Congress of Women and its Results* (New York: Macmillan, 1915), pp. 119 – 121.

that Napieralska had espoused. Clearly, the Alliance sympathized with the noble aim of ending the war as soon as possible. But the organization could not in good conscience support the cause of a peace achieved without justice for the oppressed peoples, especially the people of Poland.

The PWA of A general administration then went ahead to authorize a public statement defining the fraternal's position. This statement was sent to the president of the United States, the Holy Father in Rome, and to government officials in America and abroad. In it, the Alliance again repudiated the "propaganda" of peace at any price and called for a peace settlement that would bring freedom and justice to the oppressed people of Poland:

> Create a peace for the world, but a new kind of peace lasting and holy – not as heretofore founded on injury, misery and violence, on the breaking of laws and enslaving the weaker nations. Such a peace must be compensated for by the bloodiest wars, oceans of fire, smoke and annihilation. Create a new peace, a peace that will declare to all the world that violence and injury are no more, a peace that will hail a new world order. Such a kind of peace, founded on humanity and justice, will honor law and order and promote the happiness of all humankind. It will end strife and violence among cultured nations and will for all time stop the cruel torture of the weaker by the stronger.

> We, the daughters of a nation whose freedom was seized by force and most brutal violence, what was in reality a robbery in broad daylight, with one united voice protest with all our souls against the false peace activity whose ultimate aim is "peace at any price."[9]

---

[9] In Frank Renkiewicz, compiler and editor, *The Poles in America, 1608 to 1972. A Chronology and Fact Book* (Dobbs Ferry, NY: Oceana Publications, 1973), pp. 82 – 83 and in Karłowicz, *Historia Związku Polek* pp. 93 – 94.

In the United States, the PWA of A stance won favorable responses from various government leaders, and President Wilson was informed of its contents. Soon afterward, Wilson issued a proclamation that January 1, 1916, be set aside for the collection of donations for Polish relief. Once gathered, these monies were to be expended under the auspices of the International Red Cross organization.

In August 1916 the Great War in Europe entered its third year with no end to the carnage in sight, and the United States doing its best to maintain its neutrality. In November 1916 Wilson won reelection with the campaign slogan "He Kept Us Out of War." At this point, the leaders of the Polish Central Relief Committee, with President Neumann concurring, decided it was a good time to establish a political action subcommittee to present the Polish case to America. This subcommittee, known as the Polish National Department (*Wydział Narodowy*), was headed by John Smulski, a respected Chicago Polonia leader, banker, and politician.[10]

Smulski possessed excellent political contacts in Washington, D.C., and enjoyed a solid working relationship with Paderewski, by then the representative of Dmowski's Polish Committee headquartered in France. That body was already acting as a kind of provisional government in exile on behalf of a Polish state that did not yet exist. Its members remained confident, however, that their cause would soon win the official backing of Britain and France.

The creation of the Polish National Department signaled the true beginnings of the politicizing of the independence issue in Polonia. That November, only three months after the department's formation, the governments of Germany and Austria-Hungary issued a joint proclamation promising an autonomous postwar Polish state linked to them in return for broad Polish support in

---

[10] On the Polish Central Relief Committee, the Polish National Department, and other World War I Polonia organizations, see Donald E. Pienkos, *For Your Freedom through Ours: Polish American Efforts on Poland's Behalf, 1863 – 1991* (New York and Boulder: Columbia University Press and Eastern European Monographs, 1991), pp. 53 – 63.

their struggle against tsarist Russia. Presumably, this state was to be carved mainly from the Polish territories under Russian rule prior to the war, lands that had come under German and Austrian occupation during the conflict.

The National Department echoed Dmowski's position in support of the British-French-Russian allied cause and repudiated the German-Austrian proposal. Polonia's aim, its leaders maintained, was that their victory alone would result in an independent, reunited, and democratic postwar Poland.

Things changed dramatically in 1917 as a result of two major developments. In March the tsar was forced to abdicate his throne in the face of growing popular discontent with his failed leadership of Russia's war effort. In the months that followed, the reeling empire experienced a crisis that caused its military defeat. In November, the capital of St. Petersburg was seized by revolutionaries calling for the creation of a Bolshevik communist regime. Led by Vladimir Ilyich Lenin, the Bolsheviks sought an immediate end to Russia's involvement in the war and were willing even to accept the loss of the empire's western provinces, including Poland, to terminate the conflict, at least for the time being. Given this radically changed situation, France and Britain were for the first time free to formally agree to Dmowski's position and support the restoration of a postwar Polish state.

A second development involved America's entry into the conflict in April as an ally of Britain and France. This move had particular relevance for the Polish cause in that President Wilson was already on record in favoring the right of independence for the nationalities under foreign domination throughout Eastern Europe.

The president's most explicit statement on Poland's behalf, influenced by the persuasive words of Paderewski, would come later, on January 18, 1918. That day, Wilson presented his "Fourteen Points" speech outlining America's goals in fighting the war. Point thirteen declared that "an independent Polish state should be erected which should include the territories inhabited by indisputably Polish populations, which should be assured free and secure access to the sea, and whose political and economic independence and territorial integrity should be guaranteed by covenant."

America's entry into the conflict proved decisive; less than twenty months after Congress's declaration of war an armistice was reached with the heads of the exhausted German empire. On the same day, November 11, 1918, Józef Piłsudski declared Poland's independence in Warsaw. After 123 years of foreign dominion over its partitioned lands, Poland had been restored.

Polonia's part in the U.S. war effort and in Poland's rebirth was a real, if generally unacknowledged one. Between 190,000 and 300,000 Polish Americans volunteered or were drafted for military duty in a U.S. military force of two million, a fraction that was far higher than the proportion of Poles in America, which was then about three percent of the country's population. Whatever the exact numbers may be, it is obvious that as a body, young men of Polish origin and extraction displayed extraordinary devotion to their adopted homeland.

Further, when Poles were permitted to form their own contingents in order to participate in a distinct Polish army under the authority of Dmowski's national committee, more than 38,000 did so. Over 22,000 of them saw active duty, first in France in 1918, then in Poland in 1919 to 1920. Known as the Blue Army (*Armja Błękitna*) after the distinctive color of their members' uniforms, this force operated under the command of General Józef Haller in France and Poland as part of an international fighting force of nearly one hundred thousand Poles from North and South America, Britain, France, Belgium, and the French prisoner-of-war camps.

The organizations of Polonia, largely through the *Wydział Narodowy*, lobbied hard in Washington and did their best to mobilize the members of the American Polish community in support of the independence cause. In August 1918 the *Wydział Narodowy* successfully organized a massive convention of Polonia organizations, or *Sejm Wychodźstwa*, to further manifest their concerns for Poland to U.S. government leaders. The convention, held in Detroit, brought together more than nine hundred delegates who attended as representatives from fraternal organizations, parishes, business, cultural, labor, and the press from around the land.

Both Paderewski and Dmowski addressed the conclave. Each praised Polonia for its many wartime activities for Poland. Looking ahead, Paderewski appealed for Polonia to initiate a ten million dollar fund drive to support the work of rebuilding the postwar Polish independent state. Eventually more than five million dollars were collected in this drive, but the end of the war only ten weeks after the *sejm* took the wind out of the effort's sails.

Many members of the Polish Women's Alliance of America attended the *Sejm Wychodźstwa*, including its corps of national officers. President Neumann was named to a seat on the executive board of the National Department in the elections that were held at the gathering.

PWA of A officers and activists also played salient roles in recruiting young men for the Blue Army and young women for two new groups of volunteer nurses working in war-ravaged Poland. One of these, the Gray Samaritans, was created to help organize and distribute relief assistance after the war. A second, the Polish White Cross, was assigned initially to serve the medical needs of the Haller army. After arriving in Poland, they also became engaged in relief assistance on behalf of orphans and in providing hospital care.[11]

The twelfth Polish Women's Alliance of America convention in September 1918 witnessed the thirty-six-year old Napieralska's election to the presidency following Neumann's decision to retire. Although Napieralska demonstrated the same patriotic dedication and high energy level as her predecessor, the succession signaled a major changing of the guard for the Alliance. Twenty-two years

---

[11] Józef Orłowski, *Helena Paderewska w pracy narodowej i społecznej, 1914 - 1929* (Helena Paderewska's patriotic and social work for Poland, 1914 – 1929) (Chicago: privately published, 1929); Robert Szymczak, "An Act of Devotion: The Polish Gray Samaritans and the American Relief Effort in Poland, 1919 – 1921," *Polish American Studies* 43, no. 1 (1986): 13 – 36.

Neumann's junior in age, the American-born Napieralska was at ease as a public speaker in both the Polish and English languages.

With the war's end two months later, a distinctive period in the development of the PWA of A was also brought to a close. The Polish independence cause, which for the previous twenty years had occupied the attention of so many in Polonia, was seemingly realized, although the new Poland would be obliged to battle its various new neighbors for the next two years to settle its national borders.

And while some American Poles did return to their newly independent homeland, among them *Głos Polek* editor Stefania Laudyn-Chrzanowska, more than 95 percent chose to remain in America. Such a development might well have been expected, given the many millions of dollars Polish Americans had invested in U.S. liberty bonds. This was a far greater amount than what they donated to Polish relief and independence drives directed by Polonia's organizations. In the PWA of A alone, nearly $1.2 million in such bonds were sold to members from its home office.

The earliest motto of the Polish Women's Alliance of America, one adopted in the first decade of its operation and used throughout the war years, was simply *czyn,* a word that can be translated as action or service. One could hardly find a word more appropriate in describing what the PWA of A stood for in its first two heroic decades in peace and war, for this was a time when the organization grew from a few women in a single group to a fraternal society of twenty-one thousand members in 272 local groups in ten states around the country. Their efforts had made possible a weekly newspaper to carry forth the Alliance's message and an education department that succeeded in deepening awareness of the Polish heritage in the larger community. Moreover, the PWA of A had evolved into a solid business enterprise, one with assets of nearly $400,000.

GROWTH AND CHALLENGES:

THE NAPIERALSKA AND WOŁOWSKA PRESIDENCIES 1918 – 1947

We are moving forward, always with good will, and always with a loving spirit towards our fellow fraternal organizations, towards the entire society of which we are part, towards the ideals that are the foundation of the beloved Polish republic, and our own country, the wonderful United States of America. We, activists of Polish birth and Polish extraction, are moving forward and we will remove the thorns of destructive discord, bringing near to ourselves the fruits of our constructive work.

Emilia Napieralska, 1923

I ask sincerely of all of you, my sisters of the Polish Women's Alliance, that you give yourselves over to honest, sincere work together. Without fraternal cooperation among us, our best and most noble intentions will come to nothing.

Honorata Wołowska, 1935[1]

The war's end in November 1918 coincided with Poland's rebirth as an independent state and, almost precisely, with the beginning of a new regime in the Polish Women's Alliance of America. It was one headed by a thirty-six-year-old Chicago-born activist of Polish and Czech parentage named Emilia Napieralska. Despite her youth, Napieralska was already a seasoned veteran of the Alliance, having joined the movement in 1901, a year after its first national convention.

---

[1] Napieralska's words appear in Napieralska, *Związek Polek w Ameryce*, 1898 – 1923, p. 17; Wołowska's are from her presidential acceptance speech in 1935, quoted in Karłowicz, *Historia Związku Polek* p. 158.

In 1910 Napieralska was elected national secretary of the PWA of A at the age of twenty-eight. Her victory showed that she was already a powerful force in the organization. During World War I, she rose to new prominence, representing the PWA of A and Polonia at meetings with President Woodrow Wilson in the White House. She was an assertive, eloquent spokeswoman for the Alliance at the Women's International Peace Conference in the Netherlands, where she made an impassioned and dramatic address on behalf of Poland's independence. Still later, in August 1918, she took an active part in the proceedings of the massive Congress of the Polish Emigration in Detroit that proclaimed Polonia's identification with Poland's independence, as personified by Paderewski and Dmowski.

In some ways, Napieralska was the ideal PWA of A leader. Young, intelligent, attractive, she was a dynamic public speaker who could express herself fluently in both English and Polish, this at a time when many leaders of the Polish American community were still "fish out of water" when called to speak publicly in the English language.[2]

Napieralska represented well the progressive spirit that infected the Polish Women's Alliance of America. Indeed it would not be until 1928, ten years after she was first elected president, that another major Polonia organization would be headed by a person born in America. This occurred when the Polish Roman Catholic Union fraternal elected John Olejniczak of Indiana as its president. Similarly, the first American-born president of the Polish National Alliance, Charles Rozmarek of Pennsylvania, did not assume office until 1939. In the case of the Polish Falcons of America, its first American-born president, Walter Laska, did not take the reins of leadership until 1952.

Napieralska possessed a considerable commitment to public service. She was also an avid traveler, both throughout America and Poland, and organized the first formal PWA of A's sponsored

---

[2] Napieralska was already recognized for her work and leadership skills by an observant reporter from Milwaukee's Polish language daily who was covering the 1906 PWA of A convention. The meeting was a stormy one, and the then twenty-four year old Napieralska won high grades for her grace under fire as its recording secretary. *Kuryer Polski*, July 1, 1906.

trips to the homeland in the 1920s. Her travel interests were also a target for criticism, because of her frequent absences from the home office. To such comments Napieralska would reply that the Polish Women's Alliance of America was a growing organization and required dynamic leadership to promote its development.

A look at the condition of the Alliance, especially in the first decade of Napieralska's administration, shows that the fraternal did indeed enjoy a period of rather spectacular growth. This was only reversed by the onset of the Depression in 1929. [3]

The Expansion of the Polish Women's Alliance of America, 1918 – 1931

Date	Adult Members	Youth Members	Groups	Assets
1918	21,109	None	272	$ 277,975
1931	52,717	12,604	657	$3,090,207

As shown in the table above, never prior to Napieralska's presidency had the PWA of A achieved such dramatic success in sustained growth. Yet when Napieralska left office in 1935, it was under a welter of criticism about the decline in membership, even though this was a problem that was hardly unique to the Alliance. All Polish fraternals suffered substantial membership losses because of massive unemployment that in many communities exceeded 25 percent, chronic underemployment, and sharp declines in real household income.

But during her glory years as president in the 1920s, Emilia Napieralska proved to be very much the leader in the America-centered Polonia life of the time. With Poland finally independent and seemingly off the ethnic community's agenda for the first time in decades, most members of the Polish community focused on improving their lives in America. The economic prosperity of the

---

[3] The PWA of A's record of growth (310 percent between 1918 and 1931) was even greater than that of the PNA, which rose 216 percent, from 133,000 to 287,000 members in roughly the same period and that of the PRCUA which rose 200 percent, from 85,000 to 169,000 members.

roaring twenties benefited many Polish Americans and helped make the primary objective of Polonia's fraternals the expansion of their memberships. Napieralska and her PWA of A colleagues proved very adept at this work.

At the same time, Napieralska's prominence during the war years gave her unassailable credentials as a leader in the still heavily immigrant community's patriotic activities. Significantly, in the 1920s she worked inventively to maintain the PWA of A's ties to the newly independent homeland. One idea was to head the first pilgrimage by the organization's members to Poland. This memorable tour of the "old country" took place in 1928 and was repeated a number of times in the following decade.

In America, Napieralska encouraged Alliance members to be proud of their heritage. An early opportunity to do this came in 1921 when Napieralska led the PWA of A effort to form a relationship with the renowned scientist Maria Skłodowska Curie on the occasion of her first visit to the United States. This effort was repeated in 1929 during the two-time Nobel laureate's second trip to America. In June 1921 Napieralska and Treasurer Łucja Wołowska traveled to New York to welcome Madame Curie on her arrival. They even went so far as to invite her to the PWA of A home office while she was in Chicago, an invitation that was, however, declined.[4]

Undeterred, Napieralska saw to it that the eminent scientist was made an honorary member of the Alliance. She arranged for a gift of one thousand dollars to be awarded by the general administration to Skłodowska Curie, to be used in purchasing a

---

[4] While Skłodowska Curie did visit Chicago in 1921, her appearances there were organized by the wives of prominent business and professional leaders. A Polish women's committee was involved with them and made a donation of $1,000 to support the research of the renowned scientist. On the committee were former PWA of A president Anna Neumann and past *Głos Polek* editor, Stefania Laudyn Chrzanowska. Krystyna Kabczynska, *et al.*, editors, *Korespondencja Polska Marii Skłodowskiej-Curie: 1881 – 1934* (The Polish correspondence of Maria Skłodowska Curie: 1881 – 1934. Warsaw: *Instytut Historii Nauki* P. A. N., 1994), pp. 160 – 161, 163 – 165, for Napieralska's July 2, 1921, letter to Skłodowska-Curie, the Polish Women's Committee invitation of May 21, 1921, to meet the Nobel Laureate during her June 15, 1921, visit to Chicago, and Skłodowska Curie's letter of thanks on July 29, 1929, to the PWA of A.

gram of radium for her future research. The scientist thanked the PWA of A for the gesture in a letter in which she declared that its gift would be used in her establishing a radiology clinic in Warsaw.

During her second trip to the United States in 1929, one specifically aimed at raising more research funds for her work, Skłodowska-Curie was again invited to Chicago to visit the PWA of A home office. This time, however, fatigue obliged her to cancel the entire trip to the Middle West; already the great scientist was experiencing the symptoms of the radium poisoning that would cause her death five years later at the age of sixty-seven. Once again, however, the PWA of A leadership approved a gift of one thousand dollars for another purchase of radium for her Warsaw radiology clinic.

A Madame Curie would in fact pay a visit to the Alliance's national headquarters. But this would come much later, in 1939, when Eve Curie, the Nobel laureate's daughter and biographer, paid her respects to the organization that had honored her mother.

Napieralska seemed constantly able to find new ways to promote the Alliance's mission. A look at the PWA of A silver jubilee album published in 1923 offers a good example of her efforts in this direction. On the cover of this publication is the fraternal's new emblem. The evocative design shows two women, one from America, the other from Poland, clasping hands. Between them is a shield vividly displaying the symbols of their two countries. In the background a bright sun heralds the new day for both lands. This stunning piece of artwork made a very favorable impression at the time and has continued to be used by the Polish Women's Alliance of America.[5]

At the 1927 PWA of A *sejm,* the delegates accepted a special banner as a gift from John Smulski, leader of the World War I-era Polish National Department. This banner included the organization's emblem and its name in both Polish and English. In 1931, at the Alliance's sixteenth convention in Washington, D. C.,

---

[5] The original banners used by the Polish Women's Alliance of America at patriotic and religious events had very much resembled the banner of the Polish National Alliance. The PWA of A's new emblem maintained its traditional patriotic focus while underscoring its character as an American and women's organization.

delegates approved a resolution to place a picture of the icon of the Częstochowa Madonna on the obverse side of its banner. In so doing, they asserted their identification with the Roman Catholic Christian religious tradition. Until this time, this orientation, while informally very deeply felt among the membership, had never been made explicit. Under Napieralska too, the motto of the Women's Alliance was also changed, from *Czyn,* (service) to *Bóg i Ojczyzna* (God and country).

Napieralska's presidency was marked by several other organizational moves that helped further strengthen the Alliance. Perhaps of greatest significance was the formation and expansion of its youth division. This not only meant an increase in the fraternal's membership, but it also opened up new avenues of activity for the organization at the local level.

The idea of a PWA of A youth division, or *Dział Małoletnich*, composed of youngsters under age fifteen, went far back in time. Indeed, the first youth circle of the Alliance, named *wianek* (garland) by local activists, was established in 1910 in the town of Ironwood, Michigan. Among its aims was the organizing of educational and cultural activities for youngsters, activities believed to be important in deepening their knowledge and interest in the Alliance later on.

In 1916 the Illinois legislature approved a bill allowing fraternal societies chartered in the state to enroll persons under age sixteen as insured members. The decision was greeted enthusiastically by PWA of A members; at the Alliance's eleventh convention later that same year, a resolution to create a youth division was approved.

Initially this resolution limited insured membership in the Alliance's youth division to the daughters or sisters of PWA of A members or to female minors under their guardianship. Youngsters admitted into the Alliance were assigned to the youth circle (*wianek*, the plural form is *wianki*) attached to the group to which their adult relatives belonged. During the early years of the program, membership was restricted to girls between the ages of eight and fifteen and juvenile members could only be insured for up to $100. These limits reflected the Alliance's concerns about childhood mortality and its financial implications for the fraternal.

The PWA of A youth division was approved at the Alliance's twelfth convention in Detroit in 1918. There, the rules for admission were considerably liberalized. Accordingly, girls between the ages of two and seventeen were made eligible for admission and for amounts of insurance rising to a maximum of five hundred dollars. These decisions contributed to the rapid growth of the Alliance over the next decade.

In 1921, 1,422 girls belonged to the PWA of A youth division, or 5.8 percent of the organization's membership. Already at this early date, forty-three *wianki* were in existence, one for every seven adult groups in the Alliance. By the fifteenth convention in 1927, some 248 groups (out of 479) possessed their own *wianki*. Some 6,708 youngsters belonged to the organization and comprised 15.5 percent of the total membership of 43,249. And despite the Depression's adverse effects on overall membership and on the number of youth circles, some 7,343 children and young teens remained in the *wianki* at the time of the Alliance's seventeenth convention in 1935. By then they accounted for 12.5 percent of the total membership of 58,616. Thereafter, while the number of *wianki* continued to raise, juvenile membership in the PWA of A declined for the next decade. It was only after World War II that the situation was reversed. One reason for the fall-off in the war years had to do with the entry of masses of women into the labor force, many for the first time, as replacements for young men entering the armed forces. The absence of younger women of Polish origin from the domestic scene was felt in the *wianki*, which depended on them as youth leaders.

A second initiative early in Napieralska's presidency involved the forming of local networks of PWA of A groups, units called *komisje* (councils) whose mission was to promote membership and fraternal life and *wianki* activities. In point of fact, the first council formed in Milwaukee in 1911, when five PWA of A groups agreed to work together more systematically to promote its activities in that city. Maria Kryszak, later the editor of *Głos Polek,* was elected to chair this first council. But until Napieralska's accession to the presidency in 1918, the Milwaukee experiment remained the only such body within the PWA of A.

Thereafter, between 1918 and 1935, twenty-five councils were formed. They were located in Pittsburgh (1919); Detroit, (1920); Buffalo, and Holyoke, Massachusetts (both in 1921); Cleveland, (1922); Hartford, (1923); Dunkirk, New York (1925); South Bend, Indiana (1927); St. Louis, (1928); Newark, and Niagara Falls, New York (both in 1930); Weirton, West Virginia, and Hamtramck, Michigan (both in 1931); East Chicago, Indiana (1932); Erie, Pennsylvania (1933); Philadelphia, (1934); and Omaha, (1935). In addition, six councils were formed in the Chicago area, in 1925, 1929, 1930, 1931, 1933, and 1935, with two others in eastern Pennsylvania in the Wilkes-Barre area (in 1921 and 1929). The councils not only stimulated the recruitment of new members but also offered valuable opportunities for leadership.

Believing that the Polish Women's Alliance of America ought to build more contacts with other American fraternals and in this way be better attuned to developments in the insurance industry as a whole, Napieralska promoted the Alliance's entry into the National Fraternal Congress in March 1922. Since then the PWA of A has remained a staunch participant in the NFCA, an umbrella association bringing together a wide variety of fraternal benefit societies – some based on their members' religious affiliation, others on the nationality principle, some large and even nationwide in scope, others regional or local in character. Over the years, Alliance members have been active in its organizational affairs, both at the national and state levels.

Through meetings and publications, the NFCA has greatly advanced the fraternal mission. Especially in the past two decades, the NFCA has kept its member organizations well informed about the many legal issues that affect their operations as not-for-profit associations.

The vitality of the Polish Women's Alliance of America during Napieralska's tenure was perhaps best demonstrated by the growth of the movement at the local level. In 1918, a total of 272 local PWA of A groups were in existence, half of which were located in the Chicago metropolitan area. While PWA of A groups also operated in nine other states as well (Connecticut, Indiana, Massachusetts, Michigan, Nebraska, New York, Ohio, Pennsylvania and Wisconsin), Illinois was home to 60 percent of the Alliance's local units.

A look at the Alliance twenty years later presents a much different picture (see table below). By then, the PWA of A was operating in fifteen states and the District of Columbia. Even more dramatically, the fraternal had grown to include 639 local groups, a 235 percent increase. And while the largest number of groups, 212, were located in Illinois in 1938, more than two-thirds of the groups in the Alliance were located in other states.

Number and Location of PWA of A Groups 1918 and 1938

	1918	1938	Rate of Increase (%)
Illinois	163	212	130
Pennsylvania	28	152	543
Wisconsin	22	26	118
Connecticut	14	29	207
Indiana	11	21	191
Ohio	11	21	191
New York	11	60	545
Michigan	9	57	633
Massachusetts	2	20	1000
Nebraska	1	5	500
New Jersey	-	23	
Missouri	-	6	
Maryland	-	3	
West Virginia	-	2	
California	-	1	
District of Columbia	-	1	
Total	**272**	**639**	**235**

Chicago's place in the PWA of A, while still dominant, was less significant by the late 1930s than it had been in the Alliance's first two decades. In 1938, 28 percent of all PWA of A groups (176) were located in the windy city, compared to 50 percent (136) in 1918. Moreover, in 1938, 55 percent of the groups (348) were in the Midwestern states of Illinois, Indiana, Wisconsin, Michigan,

Ohio, and Nebraska compared to 80 percent (217) twenty years earlier.

The growth in membership, combined with the Alliance's organizational expansion, gave rise to discussions about the need for a new and larger fraternal home office. These culminated at the sixteenth convention in 1931, when a proposal was approved to expand the existing national headquarters. This building which dated back to 1912, was deemed to be too small to serve the Alliance's current needs. The resulting expansion and remodeling of the facility was placed in the hands of a blue ribbon committee composed of the members of the general administration, joined by Illinois State President Anna Klarkowska, former vice president Angelina Milaszewicz, former director and vice president Stanisława Szeszycka, former directors Valeria Chojnacka and Clara Rybak, and local activists Maria Łagodzinska and Wanda Wleklinska.[6]

The project resulted in the quadrupling of the structure's original size, the addition of a fourth floor, and the refinishing of the facade in white marble. The completed renovation proved to be such a success that the modernized home office would satisfy the Alliance's needs for the next forty-six years.

The dedication ceremonies of April 30, 1933, were memorable and well attended. Presiding at the event, the Reverend Thaddeus Ligman expressed the hope that the remodeled home would serve to "deepen knowledge, understanding, respect, and a favorable opinion about the Polish cultural heritage." In later years, the Alliance's national office continued to serve, as it had in the past, as the locus for a multitude of major meetings and significant events in the Polish American community.

---

[6] Milaszewicz, vice president between 1914 and 1916 and again from 1921 – 1931, went on to serve as PWA of A Illinois state president from 1935 – 1943. Łagodzinska's daughter Adela was vice president of the Alliance from 1939 – 1947 and president from 1947 – 1971. Wleklinska came from a family with roots in the Alliance extending to its earliest years. On the building expansion project itself, see Karłowicz, *Historia Związku Polek*, pp. 145 – 151; *Pamiętnik Poświęcenia Domu w Czasie 35-tej Rocznicy, 30-go Kwietnia, 1933* (Memorial album covering the dedication of the home office at the time of the thirty-fifth anniversary, April 30, 1933) (Chicago: Polish Women's Alliance of America, 1933).

Napieralska and her colleagues and fellow officers began training their sights on a number of other matters that had been overshadowed in the past by the work for Poland. The new priorities involved strengthening the fraternal's financial base and expanding its insurance program.

The first of these dealt with a basic question, the pricing of PWA of A insurance, which, the Alliance was advised, was too low. This matter was brought to the delegates at the thirteenth convention in 1921; there they approved Napieralska's recommendation, made in the name of the general administration, to raise all insurance premiums to meet the requirements of the departments of insurance in the states where the fraternal was licensed. As a result, the PWA of A adopted the American Experience Table of Rates in setting its future insurance premiums.

This rating system, already followed by other associations, served as a persuasive reason for the Alliance to join the National Fraternal Congress, something it did in 1922. The rate increase itself was a modest one, only four cents for every hundred dollars of insurance held by each member. But it substantially strengthened the Alliance's financial base and helped it better meet the challenges of the "leaner years," which, it turned out, arrived with a vengeance in the Depression.

The rate increase was further justified by the Alliance's experience in 1918, when a nationwide influenza epidemic caused the deaths of more than one hundred members. The PWA of A managed to handle the extraordinary financial burdens these obligations placed upon its insurance program by requiring each of its groups to charge a temporary assessment on its members. But this action was only a provisional way to handle the problem.

A second change, this one on the products side of PWA of A operations, also came into effect during Napieralska's administration. In 1930 the Alliance received Illinois state authorization to offer a new plan of permanent life insurance. This plan, a twenty-year payment-benefit certificate, complemented the Alliance's traditional ordinary life insurance program, wherein a member paid insurance premiums throughout her lifetime. The new plan enabled the policy owner to fully pay for her insurance coverage over a period of twenty years.

In 1935 the delegates to the seventeenth convention went further and approved a new table of rates. The table, besides revising the cost of the twenty-year whole life insurance certificate, included a provision enabling the Alliance to offer another new plan of insurance as well. This was a seven-year term insurance policy, one that offered life insurance protection for a limited period of time.

These additions to the existing PWA of A program substantially broadened the fraternal's offerings to adult and child members. Since then these too have been modified, sometimes substantially, over the years.

Although different in certain respects from her predecessors, President Napieralska shared the same dedication to the fraternal's mission. As such she proved to be an ideal spokeswoman for the Alliance at a time when many Americans were turning away from the aims of the progressive era.

The socially oriented and reform-minded progressive movement peaked in 1919 and 1920 with the ratification of two amendments to the U. S. Constitution. These were the eighteenth, which prohibited the sale of alcoholic beverages, and the nineteenth, which gave women the vote. Ironically, these twin triumphs, both of which had long been advocated by the women's movement in America (and supported by many in the PWA of A), brought the progressive era to a speedy close. In like manner, Józef Piłsudski's declaration of Polish independence on November 11, 1918, the last day of World War I on the western front, brought a climax to the decades-long Polonia effort on behalf of freedom for the homeland. Thereafter, while Poland was left to resolve a mass of complex issues, among them the delineation of its contested national borders, the building of a stable political life in a polyglot society with no experience in democratic government, and the development of an economy after years of bitter conflict, independence was never seriously doubted after the decisive Polish victory in August, 1920 over the Bolshevik army at the Battle of Warsaw.

In the 1920s, new issues took center stage. On the international scene, the United States, after winning "the war to end all wars" to "make the world safe for democracy," rejected the very Versailles peace treaty that had been the handiwork of its own chief of state, Woodrow Wilson.   Further, when presidential elections were held in 1920, Wilson's Democratic party successor suffered a landslide defeat.   The message of the victorious Republican party standard-bearer, Warren G. Harding, was one of isolationism rather than engagement on the foreign policy front and a commitment to the vague but anti-progressive notion of "normalcy" at home.

To the extent that economic conditions in the 1920s gradually improved under Harding and his successor, Calvin Coolidge, the times were generally good for ordinary citizens.   New forms of mass entertainment became popular, among them radio features, athletic events, dance crazes, and talking motion pictures.   The prohibition of the sale of alcoholic beverages was widely criticized (and often ignored in immigrant communities like those inhabited by Polish Americans) and the controversial amendment was repealed in 1933.

For large numbers of working people, many of them immigrants and their offspring, incomes remained fairly stable in the 1920s even as the country reached "full employment" by 1927. At the same time, support for trade unionism as a means of winning better wages and working conditions waned considerably with the end of the progressive era.   (The union movement would not experience a revival until the passage of the Wagner Act in 1935.   This Depression-fighting legislation was an important element of the "New Deal" Democratic administration of Franklin Delano Roosevelt.)

Congress's action in 1921 approving a law to end "open immigration" from Europe to America was another sign of the new normalcy of the post progressive era.   Earlier attempts had been enacted to prohibit the immigration of criminals, anarchists, prostitutes, and the mentally infirm and physically handicapped, people from Asia, and other "undesirables".   But broad legislation to limit immigration had been derailed, either in Congress or by presidential vetoes.   Yet the new bill not only passed in Congress, it won the president's endorsement, an achievement that paved the way for even more far-reaching immigration restrictions in 1924.

The landmark Immigration Restriction Act of 1924, which remained on the books for forty-one years, was notable in two ways. It reinforced the 1921 law's annual limits on the total number of immigrants permitted to enter the United States. As eventually implemented after 1927, annual immigration was limited to 154,000, a precipitous drop from the years of open immigration. In 1913, the last full year of open immigration before World War I, more than one million persons had been admitted into the country. Overall, between 1901 and 1910, some 8,795,386 persons had entered the United States. Between 1930 and 1940, total immigration declined to 580,644.

Second, the 1924 act reaffirmed the 1921 law's idea of setting immigration quotas based on the principle of national origins but used the 1890 census year as a measure in determining those quotas. In 1890, the U.S. population contained relatively few immigrants from eastern and southern Europe – the homelands of Poles, Jews, Czechs, Slovaks, Hungarians, Balts, Ukrainians, Romanians, Bulgarians, Greeks, and Italians – compared to those who hailed from northern and western Europe – including the British Isles, France, Germany, Switzerland, the Netherlands, Belgium, Austria, and the Scandinavian countries. As a result, the quotas set for future immigration from eastern and southern Europe were made extremely low, while the rules for newcomers from northern and western Europe remained far more liberal.

Although the 1924 law was subsequently modified, 83 percent of all future immigration continued to be allotted to northern and western Europe and only 15 percent to eastern and southern Europe. For Poles seeking to enter the United States after 1924, the change was especially dramatic. In 1913 alone, some 170,000 people from the Polish lands had come to this country. The 1921 quota set a ceiling of 31,000 per year for Polish immigrants. The 1924 law further reduced this number, with the annual total of allowable Polish immigrants adjusted after 1927 to 6,524.[7]

---

[7] On the efforts to restrict immigration after World War I and the story of immigrant reform after World War II, see John Higham, *Strangers in the Land: Patterns of American Nativism, 1860 – 1925* (New York: Athenaeum, 1975); and John Higham, *Send Them to Me: Immigrants in Urban America,* revised edition (Baltimore and London: Johns Hopkins University Press, 1984).

The immigration acts' intent was obvious: to preserve America as a country of inhabitants having a national heritage from northern and western Europe and a religious tradition that was Protestant in character, aside from the Catholic Irish migration. What is more, the mainly east central and southern European Catholic, Jewish, and Orthodox immigrant populations already in America were expected to assimilate into the dominant culture.

The result of these enactments was, as expected, a drastic curtailing of Polish immigration from the 1920s until the 1960s. There was but one major exception to this rule, Congress's passage of the post-World War II Displaced Persons Act in 1948. This legislation enabled more than 140,000 Polish newcomers to be admitted under a special dispensation.

For Polonia, the impact of immigration restriction was enormous. The ethnic community continued to exist, of course, but it gradually lost it's heavily immigrant profile. In time, Polonia developed two faces, one that was foreign born, aging and gradually shrinking in size, the other American born, younger, burgeoning, and largely assimilated into the dominant English-speaking culture.

There were other societal threats to the Polish ethnic community and others like it. One came, briefly, from the Ku Klux Klan, which had initially formed after the Civil War as a protest movement against federal military rule over the conquered Southern confederacy. As reconstituted after 1915, the Klan retained its virulent hostility to African Americans but extended its hatred to Catholics, Jews, and immigrants. But the Klan remained strongest in the South and in rural parts of the Midwest and Northwest. Relatively few Polish Americans resided there so its impact on Polonia was not particularly pronounced.

More significant were the actions of Roman Catholic Church leaders such as Cardinal George Mundelein, archbishop of Chicago from 1915 – 1939, who sought to end the nationality-based parishes in his far-flung diocese and opposed the teaching of foreign languages, among them Polish, in the parochial schools in his domain. His aim was to establish an American Catholicism fashioned in the popular image of the melting pot.

Significantly, by the 1920s Americans of Polish birth and ancestry had largely come to see themselves as Americans first and foremost, though most were very familiar with the language, customs, religious traditions, and folkways of Poland. To them, criticisms that they were "hyphenated" Americans and thus somehow divided in their national loyalties had little meaning. Indeed, they and their parents had already demonstrated their loyalty by serving in the U.S. armed forces in World War I, by purchasing liberty bonds, and by remaining in America following Poland's restoration to independence in 1918.

In places like Chicago, with its heavily immigrant and ethnic character, few Polish Americans were much bothered by the rantings of nativists or even the actions of churchmen like Mundelein. Polonia's Roman Catholic parishes remained bastions of Polish culture. In Polonia's organizations too, activists like Napieralska weren't much distressed by these issues either. To them, there was no question of divided loyalties. Indeed, they were at the same time strongly patriotic toward America, loyal to the Church, and devoted to upholding their Polish heritage and the organizations that reflected its values.

Thus, the Polish Women's Alliance of America in the 1920s and 1930s fervently maintained its identification with the Polish language. For instance, the PWA of A organ, *Głos Polek*, continued to publish solely in Polish, and the Alliance's conventions were conducted in the ancestral tongue. Organized PWA of A tours to Poland were called "pilgrimages." And celebrations in Polonia dealing with Poland, such as the annual May Third Constitution Day commemorations, were as enthusiastically and widely supported as the Fourth of July.

A glance at the resolutions approved at PWA of A conventions provides another indication of the organization's focus. In 1927 the first four resolutions approved at the fifteenth convention of the Alliance were as follows:

We pay homage to our noble country, the United States, with its starry standard, and promise to it our constant and sincere loyalty.

We affirm our impassioned love for our Mother – Poland and our attachment to the Catholic Church.

We commit ourselves to maintain and promote our ethnic values, to show solidarity with our Polish fatherland, to foster the Polish language and to induce in our young generation a knowledge and love of our beautiful Polish language.

We recommend that our leadership work in cooperation with other Polish fraternals. . . . and that our members engage themselves in harmonious work for the benefit of the Polish Women's Alliance in America and the entire Polish emigration.[8]

Among the resolutions approved at the Depression-era sixteenth convention in 1931 were two that again spelled out what America and Poland meant to PWA of A members:

As citizens of this country, we stand loyally by the starry standard and in these difficult economic times, commit ourselves to work on one another's behalf and to provide help to our society, so that we can do our part to meet this crisis and direct our cooperative efforts to bring about a brighter future.

We are daughters of the great and noble Polish nation, which after so many years of foreign oppression, has at last regained its independence, not just by diplomatic means but through the blood shed by its people, and by their loved ones too, those who served in the ranks of the Polish Army in France, which we in the Polish Women's Alliance devoted ourselves to create. Let us never forget our unifying ties with Poland, our motherland, and while we will not ever interfere in her internal politics, let us always

[8] *Protokóły XVgo sejmu, 1927* (Minutes of the Fifteenth PWA of A Convention in 1927), p. 64.

be ready to cooperate with Poland, whose imprint we will never permit to be effaced from our hearts.[9]

With respect to Poland, the end of World War I had meant independence after 123 years of foreign rule and partition. The United States had played the decisive role in the Allied victory and its president had worked for Poland's rebirth; the Poles in America and their organizations had done more than their part to support both causes.

After 1918, the overwhelming majority of Polish people in the United States chose to remain here, a sign of their growing attachment to their adopted country and their wary recognition of the new Poland's unsettled situation. Once again, their attention was focused upon providing for their families in America. Evidence of this was the trend in rising rates of home ownership in the postwar Polish community and the increase in the number of Polish Americans purchasing large-ticket items such automobiles and household appliances. Parish membership and involvement in fraternal organizations such as the Polish Women's Alliance of America continued to be very important as well.

There were those in Polonia who continued to be interested in post-war Polish matters and its concerns. For some the issue involved pride in Poland's new independence. For many more, the ties with relatives in the old country were most important. Thus, many thousands of Poles in America maintained their contacts with the families back home through the mail and by forwarding money and goods to them. The widely read Polish language press of the day was yet another important link to Poland.

But post-war Polish domestic politics were extraordinarily complex and very different from what Polish Americans had grown used to in this country. As such, developments in the old country proved to be increasingly difficult for Polish Americans to follow. What is more, Poland's economic problems from the start were daunting, and these only further distanced most of Polonia's

---

[9] *Protokóły XVIgo sejmu, 1931* (Minutes of the Sixteenth PWA of A Convention in 1931), p. 62.

population from maintaining an in-depth interest in life in the old homeland.

Prior to and during the war Polonia's secular and religious leadership, organizations, and institutions had generally identified with the nationalist movement in Poland as it was represented by Roman Dmowski and Ignacy Paderewski. As a consequence, most Poles in America had been opposed to their main rival, Józef Piłsudski. However, as things developed in the 1920s and after, it was Piłsudski, not Dmowski, who played the more influential and ongoing leadership role in Polish affairs. In May 1926, Piłsudski and his followers seized power in a military *coup d'etat* and then overturned the elected parliamentary government.

Piłsudski's regime was really a dictatorship. Yet his new government did enjoy a substantial amount of popular support. Clearly, a large part, perhaps most, of the citizenry agreed to some extent with his support for strong national leadership, order, and honesty in government. At the same time, Piłsudski's seizure of power (he would rule until his death in 1935) meant the end of Poland's brief, seven-year, experiment with democratic governance, to the consternation of many Poles and Polish Americans. Moreover, Piłsudski's regime continued on after his passing until 1939 under his colleagues, who were derisively labeled the "colonels' clique" by their critics. Through these years, the authoritarian system he had fashioned, its accomplishments and its limitations, made it, and Piłsudski, subjects of broad public ambivalence. It collapsed in September 1939, when Poland was invaded, partitioned, and destroyed by Nazi Germany and Soviet Russia. On August 23, 1939, Hitler and Stalin had secretly agreed to dissolve the Polish state born in 1918. In the years that followed the two aggressors would attempt to destroy the Polish population as well.

In Polonia, interest in maintaining the World War I-era Polish National Department waned after 1918. In 1925 the political action federation held the last of its conventions. It was followed by a new association of Polish American organizations, the Polish Welfare Council of America (*Polska Rada Opieki Społecznej w Ameryce, PROSA*), which included in its ranks the Polish Women's Alliance of America. Unlike its predecessor, *PROSA* restricted itself to promoting the cultural and societal causes of the Polish community in America and sought to steer clear of Polish politics. In any event, it enjoyed little success during its five years of existence.

Following Piłsudski's rise to power in 1926, his followers in Poland encouraged his enthusiasts in other countries to initiate concerted efforts of their own to build support for the new regime. A major undertaking in this vein involved the establishment of an international association of the organized Polish *diaspora* aimed at advancing Poland's interests abroad. The Polish government backed this effort and assisted a number of Polonia communities in promoting knowledge of the ancestral cultural heritage and language and in facilitating greater opportunities for Polish people living abroad to visit the old homeland. Emphasis was given to building ties with the organizations of the American Polonia, by far the largest and best organized of all the Polish emigrant communities.

The first efforts in this direction came in 1928 and 1929, when meetings were held in Warsaw to establish the Organizational Council of Poles from Abroad, or *Rada Organizacyjna Polaków z zagranicy*. But few Polonia representatives attended these gatherings, and they proved to be ineffectual. In August 1934, a much-better-organized congress was held in Warsaw to set up a more permanent World Union of Poles from Abroad (*Światowy Związek Polaków z zagranicy*). This organization came to be known in Polonia by its acronym, *Swiatpol*.

This time, 131 representatives from twenty-seven different national Polonia communities attended the congress. Significantly, thirty-three Polish government officials also took part in the proceedings.[10]

By far the largest delegation at the congress, one numbering thirty-eight men and seven women, came from the United States. But most of the members of this group, which was headed by Censor Francis X. Swietlik of the Polish National Alliance, were not especially enthusiastic about *Swiatpol's* aims and the congress.

---

[10] For the list of delegates and the countries they represented, see Światowy Związek Polaków z Zagranicy: *II-go Zjazd Polaków z Zagranicy, 6 – 9 Sierpnia, 1934 roku* (World Union of Poles from Abroad: Second Congress of Poles from Abroad, August 6 – 9, 1934. Warsaw, 1935).

Moreover, after speaking with the U.S. ambassador in Warsaw, they became even more dubious.

When the first session of the congress was called to order, all of the Polish Americans were in attendance. They declined, however, to take part in the initial ceremonies of the gathering. There, all delegates were called upon to swear their fidelity to *Światpol,* which was an agency of the Polish government. In defending this action, Swietlik presented his delegation's position in fairly blunt terms. He declared that "American Polonia is neither a Polish colony nor an ethnic minority, but a component part of the great American nation, proud, however, of its Polish origins and careful to make the young generation love everything that is Polish." [11]

Having made their point, the members of the American delegation remained in attendance and even expressed a willingness to cooperate with *Światpol* in cultural matters. Maria Kryszak, the editor of *Głos Polek*, was the sole member of the PWA of A general administration at the congress, although several other members of the Alliance were also present at the meetings. All members apparently agreed with the positions taken by the American delegation. Still, the delegation's refusal to join *Światpol* proved to be controversial and was subjected to some sharp criticisms in the United States. Interestingly, there is no mention of the Warsaw congress in the proceedings of the seventeenth PWA of A convention, which was held only a few weeks later.

What did occur at the 1935 convention was nevertheless significant, since it resulted in the sudden end to Emilia Napieralska's career as president of the Polish Women's Alliance of America. This was particularly surprising because the fifty-three year-old Napieralska had held the presidency of the Alliance for the past seventeen years, was vigorous and seemingly popular, and looked to be in a very strong position to win reelection to another

---

[11] Brożek, *Polish Americans, 1854 – 1939*, pp. 190 – 192. See also Tadeusz Radzik, *Polonia Amerykańska wobec Polski, 1918 – 1939* (American Polonia and Poland, 1918 – 1939. Lublin: Wydawnictwo Polonia, 1990); and Bóguslaw Winid, "Dreams of Trans-Atlantic Brotherhood, Warsaw and the Polish American Community 1919 – 1939," *Gwiazda Polarna* (Stevens Point, WI) English-language supplement, February, April, June, August, and September 1997.

four-year term. Her reputation as "undoubtedly one of the most remarkable women that Polonia in America ever produced" also seemed to make her a seemingly invincible presence at the convention.[12]

Questions had been raised about Napieralska's leadership going back many years. One might recall that her participation at the International Women's Peace Congress in Europe in World War I had sparked some complaints; in fact, her remarks at the gathering had not been printed in *Głos Polek*. Later, she had been criticized for an extended visit she made as president to Poland. Notably, at the 1931 PWA of A convention, Napieralska had surprised everyone by suddenly stating she would not be a candidate for reelection, although she had not faced any opposition for the presidency. It was then left to Honorata Wołowska, the veteran Pennsylvania PWA of A activist who was presiding as chair of the convention, to take the extraordinary step of nominating Napieralska herself. It was in this unexpected and extraordinary fashion that Napieralska was thus reelected without opposition to a fifth consecutive term.

In 1935 Napieralska came in for new criticism. The main complaint was that she had not been giving her full attention to the PWA of A home office because of her work as county civil service commissioner, a post she had held for some time. (One of her more notable political activities had involved working for local approval to rename Chicago's Crawford Avenue after the American Revolutionary War hero Casimir Pulaski.) But such outside work had been banned by the PWA of A at its 1927 convention, when the Alliance's by-laws were amended to require persons holding the offices of president and national secretary to serve on a full-time basis. This clear conflict had not prevented Napieralska's reelection in 1931.

But in 1935 conditions had changed. By then there was growing concern over the fortunes of the Alliance because of the Depression's impact on the fraternal. The decline in PWA of A membership, after decades of growth, was especially

---

[12] Karol Wachtl, *Polonia Amerykańska: dzieje i dorobek* (American Polonia: Its history and legacy. Philadelphia: privately published, 1944), pp. 172, 396.

disheartening. And this time, Napieralska found herself facing a serious rival for the presidency in Honorata Wołowska.

The end began on September 24, 1935, the convention's second day, at a session at which changes in the Alliance's constitution and by-laws were being considered. Rising to make a motion was a delegate from Detroit named Elizabeth Zajączkowska. In it, she added new language to Article 8 of the by-laws. This lengthy provision dealt with membership in the PWA of A general administration, namely the offices of the president, vice president, secretary general, treasurer, the directors, along with the legal counsel, medical examiner, editor of *Głos Polek*, and the presidents of the state divisions. It included language about the process of nominating and electing qualified PWA of A members to national leadership.

The final paragraph of Article 8 stated that "the terms of office for members of the general administration are without limitations." Delegate Zajączkowska now proposed that "officers of the general administration cannot serve in the same office for longer than two terms." Several delegates took the floor in the ensuing debate, including Barbara Fisher of Group 556 of Chicago and Łucja Wołowska, one of the most senior members of the Alliance and a veteran past officer. After some discussion, Fisher moved for a secret ballot on Zajączkowska's amendment.[13]

A good deal of parliamentary maneuvering followed. A vote was at last taken, and the amendment was approved by a margin of 310 – 113. Łucja Wołowska then rose to declare that since more than two-thirds of the delegates had approved the motion, the rules of parliamentary procedure required that the change in the by-laws take immediate effect. Napieralska had suddenly become ineligible to run for reelection.

Over the next two days, discussions continued over the implementation of the new two-term limitation. This was further complicated by the new ruling's impact on several other national officers besides Napieralska. Two incumbents, Treasurer Joanna

---

[13] *Konstytucja i Ustawy Związku Polek w Ameryce, 1931* (Constitution and by-Laws of the Polish Women's Alliance of America, as revised, 1931), p. 17. For the debate, see *Protokóły XVII Sejmu, 1935* (Minutes of the seventeenth PWA of A convention in 1935), pp. 60 – 74 and *passim.*

Andrzejewska and Secretary General Victoria Latwis, did succeed in resolving their problem in an ingenious fashion. They simply agreed to run for each other's office.

The popular Andrzejewska thus ran for secretary, and was elected without opposition, just as in 1931 when she had been reelected treasurer. For her part Latwis won the post of secretary general over Maria Porwit, the same opponent she had beaten for the office of treasurer in 1924, 1927, and 1931.

Napieralska, however, rejected the option of becoming a candidate for vice president. That would have placed her opposite the popular Helena Sambor of Indiana, who was running for her second term and was thus not affected by the rule change. On Saturday morning, the convention's sixth day, Napieralska took the floor just before the election of national officers. Speaking with great emotion, she criticized the decision preventing her from even becoming a candidate for reelection. She then expressed her anger over allegations that she was motivated by financial reasons for seeking the presidency.

"Let the Convention decide when I should leave office," she declared. "I knew how to be the general of this organization and I will find my way as a member in its ranks, if I am granted a mandate to attend the meetings of the convention." One of her supporters then demanded another secret ballot on the by-laws revision, but this time Napieralska accepted her defeat, "for the sake of holy peace, harmony, and the good of the Polish Women's Alliance of America."

In the subsequent balloting for president, Honorata Wołowska was elected over Clara Swieczkowska of Detroit by a margin of 222 – 175. In taking the podium, Wołowska promptly entertained a motion naming Napieralska and Anna Neumann honorary presidents of the Polish Women's Alliance, thus having them join Stefania Chmielinska in receiving this distinction.

But Napieralska was absent for the swearing-in ceremonies at the convention's close. Afterward, she played no further role in the Alliance and did not attend the 1939 convention. In 1943, she suffered a fatal heart attack at age 61 and was laid to rest in Chicago's Saint Adalbert Cemetery following a funeral attended by several thousand people.   The two-term limitation was itself removed from the PWA of A constitution and by-laws not long after.   This permitted Honorata Wołowska to serve a third consecutive term as president.   (Already, she had won reelection without opposition in 1939.)

HONORATA WOŁOWSKA:
PRESIDENT OF THE WOMEN'S ALLIANCE

Honorata Wołowska could not have been more different from her predecessor, although both she and Napieralska had shared a lifelong involvement in the fraternal and an equally deep commitment to its mission. The Polish-born Wołowska was seven years older than her predecessor and had been a widow with four children for seven years when she became head of the Alliance. Her presidency would last twelve years and coincide with the years of World War II. Not surprisingly, the war would be an all-consuming concern of the Alliance from the moment it began on September 1, 1939, the day Nazi Germany invaded Poland, until Germany's surrender on May 7, 1945.

That Honorata Wołowska would lead the PWA of A in these years was fortuitous, for she was a person whose life had been defined by her deep-felt patriotism for Poland. Wołowska was an immigrant who in 1891, at the age of sixteen, came with her parents to the United States. Between 1891 and 1935, Wołowska spent most of her years in western Pennsylvania, where she taught school, married and raised a family. Nonetheless, she remained focused on the Polish cause and the place of women as rightful participants in the leadership of the organizational life of the Polish immigration.[14]

The Polonia of a small coal-mining town in Pennsylvania also made its mark on Wołowska. In her years there, she was ever the apostle of her causes in the Polish organizations to which she belonged, and this fervor distinguished her from the more cosmopolitan Napieralska. Appearances notwithstanding (in the years of her presidency Wołowska certainly looked the part of a petite, grandmotherly lady), she was a tough, longtime veteran of voluntary work in Polonia who viewed the mission of the PWA of A as that of a patriotic force working for Poland's cause. Membership

---

[14] A brief biography of Wołowska, written by Hazel McDonald in an undated 1935 English language news story found in the PWA of A archives, states that she had been a volunteer social worker in her earlier years for Jane Addams in Chicago, that she had gone to Poland in 1920 to organize the Gray Samaritans there, and that she had been involved in the resettlement of Polish orphans in America.

work, though certainly important, was mainly significant in making the PWA of A, a greater force in the ethnic community's work for Poland and the preservation of the Polish culture in America. The sale of insurance was more a means to this end than an end in itself.

Wołowska's perspective had its roots in her youth. Already in the mid-1890s, she had risen to leadership in the Polish Falcons Alliance as one of its first female gymnastics instructors. The Falcons Alliance was clearly a movement with which she identified, one that sought to link the pursuit of physical fitness and patriotic identification with Poland's independence. Its motto, "a healthy spirit in a healthy body," underscored its conviction about the tie between physical fitness and patriotic service. A second was more militant in tone: "hail to our Fatherland, talons to our enemy!" Moreover, the Falcons were unique among the Polish immigrant organizations of the day in their willingness to admit women into their ranks.

But Wołowska's initial involvement in the Falcons Alliance came, at least for a time, to an abrupt end when she and several other young women, including Stefania Chmielinska, were refused full membership equality with men. Not long after, she joined the newly created Polish Women's Alliance of America and was a delegate in 1900 from Braddock, Pennsylvania, to its first national convention. This PWA of A group was also the first in the Alliance to be formed outside of Chicago.

Wołowska did not seek to become a PWA of A officer largely because she lived so far away from Chicago, where the general administration of the Alliance was centered. Nevertheless, she maintained close contact with Łucja Wołowska (no relation) and Chmielinska. At the same time she continued to be closely associated with progressive and nationalist activists in the Falcons movement in Pennsylvania. One of these was Teofil Starzynski, an immigrant who had become a physician in Pittsburgh. In 1912 Starzynski was elected national president of the Falcons Alliance and moved its headquarters from Chicago to Pittsburgh. In the years that followed, Wołowska's activities in the organization increased. In 1918, she was elected the Falcons' women's national vice president. At the same time, she continued to serve as president of the western Pennsylvania district of the PWA of A, a responsibility she held between 1916 and 1935.

Upon her election as Falcons vice president, Wołowska promised to work aggressively to advance its traditional aims among women declaring that she had no intention of being a mere figurehead in office. She asserted that "those who know me from my local district work understand that I do not know how to sit back with my hands folded" and predicted that her fellow national officers would soon see this for themselves.

Wołowska's tenure as a Falcons leader was brief but eventful, since it coincided with America's entry into World War I and Polonia's active support of the Polish independence cause. An early activity involved recruiting volunteers for the Polish army being raised in America. This force was officially approved in October 1917 by the U.S. War Department, predecessor to the Department of Defense. Eventually more than 38,000 men volunteered for the army with over 22,000 serving in Europe. More than 5,000 of these were members of the Falcons Alliance.

As a Falcons officer, Wołowska chaired the Polish Women's Committee of National Assistance and the Polish Army (*Komitet Polek Pomocy Narodowej i Armii Polskiej*). Its work included recruiting young female volunteers to serve as nurses in support of the Polish army being raised in the United States. This effort, known as the Polish White Cross, was spearheaded by Helena Paderewska, wife of Ignacy Paderewski. The committee also supported the creation of the Polish Gray Samaritans nursing corps, a body of more than thirty young women sent to Poland in 1919 to help the seemingly countless destitute people in the war-ravaged country. The Gray Samaritans served under the general auspices of the American Relief Administration headed by Herbert Hoover. Still later, Wołowska became involved in organizing resettlement efforts in America on behalf of scores of Polish orphans who had been permitted to come to the United States from Siberia.

As a Falcons leader, Wołowska pressed for the twin causes of patriotic service to Poland and an equal place for Polonia's women on behalf of the Polish cause. At Falcons' gatherings, she called on women to take part as equals with men in the organization's physical training programs and its patriotic work. She railed against the second-class treatment of women in Polonia's organizations and won warm applause at the 1918 Falcons convention when she declared she would make no report to the conclave so long as women were denied any of the rights of membership enjoyed by men belonging to the Falcons Alliance.[15]

At the 1920 Falcons convention, Wołowska won the rights of women's equality that she had demanded earlier. In her remarks to the delegates, she proposed that women be given leadership duties in the Falcons Alliance and that they use these opportunities to preserve Polish ethnic consciousness and the Polish language in America.

Only a few months later, in February 1921 Wołowska resigned her Falcons post, giving no reason for her decision. (She may have been in Poland at the time.) She was, however, a delegate to the 1922 Falcons convention and there served as one of its deputy chairs. But by this time she was again devoting her time primarily to the Polish Women's Alliance of America. In November 1925, when the University of Pittsburgh held a ceremonial grand opening of its Polish Room, Wołowska attended the event as state president of the PWA of A, not as a Falcons leader.

From this point on, Wołowska focused entirely on the work of the PWA of A as a district president of its western Pennsylvania organization. It was in these years that she advanced her reputation as a believer in conducting business in a strict, procedural fashion. This was especially evident in 1931 at the Alliance's sixteenth convention, which she was elected to chair. There, her emphasis upon adherence to procedure may well have ruffled some feathers and helped bring about her defeat, by a vote of 217 – 196, when she was nominated for the vice presidency.

At the same time, Wołowska was very busy recruiting new members to the PWA of A in the eastern states. A list of all local groups that appeared in the Alliance's 1938 official history offers some good evidence of the extent of her effort. In the book forty-

---

[15] Arthur L. Waldo, *Sokolstwo Przednia Straż Narodu* (The Falcons movement: Vanguard of the Polish nation, vol. 4. Pittsburgh: Polish Falcons of America, 1974), pp. 409, 486, and *passim*.

three different groups are identified as having been organized through her initiative, most of them in Pennsylvania. No other single member of the Alliance is identified as having come close to Wołowska in this work, with Maria Porwit a distant second as an organizer of twelve groups, followed by Anna Neumann with five, and Stefania Chmielinska, Maria Szakalun, Leokadia Kadów, and Bronisława Wawrzynska with four each.[16]

Once Wołowska was elected President in 1935, membership in the Alliance began to increase after the declines of the early 1930s. Between 1935 and 1939, the organization registered a gain of more than four thousand members, from 60,666 to 64,818. Here, a notable contribution was made by Vice President Helena Sambor. Wołowska also focused on expanding the young people's circles, *Wianki*. As a former schoolteacher, Wołowska believed that a strengthened *Wianki* was an excellent way both to deepen the young people's appreciation of their heritage and to build the Alliance in the years to come.

Throughout the Polonia of the 1930s, many fraternalists shared a concern about the future loss of ethnic feeling among the American born. One way to deal with the problem involved a growing interest in transplanting the Polish scouting movement, or *Harcerstwo*, to America. Worries about the future generation were also a factor in the popularity of Poland's *Światpol* organization. Undoubtedly, the matter was on the minds of many Polish Americans. In the PWA of A, Wołowska's emphasis, not surprisingly, was to promote youth participation in the Alliance's dance, choral, and cultural activities – both at the national level and in programs sponsored by its local groups.

One initiative involved training cultural instructors to lead a six-week educational program under the auspices of the Alliance. The first of these took place in summer 1940 and was directed by Adeleine Preiss. The effort produced a number of youth instructors who went on to organize *Wianki* dance and choral activities for years after, both at the local group level and at larger gatherings. Another initiative was the PWA of A youth conference, a kind of

---

[16] Karłowicz, *Historia Związku Polek*, pp. 203 – 340, lists all PWA of A groups that were active at the time of the Alliance's fortieth anniversary, including the name of its founder.

weekend jamboree that brought together many of the *wianki* units. Two such early conferences took place in Cleveland in September 1941 and in Pittsburgh in September 1942. More than one thousand youngsters took part at each event. However, because of America's entry into World War II in 1941, these large events turned out to be the only ones that were held for a number of years.

With Wołowska's backing, the Alliance published its first full-length history in 1938 on the occasion of its fortieth anniversary. Authored in the Polish language by Jadwiga Karłowicz, the work offered a competent chronological narrative of the PWA of A's evolution from the time of its founding. Five thousand copies of the book were distributed in a major effort by the general administration to enlighten both members and the public about the organization and its mission.

The Alliance's fortieth anniversary was observed in other ways, too. Many historical articles were published in *Głos Polek* throughout 1938 and 1939, and there were numerous events around the country celebrating the PWA of A's achievements. A special moment came in February when the PWA of A hosted a visit by Eve Curie, the daughter of the recently deceased Nobel laureate and honorary member, Maria Skłodowska Curie, at its Chicago home office. For the occasion a room was named after the great scientist, and a portrait of Madame Curie was unveiled, the work of the outstanding Chicago artist Walter Krawiec. Six decades later, this esteemed portrait still hangs in the Alliance's national headquarters.

But PWA of A pride in its heritage extended beyond its home office walls. On October 9, 1939, on the eve of the 160th anniversary of Casimir Pulaski's death at the battle of Savannah in the American War of Independence, Wołowska and her fellow officers participated in a ceremony held at the newly enlarged Polish Museum of America next door to the headquarters of the Polish Roman Catholic Union of America fraternal in Chicago. For the occasion, the PWA of A leadership made a special gift to the museum on behalf of its entire membership. It was a massive painting that dramatically depicted Pulaski's heroic end. The work of artist Stanisław Batowski of Lwów, Poland, the painting remains a prized possession of the Polish Museum.

PWA of A interest in memorializing Pulaski was by no means new. Back in 1910, members of the Alliance were conspicuous participants at the dedication of the Pulaski and Kościuszko monuments in Washington, D.C. On October 12, 1929, the one hundred and fiftieth anniversary of the hero's death, PWA of A representatives took a prominent part in the dedication of the Pulaski monument in Savannah, Georgia.

Wołowska well appreciated the importance of engaging the PWA of A in cooperating with other organizations, both to promote fraternalism in America and to strengthen the ethnic community's ties with Poland. But like most leaders in the Polish community of her day, she was wary of too close a connection with the Warsaw-based *Światpol*. In 1936, she joined with the heads of the Polish National Alliance and the Polish Roman Catholic Union of America to form the Polish American Inter-organizational Council (*Rada Międzyorganizacyjna Polonii*). The council, while uniting the resources of its members in the spirit of *Światpol*, nevertheless followed an avowedly apolitical and humanitarian agenda. Significantly, though she headed the smallest of the three fraternals belonging to the Council, Wołowska carried on the PWA of A tradition in making the Alliance's home office the place where its meetings were held and major community events were hosted.

On September 1, 1939, everything changed for Polonia. Early that morning, Poland was attacked without warning by Adolf Hitler's Nazi German *Wehrmacht*. Though overmatched in every respect, Poland's military forces joined with the citizenry in a valiant fight against the invaders. But their cause proved hopeless, as Poland's western allies, Britain and France, took no action in the field after declaring war against Germany on September 3. Compounding Poland's disaster, the Soviet Red Army invaded from the east on September 17. Stalin's move to divide Poland, and all of Eastern Europe, with Germany was based on the secret pact he and Hitler had agreed to on August 23.[17]

---

[17] In the face of this tragedy, the Poles nonetheless mounted a substantial, well-organized resistance, both inside and outside their conquered land. A government in exile was soon created in France led by General Władysław Sikorski, a respected military figure long identified with the democratic cause. His stature was enhanced by his command of a substantial Polish military force that formed quickly in the West and eventually, with the inclusion of forces liberated from Soviet Russia in 1941, numbered 200,000 fighting personnel.

The country now fell into the blackness of a six-year alien occupation worse than any Poland had ever experienced in its thousand-year history. By war's end in spring 1945, some six million people, 20 percent of the population, had perished, including thousands of its civil, military, religious, intellectual, and professional leaders. Material losses were horrendous – 60 percent of the economy was destroyed, including many of its major cities, and nearly all of its railways, roads, and ports.

Practically the entire Polish Jewish community, which before the war had numbered more than 3.6 million members, was brutally and systematically annihilated by the Nazis. As a consequence of this holocaust, eight hundred years of Jewish life was abruptly erased in a Poland that in the best of times had been called a paradise (*paradisus judeorum*) by many Jews themselves.

The German invasion came only a few weeks before the opening of the eighteenth PWA of A convention on September 24, 1939, in Niagara Falls, New York. Understandably, the news from Europe dramatically affected the atmosphere of the gathering and gave it an almost funereal character. But the outbreak of war came as no particular surprise to many members of the Alliance. In fact, Vice President Sambor had just returned from having led a PWA of A pilgrimage to Poland that was cut short because of growing concerns over the ever worsening situation.

Informed PWA of A members well understood the gravity of the crisis and had begun to prepare the Alliance to act in solidarity with the embattled Polish people. On the news of the Nazi attack, a Polish national defense fund already set up by Polonia's organizations swung into action, its aim that of collecting money to support Poland's military needs. The defense fund, while soon terminated on U.S. government orders because America itself was not at war, was backed by the general administration of the Alliance, which voted $20,000 for the cause. Afterward, on the eve of the PWA of A convention, President Wołowska issued a series of

---

In occupied Poland, an underground movement numbering as many as 350,000 men and women was also formed. Known as the Home Army (*Armia Krajowa*), it subordinated itself to Sikorski's exile government, and did extensive damage to the Nazi occupiers. Yet another Polish army, this one under Soviet command, would operate out of Russia and take part in the capture of Berlin in 1945.

appeals "to all women and mothers of the world" and to the governments of the United States, Britain, and France. In these, she called on the democracies to do whatever they could to bring about a speedy end to the fighting.[18]

The Niagara Falls convention began with Mass celebrated by the bishop of Buffalo. In his homily, the prelate urged his listeners to keep faith that Poland would someday again experience a better future, despite its people's "Golgotha-like" trials. In response to the bitter news from Poland that weighed heavily over the convention participants and their proceedings, the Alliance's traditional gala banquet was canceled and replaced by a modest luncheon.

Collections for Polish relief were held throughout the conclave, and the delegates voted to set up a special fund for the war victims under the auspices of the general administration. By mid-October nearly thirty-three thousand dollars had been collected. The delegates also approved a voluntary assessment of each PWA of A member amounting to five cents per month for the duration of the war. Furthermore, just prior to its traditional mid-October ceremonies to install the Alliance's team of national officers, the general administration voted an additional donation of ten thousand dollars to the organization's relief fund. These actions were in keeping with those taken by the other Polonia fraternals, all of which made sizable donations of their own on behalf of the Polish relief cause.

But commitments of money comprised only a small part of the PWA of A effort to aid Poland. Drives were soon underway throughout the country to collect shoes, clothing, and food for Polish children and infants – at the local group level, in the Alliance's councils and districts, and at the Chicago home office. There, Wołowska and Secretary General Maria Porwit took lead roles in transforming the building into a beehive of volunteer activity. The mountains of boxes and packages they put together were earmarked for shipment to Europe under a variety of sponsors, among them the American Red Cross and the Polish American Council, (Rada Polonii Amerykańskiej, or RPA). This body

---

[18] These appeals are included in the text of the history of the Polish Women's Alliance of America by Maria Loryś, Historia Związku Polek w Ameryce.

was an expanded and renamed outgrowth of the Polish American Inter-organizational Council Wołowska had helped to establish in 1936. While it was initially nearly impossible to ship these goods to their intended destinations because of the hostility of Poland's occupiers, the relief work continued throughout the war.

On the organizational level, and particularly within the *RPA*, Alliance activists such as Clara Swieczkowska of Detroit, Rozalia Biedroń of Buffalo, and Jadwiga Karłowicz of Chicago worked unstintingly to make the voice of Polish American women heard in decisions to offer humanitarian assistance on behalf of the old homeland. In October 1939, the three took part in an extraordinary session of the *RPA* that was convened to better define the Polish community's aims. Their effort resulted in the creation of a special women's section within the *RPA*. Once formed, this body was soon running a new fundraising campaign of its own titled "Let's Save the Infants." Early in 1940, Wołowska developed another theme in the relief effort when, as both a leader in the *RPA* and as PWA of A president, she proposed that every woman in Polonia become a "godmother" to a Polish soldier interned in a prisoner-of-war camp.

In 1941 another PWA of A campaign was launched, this time to assist Polish families forcibly relocated to the harsh and distant central Asian regions under Soviet rule. These people were suffering miserably in their exile. Once again the idea was to prompt every Polish American household to take some concrete and specific action to provide clothing to aid a suffering Polish family.

Wołowska strongly backed the quick entry of every Polonia organization, national and local, secular and religious, into the *RPA*, and in one year the entire ethnic community was organized into thirty-six regional districts. By then, fundraising and the collection of goods were in full swing, and the *RPA* had established excellent cooperative relations with the two U.S. agencies working on behalf of the Polish relief cause. These were the American Red Cross and the Committee for Polish Relief. The Red Cross, which worked with the International Red Cross in Europe, directed its efforts to shipping supplies to prisoners of war. The Committee for Polish Relief headed by former President Herbert Hoover, made good use of its connections with the Polish exile government (which moved to London following the fall of France in April 1940) in transporting goods to occupied Poland.

Polonia's and the PWA of A's work during the first two years of the war was strictly humanitarian because of the United States's formal neutrality. This changed after Japan's attack on Pearl Harbor on December 7, 1941. In three short days, America found itself at war against Japan in Asia and Nazi Germany in Europe, and part of a great alliance with Britain, Poland, and a host of other nations, including Soviet Russia, which had been attacked without warning by its supposed partner-in-aggression, Nazi Germany, on June 22, 1941. Immediately following that betrayal, Britain's leader, Prime Minister Winston Churchill, had embraced the Soviets as his country's allies.

The great anti-imperialist alliance, known throughout the war as the United Nations, would be led by the president of the United States, Franklin D. Roosevelt. Eventually, by August 1945, it achieved a total victory over its foes. However, victory was by no means assured in 1941 when the United States first entered the conflict. To meet the challenge, millions of young Americans, more than five hundred thousand of them of Polish origin, were called on to serve America's armed forces. For its part, Polonia greatly expanded its activities in support of both the U.S. war effort and Poland's cause.

As in World War I, the Polish Women's Alliance of Alliance did its best to back the cause. Its *Głos Polek* printed many articles in support of the war effort. Organizational gatherings of the Alliance at the group and district levels did the same. The PWA of A strongly encouraged its members to buy U.S. defense bonds. To underscore this, the Alliance's general administration set aside $100,000 to purchase bonds as early as July 1942 in the name of the organization. A year later, at its nineteenth national convention, PWA of A delegates approved the purchase of another $250,000 in defense bonds to further reaffirmed their commitment to America's victory. Such actions were complemented by the Alliance's continued efforts to encourage individual members to buy bonds. The monies committed by the Alliance and its members were considerable enough to warrant a formal expression of appreciation from the U.S. War Department, which named two of its B-25 bomber planes in the Alliance's honor.

With respect to America's wartime ally, Poland, the PWA of A and all the organizations in the *RPA*, were given new opportunities to be of service. After June 1941 the *RPA* received permission from the suddenly beleaguered Soviet regime to begin shipping relief packages to Poles within its borders. Thanks to the *RPA's* participation in the National War Fund, a U. S. government-sponsored agency coordinating the collection of money and materials for the relief of the war victims (and the predecessor to the present-day United Fund), the scope of Polonia's humanitarian activities greatly increased.

From its entry into the National War Fund in 1942 until 1946, when the fund was dissolved, the *RPA* received almost $6.7 million in cash from the fund. This sum was three times greater than the amount the *RPA* had previously collected on its own. With this help the *RPA* and its member groups were able to concentrate on collecting canned foods, clothes, books, and hospital materials and making their own clothing and blankets, while agreeing to discontinue its own appeals for cash donations. PWA of A women took a leading role in these activities; moreover, the monies the Alliance had previously set aside for humanitarian purposes were now used to purchase goods for shipment abroad. This was done and at a very low cost.

All told, the efforts of the *RPA* and its member groups proved to be very considerable. One tally of the amount of materials it had shipped to Poles in need around the world estimated the total to exceed 18,000 tons. The *RPA's* leadership later reported that more than five million people had been assisted in some material fashion during the war, whether they were prisoners of war, fighting personnel serving the Allied cause or refugees in Soviet Russia, the Middle East, or Africa. And because of the *RPA's* voluntary character, the administrative costs of its operation amounted to only about two cents for every dollar that was spent in the effort.

The second historian of the Polish Women's Alliance of America, Maria Loryś, whose published work covered its activities from 1939 – 1959, provided details about the nature and forms of PWA of A wartime relief work. One interesting early action involved the Polish pianist and patriot Ignacy Paderewski. Nearly eighty years old when the war broke out and in ill health, Paderewski nonetheless offered his services to the Polish cause and was appointed chairman of the Polish exile government's parliament set up initially in France. In 1940, he sailed to America on Poland's behalf; there his appearances were widely recognized by a public that recalled his countless performances across the country over the years and his past devotion to the Polish cause.

Taking advantage of Paderewski's presence, Wołowska proposed a fundraising concert to celebrate the fiftieth anniversary of the maestro's debut at New York's Carnegie Hall, where he had launched his career as America's "first superstar," in the words of one of his biographers. The concert, at Chicago's Civic Opera House, took place on May 2, 1941, although it went on in the absence of the gravely ill Paderewski, who died less than two months later. Featuring the popular tenor Jan Kiepura, the event raised ten thousand dollars, part of it in the form of a contribution from the PWA of A. A year after Paderewski's death, the Alliance announced a new fund drive in his memory. This campaign generated another twenty-thousand dollars for the RPA. As a result of its various fundraising efforts, the Polish Women's Alliance of America had by June 1942 donated more than seventy-one thousand dollars to the RPA. This amount was surpassed only by the support given to the relief federation by the much larger PNA and PRCUA.

THE PWA OF A AND THE POLISH AMERICAN CONGRESS

Once the United States entered the conflict, Polonia was inevitably drawn into political work on behalf of Poland's restoration to independence. At first its activities were tentative in character and focused on registering the Polish community's support of the Polish government in exile. These were highlighted by visits to America from Poland's leader, General Władysław Sikorski. Two of Sikorski's trips brought him to Chicago; each time he visited with Polonia leaders at the PWA of A home office.

These meetings solidified the ethnic community's ties to the London government; this despite Sikorski's controversial decision to establish diplomatic relations with the Soviet state that had joined in Poland's partitioning in 1939. Sikorski's sharpest Polonia critics from the start were Polish emigres in the United States who identified themselves with the prewar Piłsudski regime. But these activists exerted little influence in Polonia until the spring of 1943. It was only then that two events arose whose impact would permanently define the politics of the Polish American community and its perspectives toward Soviet Russia. Eventually, this view would affect the wider American public, helping to shape postwar U.S. foreign policy toward the U.S.S.R. for decades to come.

In April 1943 the Nazis discovered a mass grave in the Katyn Forest district of western Russia, an area they had overrun nearly two years earlier. In this grave were found the corpses of more than four thousand Polish military officers interned by the Red Army in 1939. Nothing had been known of their whereabouts, or those of some eleven thousand of their comrades since April 1940, despite repeated inquiries by Sikorski to Stalin. To demonstrate to the world that they had uncovered an atrocity at Katyn for which they were not responsible, the Nazis called upon the International Red Cross to make its own unbiased investigation of the gravesite.

When Sikorski went along with this inquiry, Stalin summarily, and as things turned out, permanently, broke off diplomatic relations with the exile government. Instead he gave full support to communist loyalists of the Soviet Union then inside Russia. These individuals would eventually be tapped to head a postwar Polish communist state subservient to Moscow. The revelation of the Katyn massacre, followed by Stalin's reactions, could only strengthen the hand of Sikorski's Polonia critics. For its part the Soviet regime denied any responsibility for the atrocity during the succeeding fifty years.[19]

---

[19] Significantly, the Katyn massacre was not brought up as a Nazi war crime in the Nuremberg trials of 1945 – 1949, although the U. S. S. R. called for such an action. By then, Polish Americans were increasingly being joined by other critics of the Soviet regime who called for a full and impartial investigation of the atrocity. A special committee of the U.S. House of Representatives did just that in 1951. It concluded that the massacre had occurred in Spring 1940, when the Katyn district was still in Soviet hands. (Nazi Germany attacked in June 1941). The committee's conclusions were strenuously condemned in Moscow. However, on April 13, 1990, fifty years after the massacre, Soviet President Mikhail Gorbachev finally admitted the U. S. S. R.'s responsibility for the crime, although he fixed the blame upon the chief of the Soviet security police. Two and one-half years later Russia's President Boris Yeltsin went much further and released hitherto secret documents showing that Stalin had personally ordered the murders of some 14,700 interned Polish military officers, government officials, landowners, and police, along with

On July 4, 1943, Poland's cause experienced a second shock when Sikorski, together with his only child, was killed in a plane crash at the Straits of Gibraltar off the coast of Spain. Sikorski's death left an irreparable void in the leadership of his government. In Polonia, his critics grew louder in voicing their suspicions, both of Soviet complicity in the crash and of Stalin's future intentions toward Poland. The second issue was especially serious since an Allied victory in Europe was growing more likely each passing month. This meant that Stalin would be playing a major, if not decisive, role in determining the fate of east central Europe.

Less than a year later, in the Spring of 1944, the organizations of Polonia would join with the political *emigres,* by then formally established as the National Committee of Americans of Polish Descent (*Komitet Narodowy Amerykanów Polskiego Pochodzenia, KNAPP).* The result of their united efforts would be a new political action federation known as the Polish American Congress (*Kongres Polonii Amerykańskiej, KPA).* The Polish Women's Alliance of America would have a key role throughout this formative process and its members would play significant parts in its work as Polonia's political voice.

General Sikorski's death in 1943 dealt a great blow to Polonia, given the high esteem he had enjoyed as the personification of Poland's wartime cause. Within the Polish Women's Alliance of America, his death had another, distinctive, significance. In his visits to America, Sikorski had always come accompanied by his wife, Helena. Indeed, Madame Sikorska had gradually established a cordial relationship of her own with PWA of A leaders and had been invited to attend its nineteenth national convention, which was scheduled to take place in Philadelphia in September 1943.

After the tragedy at Gibraltar, Madame Sikorska canceled her visit. Her letter to the delegates was read in her absence and all stood in silence out of respect and sympathy. The convention then approved the creation of a new relief fund in her name and in the amount of $100,000. Its purpose was to provide assistance to

---

11,000 other "opponents" of his regime. Stalin's action, moreover, was formally approved by the entire Soviet Communist Party top leadership. "Russian Files Show Stalin Ordered Massacre of 20,000 Poles in 1940," *New York Times,* October 15, 1992.

Polish orphans.   After this action, a resolution was unanimously approved recognizing Helena Sikorska as an honorary member of the Alliance.

The PWA of A's patriotic work continued after the convention.   One notable event involved the enthusiastic welcome its members extended to six young women who had joined the Polish armed forces in England following their escape from a Soviet internment camp.   These individuals, who with their comrades in England were known by the nickname *Pestki* (kernels of hope), were a big hit wherever they traveled in America.   Their stories of the heroism and service of women of the Polish cause deepened general understanding of the cause throughout Polonia and were highlights of numerous PWA of A meetings.

The Polish exile government in London did its best to carry on after Sikorski's death.   Two men were chosen to succeed him: Stanisław Mikołajczyk as prime minister and General Kazimierz Sosnkowski as commander-in-chief of the armed forces.   But the two men did not work well together; moreover, while both were deeply committed to Poland's cause, neither possessed Sikorski's stature in dealing with Churchill and Roosevelt.   After Sikorski's death there is little evidence to indicate that the British and American leaders bothered to take Poland's new leaders into their confidence.   When Churchill and Roosevelt initiated their own diplomatic conversations with Stalin, the third head in the great alliance, Poland's representatives were left out of the mix.   This was perhaps most clearly the case when the big three held their first summit meeting in Teheran, Iran, at the end of November 1943.   (This get-together would be the first of many summits bringing together the heads of the United States and the Soviet Union over the next five decades.)

At Teheran, Roosevelt and Churchill each met privately with Stalin, with disastrous results for Poland.   Their conversations, held without the knowledge of the exile leadership, conceded to the Soviet chieftain the dominant say in determining Poland's postwar political fate and even the shape of its future borders.

On the military front, the tide had already turned after the Red Army's victory over the Germans at Stalingrad in 1942.   By the end of 1943, with the Teheran conference still going on, Soviet forces neared the eastern border of the prewar Polish state. In *Polonia*, this development was met with great apprehension, since it increasingly appeared that Stalin fully intended to place a pro-Moscow puppet regime in command in Poland once the Nazis were driven out.

The *RPA* relief federation, in which the PWA of A was a leading participant, had always avoided lobbying the Roosevelt administration to express its opposition to Poland's Sovietization. To have done otherwise, its leaders believed, would have jeopardized its eligibility for financial assistance from the National War Fund as a charitable agency. Whenever the *RPA* had expressed political views, it had limited itself to non-controversial statements in support of the Atlantic Charter. It was this declaration that Roosevelt and Churchill had agreed to and signed in August 1941. The words of the Atlantic Charter were certainly noble, and *RPA* leaders had remained hopeful that the Allies' commitment to its principles would amply protect Poland's interests.

According to the charter, the two leaders had made it their mission to defend the rights of all peoples to choose their own forms of government without foreign interference and to reject the making of any border changes by one state at another's expense. Taken at face value, these principles appeared to guarantee Poland's independence and its pre-1939 territorial integrity.

From the earliest days of the war, however, the *emigres* and their Polish American friends who later established *KNAPP* had questioned the Atlantic Charter's relevance. They criticized Sikorski's efforts to cooperate with Stalin, who had joined Hitler in destroying the Polish state. They interpreted the Katyn massacre, Stalin's diplomatic break with London, and Sikorski's subsequent death as indications of the Soviet ruler's real intentions toward Poland.

In early January 1944, the Red Army crossed the prewar Polish boundary in its pursuit of the badly weakened German forces. At the same time, the chairman of *KNAPP*, Max Węgrzynek, who was the publisher of the New York Polish-language daily newspaper *Nowy Świat* (The new world), met in Chicago with President Charles Rozmarek of the Polish National Alliance,

President John Olejniczak of the Polish Roman Catholic Union of America, and Honorata Wołowska of the Polish Women's Alliance of America. The aim of their meeting was to determine what actions they could take together on Poland's behalf. In the succeeding weeks, they engaged in further discussions to establish formal ties between the Chicago-based fraternals and the New York centered *KNAPP* group. These talks culminated on March 4, 1944, with a meeting at the PWA of A headquarters attended by some fifty activists from the two sides and a number of members of the clergy. President Wołowska, Legal Counsel Barbara Fisher, and Director Veronica Siwek represented the Alliance. The meeting resulted in a call for a national congress of representatives from Polonia organizations and parishes. Its purpose was to provide a forum for the ethnic community to express its concerns about the unfolding Polish situation.

At the meeting, the participants elected an executive committee headed by Rozmarek, with Wołowska as secretary and Olejniczak as treasurer. Rules were adopted to determine how delegates to the congress would be chosen. After setting up the subcommittees responsible for making substantive reports to the congress, the participants at the meeting unanimously agreed on a resolution that reads in part as follows:

> We, Americans of Polish descent, representatives of the Polish organizations, clergy, and the Polish language press around the country, gathered on March 4, 1944, in Chicago at the headquarters of the Polish Women's Alliance of America, keep in mind the need to strengthen our common efforts to accelerate the victory of the Allies over the enemies of democracy, affirm our agreement with the ideals of the Atlantic Charter and the "Four Freedoms" as expressed by President Roosevelt in his January 1941 message to Congress. (These were the freedoms of speech and worship and the freedoms from want and fear presented as universal goals to be attained once the war was won.)
>
> We seek to achieve a just peace, one that will guarantee the freedom and independence of the

United Nations, large and small, a peace that will prevent any further aggression.

We wish to come to the assistance of the Polish nation, which from the beginning of the War has fought on the side of the Allies and on every front and for our common aims, as previously stated, despite its having suffered the greatest casualties.

We wish to help a democratic Poland, which is represented by its one and only legally constituted government headquartered in London, a Poland whose borders are gravely threatened.

In closing, we recognize the need to create a central organization to defend the interests of American Polonia in all its fields of concern. We therefore unanimously proclaim the calling of a Polish American Congress in the latter half of the month of May 1944.[20]

Significantly, the statement recognized the threat Stalin and the Poles submissive to him in Soviet Russia posed to the London government. In point of fact, the Polish communists took the lead in proclaiming, on July 22, 1944, a Committee of National Liberation in the eastern Polish city of Lublin. (That day would be officially recognized as a national holiday in the communist-run Polish People's Republic until the republic's demise in 1989.)

The call for a Polish American Congress was also a response to the already substantial accomplishments of pro-Soviet activists in America. These individuals repeatedly claimed in talks with U.S. officials that their organizations, mainly the American Slav Congress and the American Polish Labor Committee, were in fact the true representatives of Polonia.

---

[20] From Pienkos, *For Your Freedom*, p. 113. For the story of PWA of A involvement in the work of the RPA and the Polish American Congress, see Loryś, *Historia Związku Polek w Ameryce*, and Pienkos, *For Your Freedom*, *passim*. On Poland's World War II struggle and its postwar fate, see Józef Garlinski, *Poland in the Second World* War (London: Macmillan, 1985), and Richard Lukas, *The Strange Allies: The United States and Poland, 1941 - 1945* (Knoxville: University of Tennessee Press, 1978).

On March 28, 1944, the executive committee of the nascent Polish American Congress met again at the PWA of A headquarters. After reviewing the latest developments (which included news of the action taken by *KNAPP* activists in New York City to attend the upcoming congress in Buffalo), they heard Wołowska's report on preparations for the event.   Hundreds of Polonia organizations throughout the country had just been sent information about the general purposes of the gathering and the procedures to be followed in choosing the delegates who were to take part in the proceedings.

The committee then agreed on four distinct and specific aims of the Congress: to further mobilize Polish American support behind the United States' war effort, to reaffirm Polonia's support of America's war aims as stated in the Atlantic Charter and the "Four Freedoms" speech, to develop greater cooperation within the ethnic community in support of Polish independence and territorial integrity, and to strengthen the life of the Polish American community and its institutions. The first of these was superfluous in that Polonia had always been committed to the cause. The second simply reiterated the opinion held universally in Polonia. The fourth was similarly rather unexceptional.

Item three was critical, because it underscored the fraternals' decision to identify with *KNAPP* on two key points. Point one underscored Polonia's objection to a postwar Soviet-dominated Poland.   Point two asserted the community's opposition to the redrawing of Poland's frontiers at its expense.

The Polish American Congress began on May 28, 1944, in Buffalo. It was, in the judgment of a key White House observer who forwarded his views to President Roosevelt, an event that would "go down in history as the most colossal piece of organizational work." More than 2,600 delegates attended from hundreds of parishes, fraternal societies, and community groups from twenty-six states. They were joined by reporters from the powerful Polish-language press of the day and by scores of politicians from every level of government. Some 25,000 people took part in the parade held prior to the congress's inaugural session; 16,000 spectators were in the convention hall for its opening ceremonies.

Among the sheaves of telegrams congratulating the participants at the gathering was one from President Roosevelt, which the delegates stood for out of respect for their beloved leader. But despite his good wishes, Roosevelt could hardly be pleased with the Congress or the prominent role played by anti-Soviet *KNAPP* activists in its proceedings. Earlier at Teheran, FDR had secretly agreed to Stalin's demands for changes in Poland's post-war eastern boundary with Soviet Russia. Furthermore, he was already deep into planning his own campaign for an unprecedented fourth presidential term in office and very well appreciated the importance of retaining his great popularity among Polish American voters in the upcoming November 1944 elections.

Fortunately for the president, Charles Rozmarek served as general chairman of the Congress. Rozmarek steered the speakers at the congress away from overt and divisive displays of political partisanship. He also did his best to limit their anti-Soviet rhetoric. This is clear from a reading of the two main documents approved at the Polish American Congress, which remained in existence after the Buffalo conclave under the same name as a political lobbying organization representing Polonia. (This served, in all likelihood, to make it literally the first "PAC".)

The "Memorial" or memorandum presented at the Congress and addressed to President Roosevelt stressed Polonia's deep support for America's military effort and appealed for the United States to "take full cognizance of the justice of the Polish cause." But a second statement adopted by the delegates in the form of a resolution singled out Soviet Russia for criticism and called on the United States to be vigilant in defending the Allies' war aims as stated in the Atlantic Charter. Failure to do this would mean problems for America in its dealings with Moscow once the war was over. Interestingly, Wołowska's signature was affixed to the second, tougher statement. The more mildly worded Memorial was signed by former PWA of A vice president, Helena Sambor.

As expected, the Polish Women's Alliance of Alliance was well represented at the Buffalo conclave. The entire membership of the general administration was active in the proceedings, and eight state presidents came as delegates. Scores of delegates from PWA of A groups and councils were present too, not to mention the many individual members who attended as delegates from other secular and parish organizations. Leading roles at the Congress were taken by Wołowska (as secretary of the planning committee), Barbara Fisher, and Veronica Siwek. PWA of A librarian Halina Paluszek served as a member of the committee on mandates, Helena Sambor served on the committee handling speeches in the English language, Rozalia Biedroń was a member of the nominations committee, and Armela Mix served on the social welfare committee; Treasurer Leokadia Blikowska, along with Helena Sala and Constance Rybinska registered delegates and guests for the gathering. As had been true with the organizing of the Emigration Congress back in 1918, the PWA of A played a key role in the event.

In the months following the conclusion of the Polish American Congress, President Roosevelt successfully avoided meeting with its leaders, who sought to present him with the Memorial approved in Buffalo. It was not until October 11, 1944, that such a meeting occurred. The occasion, which took place in the Oval Office, was a ceremonial one and was held to mark the anniversary of the death of Casimir Pulaski. Among those in attendance on behalf of the Polish American Congress were Rozmarek, Olejniczak, Starzynski, and Wołowska. All had been elected national officers of the PAC in Buffalo.

But the atmosphere surrounding the meeting was more political than ceremonial in character. With the November presidential election only weeks away, FDR found it most important to be photographed with Polonia's top leaders. At the same time, the crisis then going on inside occupied Poland cast an extraordinary and ominous shadow over the proceedings.

On August 1, 1944, the Polish underground resistance (*Armia Krajowa,* or *AK:* in English, the Home Army), rose up in massive and highly organized fashion against the Nazi occupiers of Poland's capital, Warsaw. The uprising's objective was to liberate the city in the name of the Polish exile government in London before it could be claimed by the oncoming Soviet Red Army and the weak Polish communist-led liberation committee. The plan was extremely risky because it depended on the ability of the large but poorly armed *AK* to rapidly and decisively defeat the well-equipped German forces and drive them from the capital. But Hitler refused to give up control of the city and ordered massive reinforcements to crush the uprising at all costs. At the same time, the Soviet forces abruptly halted their own advance on Warsaw.

Over the next sixty-three days, the *Wehrmacht* followed the strategy of pulverizing the city block by block, even as it suffered substantial casualties of its own. As a result 90 percent of Warsaw's buildings were destroyed and more than 200,000 of its civilian inhabitants perished. For his part Stalin contributed to the worsening catastrophe in opposing American and British attempts to provide the embattled Poles with military aid from the air. Stalin's aim was a Machiavellian one: to allow the annihilation of the resistance and the discrediting of its leaders through the destruction of the Polish capital, thus paving the way for a postwar Polish regime subservient to his rule.

By the time FDR received the PAC delegation on Pulaski Day, nothing could be done for Warsaw. But at the fifty-five-minute meeting, the president continued to put a positive face on the situation and even stated his support for a "strong and independent" postwar Poland. But he was silent about America's future backing of the London exile government and Poland's postwar eastern border. Cleverly, however, he had ordered a map of prewar Poland to be hung behind his desk. His aides made sure that photos of himself, his guests, and the prop were then disseminated widely in media outlets located in the many communities where large numbers of Polish American voters resided.

Wołowska returned home from Washington apprehensive about the president's silence on the key Polish issues. Soon after, she and Secretary Porwit addressed a letter to Roosevelt and a number of other top government officials that called on the United States to maintain a just policy stance in support of Poland. This letter was also mailed to all local PWA of A leaders, who were urged to share their concerns with the White House.

On October 28, 1944, FDR campaigned in Chicago to rally his supporters to carry the pivotal state of Illinois in the upcoming election against the Republican Party standard-bearer, New York Governor Thomas E. Dewey. There he secured Charles Rozmarek's personal endorsement in return for his assurance that Poland would not be abandoned. Rozmarek's support was then widely broadcast as the official endorsement of the PAC, which it was not. Roosevelt's reelection a few days later was helped greatly by Polish American voters, who backed him by a 9 – 1 margin. The Polish vote may well have been a decisive factor in determining the results in a number of closely-fought states.

In February 1945, Roosevelt, Churchill, and Stalin met at the Soviet Black Sea resort town of Yalta to discuss a number of issues, among them the fate of Poland. There, despite the absence of representatives of the London exile government, they agreed to drastically reshape Poland's future eastern, western, and northern borders along the lines Stalin proposed. Further, they set into motion a political process to create a Polish postwar government. This process was badly flawed and Soviet-dominated. By January 1947 it had resulted in a regime that was firmly under the grip of communists subservient to Moscow.

Already gravely ill at Yalta, FDR returned to Washington on March 1, 1945, and there addressed the Congress on the results of his summit meeting with Stalin and Churchill. In his remarks he gave great attention to Poland and assured his audience that what had occurred there was "under the circumstances, the most hopeful agreement possible for a free, independent, and prosperous Polish state." The Yalta decisions on Poland were immediately condemned by the Polish American Congress. And while Wołowska's name was not attached to the first PAC statement, she and her fellow PWA of A officers issued their own letter, which made the same points:

> As American women of Polish descent, we view the decisions made at Yalta as Americans. We are thus unable to understand how a country so committed to freedom like ours could ever give in to Soviet military might, and thus grant Russia the right to extend its influence into the whole of Europe and the world . . . .[21]

In the final years of her leadership of the Polish Women's Alliance of America – she would retire at the end of her third term at the convention in September 1947 – Wołowska continued her involvement on Poland's behalf. In March 1945 she traveled to San Francisco as a member of the Polish American Congress delegation that attempted to rally support for Poland's cause just before the

---

[21] In Loryś, *Historia Związku Polek w Ameryce,* pp. 122, 124.

founding sessions of the United Nations. Later, she and her colleagues promoted the PAC initiative to raise one million dollars so that it could consolidate into an enduring voice of Polonia in American political affairs. Her firm commitment to the principles of the PAC set a precedent that each president of the Alliance who succeeded her in office has followed.

But one could not ignore the new political realities taking shape in the months following the end of World War II. In devastated Poland, a communist-led provisional government was established, one that postponed until January 1947 the "free and unfettered elections" promised at the Yalta conference. When the elections were finally held, the results were falsified following a campaign to crush the non-communist democratic forces. According to one authoritative observer, it was Stalin himself who, before the elections, decided the number of parliament seats each party was to be allotted. By the end of 1947, what remained of the opposition had been suppressed, and its leaders were either imprisoned or had fled the country.

In the humanitarian realm, Wołowska continued to lead the Alliance in its work with the *RPA* organization. On her initiative, the *RPA* held its annual national meeting in August 1946 at the PWA of A home office. There, the delegates renamed the organization American Relief for Poland and turned their attention to providing assistance to the needy in Poland. This effort came in cooperation with the Polish Roman Catholic Church's own charitable agency, *Caritas*.

Another special postwar effort involved the Alliance's support for an American association named the Catholic League for Religious Assistance to Poland. The league was particularly busy after the war in raising money to help in rebuilding churches that had been damaged during the conflict. The Catholic league eventually drew support from more than three hundred local parish affiliates around the United States; already by 1946 it had collected more than $350,000 and was busy shipping liturgical supplies to Poland. Heading the work by the PWA of A in these drives was Florence Knapp of Pennsylvania.

Still another focus of PWA of A interest after the war involved its members' concerns over the fate of some eight hundred war refugees, many of them orphaned children. These individuals had been resettled during the conflict in the town of Santa Rosa, Mexico, thanks to the intervention of the *RPA*. The Alliance took a leadership role in collecting and shipping food, clothing, and home furnishings for these refugees during their time south of the border. In February 1946, in response to news of the Mexican government's decision to close down the center in Santa Rosa, the Alliance's general administration secured the necessary affidavits and financial commitments to enable all the refugees to enter this country. Leading this project was veteran PWA of A activist Armela Mix.

Although Wołowska was already more than seventy years old in 1946, she made the arduous trip to Europe on behalf of the *RPA* when she was asked to review the living conditions of thousands of displaced Poles in the refugee camps the Allied powers had established in and around Germany. Her experience there made her an ardent advocate for these unfortunates, most of who had been either forced or slave laborers in the Nazi Reich during the conflict, or prisoners of war. Despite the harsh conditions they faced in the camps, however, few were willing to return to Soviet-controlled Poland.

As a result of her European trip, Wołowska strongly supported cooperation between American Polonia and the many relief agencies that were then operating in postwar Europe. These included the National Catholic Welfare Conference's War Relief Service, headed by the Rev. (later Bishop) Aloysius Wycislo of Chicago. In time, this agency and its affiliated groups collected more than three million dollars on behalf of the refugees.

Following the passage of the United States Displaced Persons Act in 1948, the NCWC's relief service became a major player resettling thousands of Polish refugees. A number of members of the PWA of A contributed to this work by finding sponsors and temporary housing for the newcomers to America.

Despite her focus on relief and patriotic activities during the World War II years, Wołowska continued to promote the development of the Polish Women's Alliance of America as a fraternal society. A significant measure of her leadership was noted at the Alliance's twentieth convention in Chicago in September 1947.

At this historic gathering, which marked the Alliance's upcoming celebration of its golden anniversary, 67,899 individuals were identified as members of the fraternal, a gain of 7,233 from 1935, when Wołowska had first been elected. The number of juveniles belonging to the PWA of A had, however, declined. As a result, the convention approved a resolution to change the by-laws to permit male children to be enrolled as insured members into the Alliance for the first time. Perhaps as important, Vice President Adela Łagodzinska, who was elected president to succeed Wołowska, made the enrollment of youngsters a top priority in her new administration.

On cultural matters, Wołowska had been committed to continuing the work of the PWA of A as a champion of pride in the Polish heritage. One of the last expressions of this objective came in May 22, 1947, the day traditionally set aside by the Alliance to honor its founders. On this date, the Museum of the Polish Women's Alliance of America was dedicated at its Chicago headquarters. Performing the honors was the pastor of Holy Trinity Parish, the Rev. Casimir Sztuczko. Sztuczko had been one of the PWA of A's greatest friends over the years from among the clergy. Indeed, back in 1912, it had been Sztuczko who had blessed the cornerstone of the PWA of A headquarters, the building which was to house the new museum.

The museum project was directed by Halina Paluszek, then the librarian of the Maria Konopnicka reading room in the home office. Working with her was Jadwiga Karłowicz, editor of *Głos Polek*, and Maria Łopacinska, chairperson of the Alliance's welfare department. The museum was established to house the mementos that had been donated to the Alliance over the years, a sizable number of them from members of the organization. Many gifts came from Łucja Wołowska, and all sorts of materials from PWA of A conventions from years gone by were also part of the trove, as were the portraits of the Alliance's past presidents. There were greatly prized items from Poland, among them a collection of letters from Maria Konopnicka, one from Maria Skłodowska Curie, and two from the author Maria Rodziewicz, all of them made available through the generosity of the curator of the Polish

Museum of America, Mieczysław Haiman. Of note too was a gift from Marilyn Modzejewska-Pattison of Tucson: a statue of the renowned actress Helena Modrzejewska (Modjeska), her grandmother, in the role of *Antigone.* The ceremony proved to be a memorable start to what would be a yearlong celebration of the first half-century of the Polish Women's Alliance of America.

Wołowska retired from the PWA of A in 1947, at the age of seventy-two. She continued, as honorary president, to attend the major functions of the Alliance and remained involved in the Polish American Congress and the *RPA.* In 1949 she traveled to Poland on behalf of the *RPA* and returned home with an extensive report on the work of *Caritas.* Her report included a discussion of the problems the Polish charitable society was facing in its dealings with the increasingly hostile communist regime.

Wołowska remained a respected adviser to the Alliance for many years, in the spirit of Stefania Chmielinska and Anna Neumann, both of whom had enjoyed genuine "lives" in the fraternal long after they left elective office. Her passing in 1967 at the age of ninety-two was universally mourned.

Wołowska may best be recalled as a diminutive giant whose life was uncompromisingly focused on the causes of Poland's rebirth and the building of pride in the Polish heritage in America. Through her work in the Polish Women's Alliance of America, the Polish Falcons Alliance, the Polish American Congress, and the *Rada Polonii Amerykańskiej,* she greatly advanced the position of women, both as leaders in Polonia and in America at large.

THE ŁAGODZINSKA ERA: 1947 – 1971

Let us be grateful to God that we live in America; let us be grateful for our democratic way of life and let us ask that God provide the same for our brothers and sisters in Poland.

Adela Łagodzinska, 1951[1]

The twentieth PWA of A convention began on September 28, 1947, at the Congress Hotel in Chicago. In retrospect, it is an appropriate starting point from which to look back on the modern history of the Polish Women's Alliance of America. For one thing, this event took place only two years after the end of World War II. Those years were marked by patriotic activism on the part of thousands of PWA of A members both in their support of the U. S. military effort against Nazi and Japanese imperialism and in their concerted actions in solidarity with Polonia for the people of occupied Poland.

In the postwar years, the Alliance maintained its commitment to the Polish cause. Its members remained heavily involved in both the Polish American Congress political action federation and the Polish American Council humanitarian organization, and they continued to support charitable organizations such as the Catholic League. They also helped Polish refugees who entered this country to build new lives for themselves after passage of the Displaced Persons Act of 1948, in part the result of the lobbying work of the PAC and its member organizations, including the PWA of A. These efforts were to occupy a central place in Polonia for decades following Poland's devastating experience in World War II.

Poland had indeed paid an awful price in the war. About 20 percent of its population perished between 1939 and 1945.

---

[1] *Sprawozdania zarządu głównego i prezesek stanowych Związku Polek w Ameryce, 21– go Sejmu, roku 1951* (Reports of the members of the general administration and the state presidents at the 21st convention of the Polish Women's Alliance of America in 1951.

Moreover, the war had left many of its cities, towns, and villages destroyed or badly damaged, the country's transportation and economic systems were in shambles. The Polish nation that had emerged out of the World War I had also suffered extraordinary losses in human life and property, but these paled in comparison to the country's experience twenty years later. There was, however, another side to Poland's fate after World War II, one whose impact went even deeper.

After World War I, Poland, though devastated, had been established as an independent state for the first time in 123 years, as its foreign occupation and partition at last came to an end. Independence was welcomed in Polonia, and thousands of families returned to the homeland over the next few years. But 95 percent of the total Polish population in America elected to remain in their adopted homeland. With Poland restored, Polish Americans could rest assured that the main task before them was to achieve a better life for themselves and their children in this country. Significantly, the *Wydział Narodowy*, the World War I political action federation that had worked so hard for Poland's independence, soon dissolved. Indeed, not until Nazi Germany's invasion of Poland in 1939 was Polonia's organizations again called upon to make support for the old homeland their top priority.

The post-World War II scene was far more painful to the Polish people and Polonia. In its aftermath, Poland's people found themselves saddled, against their will, with a communist-dominated regime imposed by the Soviet Union, one that lacked any substantial domestic following. That regime was in complete control of the country, as a result of Poland's occupation by the Soviet Red Army and the acquiescence of the Western democratic leaders, Roosevelt and Churchill, to Stalin's new order in Eastern Europe. Furthermore, any hopes of a sovereign Poland with a popularly elected government were shattered by the "Big Three" chieftains' agreement reached at Yalta in February 1945.

By September 1947, the Poles, along with the inhabitants of Hungary, Bulgaria, Romania, Yugoslavia, Albania, the Eastern sectors of Germany and Austria, and the Baltic states of Lithuania,

Latvia, and Estonia all fell under communist domination, with Czechoslovakia soon after experiencing the same fate in February 1948. All were then tightly bound together politically, economically, and militarily to the Soviet Union and sealed off from the free world in the West behind an iron curtain. Their fate amounted to a new division of Europe and for Poland "a defeat in victory," the plaintive title of the book by free Poland's last ambassador to the United States, Jan Ciechanowski. Individuals associated with the Polish American Congress refused to accept this situation, and eventually they were joined in their opposition to Soviet domination of Eastern Europe by most of their fellow citizens.

The organizations of the Polish American community needed to remain active in backing Poland's restoration to full independence, democracy, and international recognition of the lands that had been transferred to Poland at Germany's expense at the "Big Three" conferences at Yalta and Potsdam. The Polish American Congress that had first met in 1944 did not soon disappear from the scene, as had been the fate of its World War I predecessor; instead, the PAC continued as Polonia's political action lobby. The PWA of A strongly backed the PAC and helped raise funds for the one million dollar drive initiated in 1946 so that it might carry on its activities in a financially stable manner.

Humanitarian aid remained a major Polonia activity. Poland's people received assistance in the early postwar years as did the hundreds of thousands of refugees who refused to return to a country under communist domination. Here, the work was handled at first by the *Rada Polonii Amerykańskiej* or Polish American Council (known after the war as American Relief for Poland). Beginning in 1948, both the Council and the Polish American Congress (mainly through one of its units, the American Committee for the Resettlement of Polish Displaced Persons) were helpful in working with agencies such as the Polish American Immigration and Relief Committee of New York. Together they did their part in helping in the resettlement of the more than 120,000 Polish refugees and military personnel who arrived in the United States from Western Europe under the auspices of the Displaced Persons Act. In all these actions, the PWA of A played a notable role.

Given the charged atmosphere of the early postwar years, the Polish Women's Alliance of America's 1947 convention was of particular note to the Polish community. The gathering was especially historic for the PWA of A, too, since the convention occurred just prior to the Alliance's fiftieth anniversary in 1948. The conclave thus provided an important opportunity for the leadership of the PWA of A to underscore the organization's commitment to its historic mission while focusing on its future priorities.[2]

The convention, the largest in the fraternal's history, drew 526 delegates from fifteen states and the District of Columbia who together represented the 666 groups then belonging to the PWA of A. Membership in the PWA of A stood at 67,899, of whom 6,424 were youngsters under the age of sixteen. As shown on the table below, 456 garlands (wianki) were in operation, meaning that 58 percent of the adult groups belonging to the Alliance had their own youth circles.

---

[2]Pamiętnik Sejmu XX-go i Złotego Jubileuszu Związku Polek w Ameryce (souvenir album from the twentieth convention and the golden jubilee of the Polish Women's Alliance of America) Chicago: Polish Women's Alliance of America, 1947); Protokóły 20 – go Sejmu Związku Polek w Ameryce 1947 (Minutes of the 20th convention of the Polish Women's Alliance of America, 1947); Loryś, Historia Związku Polek w Ameryce, passim.

PWA OF A Groups and Youth Circles in 1947 by State

STATE	PWA GROUPS	PWA *WIANKI*
Illinois	212	139
Pennsylvania	157	122
Michigan	58	44
New York	56	27
New Jersey	31	26
Connecticut	29	16
Massachusetts	29	13
Wisconsin	27	20
Ohio	23	10
Indiana	22	20
Maryland	5	5
Missouri	5	5
Nebraska	5	5
California	3	3
West Virginia	3	1
District of Columbia	1	0
Total	**666**	**456**

The Alliance's assets of $9,286,440 represented an increase of $2,083,038 from the 1943 convention. This news served as testimony to the progress made by the PWA of A over its first fifty years.

The 1947 convention included many heartfelt and solemn moments. Things began with the traditional High Mass that was celebrated at Chicago's Blessed Mary of Perpetual Help church by Bishop Stanislaus Bona of the Diocese of Green Bay, Wisconsin. More than one thousand people attended this event.

Following a reception at the church, all were invited to Chicago's Holy Trinity parish hall for a program of entertainment featuring performances by the PWA of A chorus, several of its youth dance groups, and its newly formed orchestra. That evening, another reception was held at the Alliance's national headquarters a few blocks away.

The following Monday morning the convention opened with greetings from Charles Rozmarek, president of the Polish National Alliance and the Polish American Congress; Francis X. Swietlik, censor of the PNA and chairman of the Polish American Council; and Joseph Kania, president of the Polish Roman Catholic Union of

America, among others.   That evening, President Honorata Wołowska chaired the convention banquet. The featured speaker for the evening was Wanda Grabinska, who came from London to present her views on the role of women in the postwar world crisis.

At the business sessions that followed, the most significant issue was the election of a successor to President Wołowska, who had previously declared that she would not seek a fourth four-year term in office. The choice was especially important, given the presidential tradition of strong leadership and lengthy tenures in the office. Wołowska had served for twelve years, following Napieralska and Neumann, who had been president for seventeen and twelve years, respectively.

The contest for the Alliance's top executive post was a spirited one.   It pitted the incumbent vice president, Adela Łagodzinska, who was then fifty-two years of age and who had served in that office since 1939, against two other strong candidates, Helena Sambor and Clara Swieczkowska.   Sambor had herself been PWA of A vice president between 1931 and 1939.   Swieczkowska was a widely known activist, having challenged Wołowska, unsuccessfully, for the presidency in 1935.

Sambor was a popular, veteran PWA of A leader from Northern Indiana.   She had been vice president under both Napieralska and Wołowska and had relinquished her post only because of the two-term rule that had been put into effect in the Alliance in 1935.   Sambor was widely known for her work in building insured membership in the fraternal. In World War II she was also active in the national leadership of the Polish American Congress. (Sambor continued to be active into the 1950s when she was elected to serve as a national director of the PWA of A.)

Swieczkowska, who hailed from Detroit, also possessed a solid record of service in the PWA of A going back many years. She too had played a prominent role in both the Polish American Congress and the Polish American Council during the war years.

Łagodzinska, a native of Chicago, had served as vice president since she had first won election to the post at the Alliance's convention in Niagara Falls, New York, in 1939. Born in 1895 into a family of Polonia activists (her mother had been deeply involved in the PWA of A), she joined the fraternal in 1919 at age twenty-four. Subsequently, Łagodzinska learned the Polish language and grew increasingly engaged in the work of the Alliance. In time she became a highly effective public speaker in Polish as well as in English. Dedicated to encouraging younger, American-born individuals of Polish ancestry to appreciate their heritage, Łagodzinska worked closely with President Wołowska during the eight years of her vice presidency.

In the balloting, Łagodzinska won in the first round, having secured more delegate votes, 265, than the combined total of her two rivals. In the election, Sambor won 168 votes, and Swieczkowska 84. Her victory proved to be as significant as it was decisive, and she went on to serve a record six consecutive four-year terms at the helm of the PWA of A. It was not until 1971 that she relinquished her post.

Adela Łagodzinska would never again encounter so serious a challenge in seeking the presidency as the contest she faced in 1947. In 1951 she was reelected by a comfortable margin of 387 votes to 156 over Jadwiga Karłowicz, the editor of *Głos Polek*. In 1955 she faced no opposition at all. In 1959 her two rivals won a total of only 185 votes to her 279. In 1963 she was returned to office by a 338 – 137 margin. In 1967, she won yet again this time by a vote of 343 – 96. Clearly, Łagodzinska was a formidable presence in the PWA of A throughout her long presidency.

Łagodzinska made her service to the Polish Women's Alliance of America and Polonia the centerpiece of her life. As PWA of A president, she continued to aggressively promote the Polish cause as a major facet of the fraternal's work. Here she worked well with Honorary President Wołowska, who remained a fixture in the Alliance for years after her formal retirement.

The twentieth convention, occurring as it did on the eve of the fiftieth anniversary of the founding of the PWA of A in 1898, offered an opportune moment to look back on the organization's achievements and to recognize the contributions of the women who had done so much to promote its growth, often in the face of great obstacles. Symbolizing the PWA of A's recognition of its roots was the convention book that was distributed among the delegates as a memento of both the history of the Alliance and a salute to its upcoming fiftieth-anniversary jubilee.

Featuring a golden cover emblazoned with the emblem of the Alliance, the nine-by-twelve-inch convention book was a substantial 192 pages in length. It included a host of greetings from the representatives of Polonia's organizations along with praise from religious and secular leaders of national and international stature. Among the well wishers were August Cardinal Hlond, archbishop of Warsaw and Gniezno and head of the Roman Catholic Church in Poland, Samuel Cardinal Stritch, archbishop of Chicago, Dwight Green, governor of Illinois, and Martin Kennelly, mayor of Chicago.

Prepared by a committee chaired by Rozalia Baczynska, the anniversary/convention book included contributions from President Wołowska, *Głos Polek* editor Karłowicz, Halina Paluszek (then the director of the PWA of A Museum located in the fraternal's home office), and youth program representative Constance Rybinska. There were comments as well from a variety of other activists, including Amelia Szlak, chairwoman of the preconvention committee and president of PWA of A District 1 in Chicago and Group 1 of the Alliance. Łucja Wołowska, one of the earliest national officers of the PWA of A and a lifelong delegate to its conventions, and Stanisława Petrykowska of Milwaukee, the oldest living former state district president, offered words of wisdom on the mission of the Alliance, Wołowska on its members' responsibilities toward Poland, Petrykowska on their loyalty to America. The book also included more than two hundred congratulatory messages from the groups and councils of the PWA of A.

The golden jubilee celebrations continued into the next year, culminating in a three-day celebration that began with a mass of thanksgiving on Founders Day, May 22, 1948, at Chicago's Holy Trinity parish church. This event was followed by special ceremonies chaired by President Łagodzinska at the PWA of A national headquarters. A mass in memory of all deceased members of the fraternal was also held at Holy Trinity church, and special ceremonies took place to honor the three past presidents of the Women's Alliance who were buried at St. Adalbert's Cemetery, Stefania Chmielinska, Anna Neumann, and Emilia Napieralska. Concurrent with these events, a special supplement of *Głos Polek*, featuring the PWA of A story and biographies of its honorary members, was distributed to members across the country.

At the jubilee banquet held later that day at Chicago's Congress Hotel, President Łagodzinska marked the occasion by distributing special anniversary pins to all district presidents. Former *Głos Polek* editor Stefania Laudyn-Chrzanowska, who had perished in Poland during World War II, was honored at the dedication of her portrait by Polonia artist Michał Rękucki. This work was later placed in the PWA of A Museum. Łagodzinska also expressed the Alliance's appreciation to Sofie Jerzyk, president of District 3 in Indiana, for winning the special jubilee membership competition among the state divisions. She had sold a total of $117,600 in insurance.

Adela Łagodzinska was from the outset vigorous in leading the Alliance in its support of Poland's freedom and independence. She also dedicated much of her time and energy to the resettlement of Polish immigrants who entered the United States after passage of the Displaced Persons Act in 1948.

As an American of Polish descent, Łagodzinska appreciated, perhaps even more than some of the Polish-born Polonia activists of her time, the importance of educating people about their Polish heritage and culture. Throughout her years as head of the Alliance she would pay a great deal of attention to this work. Here Łagodzinska found many allies. One was past director Albina Damsz of Chicago, who took the initiative to establish a school where youngsters could study Polish language, history, and literature. Sponsored by the Pobudka society, PWA of A group 723, the school operated out of the home office of the Alliance and enjoyed Łagodzinska's staunch support.

Łagodzinska had still another priority on her agenda. This involved her work to better define the Alliance's mission as a fraternal benefit society. Here her main objective was to expand the PWA of A membership base and to broaden participation in its activities among the younger generation.

Łagodzinska's interest in building membership was particularly timely. In the 1930s, with America reeling from the depression, the Alliance had had to concentrate its energies on retaining current members. With the onset of World War II, the focus had necessarily turned to working for America's and Poland's causes. But the war's end prompted a new emphasis on membership growth, both to help the Alliance realize its time-honored objectives as a mass membership movement of women and to bring its message to new generations in this country.

Łagodzinska's interest in making membership growth a high priority came at an opportune moment. For one thing, the postwar Polish American community was still cohesive and vital, and its members were receptive to the PWA of A's message. (Only later, beginning in the late 1950s and early 1960s, would large numbers of Polish Americans, especially those who were younger and more affluent, begin to relocate in large numbers to the suburbs or to newer parts of the city, a development that heralded a gradual withdrawal from Polonia life for many.) The decade after the war was also a time of rising prosperity and economic opportunity for many Americans. Not surprisingly, in these new circumstances more people of Polish heritage were entering the market to buy life insurance, something their depression-scarred parents had come to regard as a luxury.

Moreover, after 1948 large numbers of Poles began making their way from Europe to the United States. It was the first substantial immigration since the pre-World War I years. They settled in the existing Polonia neighborhoods and were quickly integrated into the community's still flourishing, ethnically based, organizational life. In joining Polonia, the newcomers contributed much to its revitalization. This postwar immigration of displaced persons, though sometimes disparaged as "DPs," proved to be quite interested in joining Polonia's churches and fraternals, including the PWA of A.[3]

---

[3]The entry of so many members of the post-World War II Polish migration into the organizational life of Polonia may be contrasted with the failure, at least thus far, of more than a few of the most recent "Solidarity era" immigrants to join the fraternals. This sensitive issue may be approached from several perspectives. From one point of view, the difference may be seen as temporary. After all, new immigrants, whatever their country of origin, must first find work and adequate housing in their new homeland before they can begin to think about joining organizations, even helpful beneficial organizations like fraternals. In this light, the behavior of the most recent waves of Polish newcomers is not unlike that of the Poles who settled in America before World War I. Indeed, despite the merits of the fraternals

Some of Łagodzinska's efforts to build membership were quite innovative for the time. For example, she rewarded the recruitment work of particularly successful financial secretaries by publicizing their accomplishments in the pages of *Głos Polek*. In her frequent visits to PWA of A local groups and councils, Łagodzinska and her fellow officers regularly emphasized membership development.

In January 1951, the PWA of A received a favorable evaluation of its financial standing from the Illinois department of insurance. As a result of this review, the Alliance took the unprecedented step of offering a special dividend. Accordingly, all members who had been insured for at least two years were made eligible for the dividend, which was distributed in the form of additional "paid up" (cost-free) life insurance.

Recruiting new members of all ages was a key aspect of Łagodzinska's efforts to strengthen the fraternal. She was especially interested in enrolling youngsters into the Alliance. At the 1947 convention, the delegates had approved insured membership for boys, along with girls, into the PWA of A Juvenile Department. The decision led to a substantial increase in the size of the department over the next fifteen years.

Significantly, in 1947 a total of 6,424 youngsters, all of them girls under age sixteen were insured through the Alliance. In 1951 the total, which by then included boys, reached 10,258.

---

in that era, they did not attract a truly mass membership until the 1920s, when the immigrants and their families had achieved a modicum of affluence. A second perspective underscores the effects of over four decades of communist rule on the Polish people. This was a time in which people were constantly told that the state's role was to take care of all of one's material needs, cradle to the grave style. Aside from the regime's grudging toleration of the Church, a prohibition on all genuine voluntary associations was the rule and a blackout against knowledge of their benefits. Yet a third perspective focuses on recognizing the significant changes that have occurred within American Polonia itself over the years.   On relations between members of different Polish emigrations in America, see Stanislaus Blejwas, "Old and New Polonias: Tensions within an Ethnic Community," Polish American Studies, 38, no. 2 (1981), 55 – 83; and Mary Patrice Erdmans, "Immigrants and Ethnics: Conflict and Identity in Polish Chicago," The Sociological Quarterly, 36, no. 1 (1995), 175-195. The first piece looks at the relations between the old pre-World War I Polonia and the post World War II emigration. The second deals with the post 1970 immigration and its differences with the Polonia establishment of that time.

In 1955 it had grown to 14,337, a net increase of 224 percent in only eight years. Thereafter, the rate of growth in juvenile membership did slow somewhat, peaking in 1963 at 17,489 members but declining to 15,317 in 1971, Łagodzinska's final year in office. The decline can be attributed largely to the fact that many young members had simply grown into adulthood at a faster pace than that of the enrollment of new youngsters into the fraternal over the same period.

With the increase in the number of children in the PWA of A came an expansion in the number of youth groups or *wianki* from 456 in 1947 to 565 in 1959. In the latter year, the Alliance included 620 local adult groups. This meant that nine of every ten of them possessed their own youth circle. Only twelve years earlier, barely two of every three groups had organized *wianki* units.

To further promote the involvement of youngsters in the PWA of A, Łagodzinska and her colleagues encouraged regular youth congresses for their benefit. These events had flowered briefly before World War II but had been discontinued when many local activists were pressed into other activities. The first of the revived congresses was held in 1953 and was judged a big success. More than two hundred young activists from around the country participated in the three-day event, which took place in Chicago. The theme of the gathering was the promotion of greater interest and appreciation of Poland's ethnic folk dance tradition and fourteen PWA of A dance groups participated in the congress. It was followed by similar events held around the country roughly every other year.

A second youth congress was held in September 1955 at Orchard Lake Seminary near Detroit just before the PWA of A's twenty-second national convention. More than two hundred and fifty young people took part in this event. Its theme was both thought provoking and forward looking: "How Does Your Polish Ancestry Make You a Better American?"

In June 1958, a third congress was held, again in Chicago. The themes taken up at the gathering were fresh and relevant: "What I Do and Don't like About the Daily Life of a Young Woman," "Teaching as a Career," and "Dieting." The discussions on these and other matters generated great interest and enthusiasm among the participants and helped build new optimism among Alliance activists about the Alliance's capacity to reach out to the new generation with its message. Once revived, the PWA of A youth congresses, later called youth conferences, have continued to the present time as regular events. [4]

As a result of these and other efforts to focus attention upon expanding membership, the PWA of A experienced a dramatic increase in growth in nearly all sectors of its organizational life. This was most readily observed in the 1950s.

PWA of A MEMBERSHIP AND ORGANIZATIONAL GROWTH 1947 – 1971

	Total Members	Adults	Youths	Groups	Youth Groups	Total Assets*
1947	67,899	61,475	6,424	666	456	9,915
1951	79,690	69,432	10,258	667	511	12,657
1955	87,067	72,330	14,337	661	545	15,691
1959	90,302	73,603	16,699	643	565	19,835
1963	91,101	73,612	17,489	620	558	23,665
1967	90,080	73,399	16,681	592	531	26,736
1971	86,351	71,034	15,317	559	496	28,684

*Total Assets (1000s of dollars)

The PWA of A also expanded both geographically and institutionally after 1947, especially in several parts of the country where it had hitherto had only a modest presence. Several new regional councils were established in Los Angeles, Western Pennsylvania, and New Jersey. All became centers of PWA of A activism.

---

[4] By its activities from the 1950s onward, the PWA of A proved itself to be far ahead of other organizations in focusing its attention on drawing young people to its message. Not until the late 1960s was there a significant surge in promoting cultural pluralism and the "new ethnicity" in America. Perhaps the most discussed and debated publication, among many, in this genre was written by a theologian of Slovak heritage, Michael Novak, *The Rise of the Unmeltable Ethnic* (New York: Macmillan, 1971).

In 1951, a new regional district was established called District 12. It covered the state of Maryland and the District of Columbia and was initially headed by Martha Welzant. A second, District 13, took in the state of California following its separation from Nebraska. Elected to lead this new district was Wanda Dettling. In 1967 Dettling made a spirited, if unsuccessful, challenge for the presidency.

The Łagodzinska-led efforts to promote member growth had much to do with the Alliance's expansion in the postwar years. But the impressive gains the PWA of A recorded in the years between 1947 and 1971 were also to a great degree a reflection of the period in which the organization was operating. This was an era of still vibrant Polonia life that was further strengthened by the entry of large numbers of newcomers from war-torn Europe. These individuals were often highly receptive to the message of the PWA of A and its fellow fraternal societies. But by the mid 1960s s the slow decline of the Polonia began to be reflected in PWA of A membership figures. By 1971, total membership in the Alliance fell by 5 percent from its level twelve years earlier.

This downward trend was not unique to the Polish Women's Alliance of America and was readily observed in the membership data for other Polish American fraternal insurance societies as well. A glance at the record of the two other leading Chicago-based national Polonia fraternals, the Polish National Alliance and the Polish Roman Catholic Union of America, makes this clear, though some differences in their experiences are also evident.

Membership in the Largest Polish American Fraternals, 1935 – 1978

	Polish Women's Alliance	Polish National Alliance	Polish Roman Catholic Union
1935	52,880	284,289	154,622
1955	85,407	337,829	175,502
1970	87,084	326,611	139,071
1978	78,030	302,137	114,941

One can sum up the record of the twenty-one year long administration of Adela Łagodzinska by noting that hers was a presidency that was characterized by a commitment to establish policies to strengthen the Alliance as a fraternal insurance benefit society and to expand its membership base.   Even the membership declines in the last years of her tenure, though troubling, were not unique to the PWA of A. Rather, they were attributable to broad social and cultural developments in the American society of the 1960s and 1970s.   These included significant changes in the Polish ethnic community and assimilation's impact on a population whose members were, with the exception of the post World War II newcomers, one or two generations removed from the immigration experience.

THE PWA OF A AS A FORCE IN POLONIA IN THE ŁAGODZINSKA ERA

The Chicago-born Łagodzinska quickly rose to become a leading figure in representing the PWA of A in Polonia affairs once she took over the presidency of the Alliance.   Under her leadership the PWA of A remained heavily engaged in the activities of the ethnic community's main organizations, the Polish American Congress and the Polish American Council.

Already in 1948 Łagodzinska was elected national vice president of the Polish American Congress, Polonia's political action federation, at its second national convention; she continued to serve in that capacity until 1971. Her strong-willed dedication to her work not only benefited the Congress, but cemented the bond that has continued to exist between the PAC and the PWA of A long after her own retirement.

Łagodzinska was also chosen to be deputy chairman of the American Committee for the Resettlement of Polish Displaced Persons, a major unit of the PAC. The committee was chaired by Blair Gunther, a Pennsylvania judge and national leader of the PNA. Its mission was to assist refugees who were admitted into the United States under the provisions of the Displaced Persons Act of 1948. This the committee did by identifying Americans, Polish and non-Polish, who agreed to sponsor the newcomers on their arrival and help them get on their feet in the new land.

Łagodzinska took her duties with the committee very seriously. She also headed the PWA of A's activities to set up its own committee to aid the newcomers. Taking leadership roles in this demanding work were Vice President Bronisława Karczewska,

Legal Counsel Barbara Fisher, former vice president Helena Sambor, and Director Veronica Siwek. A notable example of their efforts is discussed by PWA of A historian Maria Loryś. It is the story in which fifteen immigrant families, eighty-one people in all (of whom fifty-two were children), found new homes in Chicago through the help of the PWA of A.[5]

Although there were serious frictions between Charles Rozmarek, the strong-willed president of both the Polish American Congress and the Polish National Alliance fraternal society, and former PNA censor Francis Swietlik, chairman of the Polish American Council, Polonia's chief humanitarian federation of the day, their animosity neither involved Łagodzinska nor limited the effectiveness of her own volunteer work. Indeed, she continued for many years as both the general secretary of the council while serving as a vice president of both the PAC and its resettlement committee. Łagodzinska also worked closely with Monsignor Felix Burant of New York, who with Walter Zachariasiewicz headed another key agency of the time, the New York based Polish American Immigration and Relief Committee.[6]

Łagodzinska was also active in still another humanitarian association, the Catholic League for Religious Assistance to Poland, a Chicago-based organization formed in support of the Polish Roman Catholic Church. In the process, she deepened the Roman Catholic orientation of the Polish Women's Alliance, which had once been strong in the 1920s and 1930s under President Emilia Napieralska but had become a less salient aspect of PWA of A life under Honorata Wołowska. Because of her connection with the Catholic League, Łagodzinska was invited to represent Polonia at the planning meetings of the National Catholic Resettlement Council in the early 1950s. This body enjoyed good relations with Catholic dioceses throughout the country; its mission was to

---

[5] Loryś, *Historia Związku Polek w Ameryce*, pp. 183 – 184.

[6] For a capsule history of the Polish American Immigration Committee, see Walter Zachariasiewicz, "The Organizational Structure of Polonia," in Frank Mocha, editor, *Poles in America: Bicentennial Essays* (Stevens Point, WI: Worzalla Publishers, 1978). The dedicated Burant, a third-generation American of Polish descent and a pastor of a Manhattan parish, was succeeded upon his death by Monsignor John Karpinski. More than fifty thousand persons are estimated to have been assisted by the organization in its first thirty years of work.

coordinate the work of a variety of charitable organizations on behalf of the newcomers from Europe. In this way, the PWA of A served as a clearinghouse for Polish resettlement work.

In addition, Łagodzinska took a leading role in defending the rights of Polish immigrants to enter the United States, a position that was not especially popular in the atmosphere of rising anticommunist sentiment that accompanied the early Cold War years. This was the time of the most severe antagonism between the United States and Stalin's Soviet regime. There were understandable security concerns in this country about the threat of foreign subversion, concerns that were reflected in the passage of the McCarron-Walter Act of 1952. This law placed new restrictions on the number of new immigrants from Eastern Europe. While Łagodzinska and her colleagues in the PWA of A and the PAC understood the government's security concerns, they expressed Polonia's resentment against the use of the communism issue to restrict legitimate Polish immigration. Together with Halina Paluszek, the editor of *Głos Polek,* Łagodzinska appeared in the nation's capital to call for changes to end the act's discriminatory treatment of Polish immigrants.[7]

Łagodzinska's Catholicism was evident in various ways. In 1954, she supported the church's devotional activities during the Marian Year. This was a time of special world wide veneration of the Virgin Mary, the mother of Jesus, as proclaimed by Pope Pius XII. The Polish Women's Alliance of America was also a prominent participant at the great Mass held at Chicago's Soldier Field that same year. That memorable event brought together some 260,000 of the faithful in an extraordinary display of religious devotion. Leading one of the processions was Albina Szudarska, president of District 1 in Illinois. (Participation by PWA of A members in this event recalled their involvement in the Eucharistic Congress and Mass held in 1926 at the same arena.)

---

[7]Loryś, *Historia Związku Polek w Ameryce*, pp. 184 – 185.   A broader issue involved resentment over the Immigration Restriction Act of 1924, which remained the supreme law on the matter. Polish Americans considered the law discriminatory.   It was only overturned   due to the passage of the Immigration Reform Act of 1965, whereby the discriminatory quotas based on the national origins of immigrants were abolished.

Łagodzinska and her colleagues in the PWA of A leadership took a special interest in supporting the fundraising activities in Polonia on behalf of the construction of the great shrine of the Virgin Mother of Częstochowa, the patroness of Poland, in Doylestown, Pennsylvania. This site, not far from the city of Philadelphia, became an object of special interest, even devotion, for many Alliance groups, councils and state district units around the country. They organized numerous pilgrimages to the magnificent Basilica church that was built there. These continue to this day at what Polonia proudly calls the "American Częstochowa."[8]

Łagodzinska and the PWA of A strongly opposed the Soviet communist domination of Poland and staunchly backed every Polish American Congress initiative to rally public opposition to the regime in Warsaw. For example, in 1951 she, along with treasurer Leokadia Blikowska and Halina Paluszek, PAC president Rozmarek and other Polonia leaders, participated in the hearings of the special bipartisan committee of the U. S. House of Representatives that had been created to investigate the Katyn massacre. Roman Pucinski, a Chicago journalist, was the committee's chief investigator and led an exhaustive review of the massacre. Concluding its work in 1952, the committee found the Soviet regime responsible for the deaths of more than fourteen thousand Polish military officers in the spring of 1940. Though the committee's report was unanimously approved by Congress, it would not be until 1992 that the government of a post-communist Russia acknowledged the Stalin regime's guilt in the crime.

Łagodzinska was a dedicated anticommunist, but she was also an independent thinker who was willing and able to act on her convictions. In August 1956 she traveled to Poland as a private citizen to learn firsthand what was happening there. Her trip included a visit to the monastery of Częstochowa, which houses the famed icon of the Black Madonna. [9]

---

[8] The basilica was the dream and life's work of the Reverend Michael Zembrzuski, a priest of the Pauline order. In the 1970s, when the extraordinary burden of managing the construction and financing of the church proved to be too great, the Polish Women's Alliance of America and its members were among the first to come forward with their support.

[9] Łagodzinska's visit to the shrine came on the three hundredth anniversary celebrations in connection with the declaration of the Mother of Jesus as

Her visit to Poland occurred at a very critical and uncertain time in Polish national life. The communist regime was experiencing a major crisis, which in October led to the collapse of Stalinist control of the country and the ascent to power of a more reform-minded faction in the ruling party, one headed by Władysław Gomułka.

Following her return home, Łagodzinska was criticized for having made contact with the communist regime and somehow thereby legitimized it. But she stressed that she had traveled to Poland for humanitarian reasons and in doing so had gained the invaluable opportunity to learn firsthand what was going on in the country. In sharing her observations with PWA of A members and the leaders of Polonia upon her return, Łagodzinska accurately observed that Poland was on the verge of a political breakdown. [10]

Some virulent anticommunists in Polonia continued to demand that the Polish community in America and elsewhere refuse to deal with the Gomułka regime. However, the Polish American Congress came out in favor of a U. S. economic aid package for Poland in 1957. Backed by the Republican and conservative president Dwight D. Eisenhower, this plan eventually provided more than five hundred million dollars in assistance to Poland. Łagodzinska supported this program, just as she backed greater travel to Poland and Polonia's greater involvement in giving humanitarian assistance to the Polish people, as exemplified by new initiatives taken by the Polish American Council. [11]

In April 1957 Łagodzinska was again in Poland, this time heading a delegation of eighty-three PWA of A members and their

---

Queen and Protector of Poland. The declaration goes back to the time of the Swedish invasion of Poland, the assault on the Częstochowa monastery, and the country's liberation from its enemies in 1655. This dramatic story serves as the basis of Henryk Sienkiewicz's epic novel, *The Deluge* (*Potop*) (Philadelphia: Copernicus Society, 1991).

[10]Loryś, *Historia Związku Polek w Ameryce*, p. 218.

[11]Pienkos, *For Your Freedom*, pp. 99-102. On Gomułka and the events of 1956 in Eastern Europe, see Zbigniew K. Brzezinski, *The Soviet Bloc: Unity and Conflict* revised edition (New York: Praeger, 1961), chapters 2-3, 11, 14.

friends.   Together they made the first Alliance pilgrimage to Poland since 1939. The tour was also the first such trip to be led by a president of the Polish Women's Alliance of America since Emilia Napieralska's visit in 1928.   The theme of the 1957 pilgrimage underscored the visitors' yearnings (tęsknota) to see the old homeland again and featured trips to several of Poland's main religious sites.

While in Poland, the group traveled to the important Eastern Polish city of Lublin.   There it visited the Catholic University of Lublin (Katolicki Uniwersytet Lubelski or KUL), the only privately operated institution of higher education permitted to exist anywhere in the communist world. Following this visit, the Polish Women's Alliance of America became a strong supporter of KUL and backed a series of actions to assist the financially hard-pressed institution.

Funds were initially collected to support the development of the university's library and to purchase equipment for its biology department.   In the 1970s ten thousand dollars was donated towards the construction of new student housing. This sum plus the publicity the PWA of A regularly gave to KUL, was important, particularly because the Polish government refused to give it any assistance. (It was at KUL where a priest named Karol Wojtyła taught and did his research in theology.   Later he was named archbishop of Kraków and in 1978 became Pope John Paul II.)[12]

A highlight of the 1957 pilgrimage came with the group's visit to Częstochowa.   There the delegation met and spoke with Poland's highest churchman, Stefan Cardinal Wyszyński, the archbishop of Warsaw and Gniezno. Wyszyński had been under house arrest during the Stalinist period. Following his release, he had given his public support in December 1956 and January 1957 to the Gomułka regime, calling it the only realistic alternative to Soviet military intervention and possible bloodshed. In return, the new communist leader, an atheist himself, had been obliged

---

[12]Other examples of PWA of A projects undertaken in Poland after 1957 include its support of the Laski school for blind children near Warsaw, and the Maria Konopnicka elementary school in Żarnowice. "Our 90th Anniversary: How and Why the Polish Women's Alliance of America was formed," manuscript in the office of the Głos Polek (1988).

to make good on his extraordinary pledge to Wyszyński to allow the Polish clergy to teach catechism in the country's public schools.[13]

In 1958, Łagodzinska went to Poland for the third time in less than three years. This time she traveled in the company of Francis X. Swietlik, chairman of the Polish American Council charitable federation. On this occasion, the two leaders were able to arrange meetings with *Caritas*, the welfare society directed by the Polish Church. *Caritas* had then just recently been permitted to resume its benevolent work after having been dissolved by the Stalinists in 1949. The meetings themselves were both cordial and productive; at them Łagodzinska spoke of Honorata Wołowska's visit to *Caritas* just before the society's dissolution. Significantly, Swietlik and Łagodzinska established a new working relationship with the society, one that brought substantial material benefits to many people over the next decade.

Throughout her tenure, Łagodzinska continued to represent the PWA of A in the spirit of her predecessors. She worked effectively with Charles Rozmarek of the Polish American Congress until 1968, when he was succeeded as head of the Congress by Aloysius A. Mazewski. Mazewski had defeated Rozmarek for the presidency of the Polish National Alliance in 1967; he took over the reins of the PAC a year later. Łagodzinska worked closely with him as well.

Over the years, Łagodzinska took part in countless meetings throughout the United States to promote public support for Poland's restoration to freedom from Soviet domination. One of the most significant of these occurred in Washington, D. C. in 1959, when she spoke with Secretary of State Christian Herter to voice PWA of A support for a series of PAC initiatives. These included the winning of official American recognition of Poland's western and northern borders with Germany, which Roosevelt had accepted at Yalta but the United States had refused to ratify.

---

[13]Cardinal Wyszyński's remarks to the delegation are found in Loryś, pp. 220 – 226. Incidentally, a PWA of A gift of a piano to the Częstochowa shrine following the group's visit was still in use in the 1990s. On Polonia's stance toward Poland after 1956, see Donald Pienkos, *For Your Freedom*, pp. 99 – 102 and 139 – 149.

Łagodzinska was present, along with many other PWA of A members, at the fifth national convention of the Polish American Congress in Chicago on September 30, 1960. On this historic occasion, President Eisenhower became the first chief executive of the United States to address the organization. In his remarks the president made a special point of praising "the fierce dedication of the Polish people to the conception of liberty and personal freedom," qualities that made them "an example to the world." Another convention speaker was Senator John F. Kennedy of Massachusetts, who had just become the Democratic Party's presidential nominee.

Earlier that year, Vice President Richard M. Nixon addressed a massive Polonia audience at the annual Polish Constitution Day observance held in May at Chicago's Humboldt Park. Nixon would soon go on to become the Republican Party's presidential nominee. The year 1960 thus represented a high point in the Polish American community's significance as a factor in America's presidential politics.

There were other important occasions where Łagodzinska represented Polonia and the Alliance in connection with the Polish cause. Of particular note was her presence at the Rose Garden of the White House on July 31, 1964, where President Lyndon B. Johnson spoke to a delegation of Polish American leaders on the twentieth anniversary of the Warsaw Uprising.

Łagodzinska's loyalty and her energetic commitment to the Polonia cause were especially needed in the 1960s and early 1970s. This was a time in which the U. S. government's focus under Presidents Johnson and Nixon was on the Vietnam War. In this atmosphere, the Polish issue was for all intents and purposes placed on the back burner.

Throughout her years as PWA of A president, Łagodzinska was constant in her support of the effort to increase knowledge about the Polish immigrant and ethnic experience in America. Perhaps because she was herself American born, Łagodzinska possessed an insight that was distinct from some of her Polish-born colleagues as to the importance of educating Polish Americans about their heritage. For example, she was actively engaged in working on behalf of the fledgling Polish American Historical Association, established in 1942 under the leadership of

Oskar Halecki, a respected historian of Poland, and Mieczysław Haiman, the curator of the Polish Museum in Chicago.

Halecki had been in New York at the time of the World's Fair in 1939. Following Nazi Germany's invasion of Poland that September, he had returned to America to devote himself to writing about his homeland and promoting its cause in this country. With several fellow academic exiles, he organized the Polish Institute of Arts and Sciences in America early in 1942. The Polish Institute was established initially as a branch of the Polish Academy of Learning in occupied Poland; its aim in America was one of preserving knowledge about the embattled homeland's history and culture. Halecki and his Chicago-based collaborator, Haiman, had then gone a step further in establishing the PAHA.

Łagodzinska knew and respected both men and supported their efforts. In 1951 she proposed that that year's PAHA annual meeting be held at the PWA of A headquarters. There at the tenth gathering of the historical society, those in attendance approved its mission statement: "To meet the need for impartial and expert analysis of the contribution made by Polish Americans to the richly textured pattern of American life." Łagodzinska remained a member of the Council of the Polish American Historical Association for the next twenty-four years.[14]

Examples abound of the continued commitment of the Polish Women's Alliance of America to enlighten others about the Polish heritage during the years of Łagodzinska's presidency. In this period, the fraternal's educational department was especially active under the direction of Halina Paluszek and Monica Sokolowski. One of its major initiatives was that of distributing materials about the Polish heritage in Europe and America for the benefit of PWA of A members and the wider community. A notable example of this effort came in 1956 when the Alliance purchased seven hundred copies of Halecki's popular work, *A History of Poland,* and distributed them at no cost to U. S. church leaders, government representatives, newspapers and magazines, libraries, universities, and local PWA of A leaders.

The Alliance also paid a great deal of attention to the Polish heritage in its fraternal publication, *Głos Polek.* In many cases,

---

[14]Loryś, pp. 181 – 182.

the involvement of Łagodzinska and her fellow officers was highlighted to place greater emphasis on the importance of heritage in the Alliance.

In May 1954 a PWA of A delegation headed by Łagodzinska attended the centennial anniversary celebration of the founding of the community of Panna Maria, Texas. The little town was the home of the first settlement of Polish immigrants in America. The PWA of A representatives attending the ceremony made the most of their visit by stopping at each of the parishes that had been created in Panna Maria and the surrounding communities of Czestochowa, St. Hedwig, Kościuszko, and Pawelekville.

Another example of Łagodzinska's interest in Polonia's heritage in America came in September 1958 with the celebration of the three hundred and fiftieth anniversary of the arrival of the first Polish immigrants in America and their contributions to the first English settlement in the New World. This observance took place at the Jamestown colony in Virginia. There, a large delegation of PWA of A members that included Vice President Barbara Fisher, *Głos Polek* editor Jadwiga Karłowicz, and District Presidents Martha Welzant. Florence Knapp, Helen Robakiewicz, Aniela Jonik, and Helena Sambor were in attendance, along with many members from their districts and elsewhere too.

A third noteworthy effort came in 1966, when the PWA of A joined Poles and people of Polish origin throughout the world to celebrate Poland's *Millennium,* or thousandth anniversary of its people's acceptance of Christianity and the country's recognition as a European state. Once again, the Alliance was highly visible in commemorative events that took place in connection with the *Millennium*. President Johnson spoke at a special White House ceremony marking the event, and Łagodzinska was in attendance as the representative of the PWA of A.

Lastly, throughout her tenure, Łagodzinska continued the tradition set by her predecessors and made the PWA of A's national headquarters in Chicago a place where the supporters of the cause of a free Poland were always welcome. In November 1956, the PWA of A general administration had voted to change *Głos Polek* from a weekly to a biweekly publication. At the same time, the paper was divided into two sections, one written in Polish, the other in English. From that time on, *Głos Polek* had two managing editors, both appointed by the general administration. This decision represented a break with the past, since the editor of the publication had always been elected at the national convention. In this reorganization, longtime *Głos Polek* editor Jadwiga Karłowicz was placed in charge of the larger, ten-page, Polish language section; Melanie Sokołówska was made responsible for the English section, which was originally two pages in length.

Melanie Sokołowska's tenure was abbreviated and she was soon succeeded by Monica Sokolowski, who was not related to her. In 1971 Monica Sokolowski was herself elected a national director; it was at that point that the newly retired Łagodzinska took her place in editing the English section. She continued in this work until 1979, when at the age of eighty-three, she handed over the reins to Maria Kubiak, a member of the new generation. Łagodzinska remained interested active in the PWA of A for years afterwards. Her death in 1990 at the age of ninety-four saddened all who recalled her many years of service to the Alliance, Polonia, Poland, and America.

Of Łagodzinska's many contributions to the Polish Women's Alliance of America, two stand out. One was the work she and her colleagues performed in maintaining the organization's commitment to its founding mission. Dedication to the advancement of women, a love of the Polish heritage, and a willingness to work for the cause of Poland and its people all remained essential elements in the Alliance during and after her years in office. Second, Łagodzinska worked effectively to renew the PWA of A as a fraternal benefit society by improving its insurance products and recruiting new members into the organization. When she retired, the PWA of A was stronger than it had ever been before.[15]

A member of the Polish Women's Alliance of America for seventy-one years, Łagodzinska was always addressed as "Miss Adela" by those who came to know her. As a vice president and then as its president, she brought increased recognition to the

---

[15]Among the many honors Łagodzinska received, one of particular note was the *Fidelitas* medal that was presented to her at Orchard Lake Seminary and College in 1957 in appreciation of her dedicated services to the church and to the Polish and American peoples. Łagodzinska was the first woman to receive this honor.

PWA of A thanks to her strength of purpose, warmth, confidence, wit, and gentility. In the words of a longtime friend, Myra Lenard, she was "always energetic, full of joy, ambitious and civic-minded . . . a feminist who remained feminine . . . very elegant, beautifully groomed, astute as well as intelligent, showing a natural perception and talent for creativity and organizing . . . a natural leader who knew how to command attention."[16]

One of the kinder compliments that might well have been directed to Łagodzinska personally came from President Johnson in a speech he delivered in 1964. In talking about the achievements of the fraternal movement in America, Johnson put things beautifully when he declared:

> You have ministered to the needs of the needy. You have provided scholarships and educational opportunity for those hungering to learn. You have given to hospitals and medical services to the sick and the aged. You have brought happiness to many Americans who have not always had access to the fullest measure of the blessings of man.

---

[16] Myra Lenard, "Remembering Adela Łagodzinska: Polonia Leader and President of the Polish Women's Alliance of America, 1947 – 1971," paper presented at the fifty-sixth annual meeting of the Polish Institute of Arts and Sciences of America, Georgetown University, Washington, D. C., June 13, 1998, at a special panel honoring the PWA of A in its centennial year. Also speaking at the program were PWA of A Director Albina Świerzbińska, Theodore Zawistowski, and Donald Pienkos. PWA of A President Delphine Lytell attended the program and took part in the discussion that followed the presentations. In her remarks, Lenard also noted that Łagodzinska "paid" for her dedication to the causes of the Polish Women's Alliance of America. "In 1966 she was seriously injured in an automobile accident in Poland, one that left her with serious knee and leg injuries that plagued her for the rest of her life . . . . Her last years were spent in a nursing home where she passed away in 1990 at the age of 94 . . . . she had lived long enough to see a free and independent Poland."

NEW CHALLENGES AND ACHIEVEMENTS: THE POLISH WOMEN'S ALLIANCE OF AMERICA IN RECENT TIMES

I have been strengthened by my association with my fellow PWA of A members and by their idealism and patriotic sentiments. Their commitment to our cause guarantees a bright future for our organization . . . . Nearly all of us in the Polish Women's Alliance are born in America – but in our hearts there beats a love for Poland.

Helen Zielinski, 1975 and 1979

"It was at the turn of the last century that our noble founders established the Polish Women's Alliance of America. With your help we can carry the torch to meet the turn of the next century. We can note the past accomplishments with deserved pride, but we must also prepare for the future. We have a powerful legacy. And now we need a promise from you, to help us continue that legacy into the twenty-first century. Won't you help?

Helen Wojcik, 1995

Here we are, one hundred years after the founding of the Polish Women's Alliance of America! Surely, this very thought should evoke awe and excitement in our minds and hearts because one hundred years is a very long time. It speaks of our dedication, determination, energy, and love for the ideals of *Związek Polek* . . . . a movement seeking active participation in a fraternal setting, a voice and presence in Polonia, and an organization dedicated to maintaining the Polish cultural identity . . . . My personal conviction is that the goals of our founders became infectious. If you were a Polish woman, this was the thing to do: join the Polish Women's Alliance of America. In unity, there is strength!

Delphine Lytell, 1998

We welcome a new century with its challenges and opportunities. We have the chance to change, to begin again, and to renew our spirit.

Virginia Sikora, 2000[1]

---

[1] Helen Zielinski's words are from the president's reports to the delegates attending the 27th convention (in 1975) and the 28th convention (1979);

Adela Łagodzinska's retirement from the presidency of the Polish Women's Alliance of America at its twenty-sixth national convention in 1971 in Hartford, signaled the end of a long and important chapter in the fraternal's affairs.

Already the reins of leadership were being turned over to younger activists, who faced challenges that had begun looming on the horizon in the last decade of the Łagodzinska twenty-four year long administration, but whose full impact was not, and perhaps could not be, fully appreciated. Over the next three decades, the PWA of A would be headed by four presidents, each of whose administrations would in its own fashion confront the new and truly daunting situation.

In Hartford, Łagodzinska was succeeded by her vice president, Helen Zielinski, just as she had first won office as head of the PWA of A back in 1947 after having served for eight years as vice president under President Honorata Wołowska. Zielinski had been vice president for twelve years. During that period she had worked effectively and loyally in performing her assigned duties. These had dealt mainly with building up membership in the Alliance and promoting participation in its youth circles. As an enthusiast on behalf of these causes, Zielinski had traveled about the country many times to meet PWA of A members. She had established a personal popularity that helped to make a great success of her run for the presidency. Thus in the 1971 election, she easily outdistanced her rival, Genevieve Zaczek, by a vote of 303 to 79. Following the convention, Zielinski backed Zaczek's nomination to serve as PWA of A legal counsel, an office Zaczek then held for the next eight years. [2]

Helen Wojcik's words are from the 32nd convention (1995). Delphine Lytell's words are from her greetings at the one hundredth anniversary banquet of the PWA of A, May 16, 1998 in Chicago and were published in *Polish Women's Alliance of America Centennial Celebration, May 16 – 17, 1998* (Chicago: Polish Women's Alliance of America, 1998), a commemorative publication distributed at the banquet. Virginia Sikora's words appeared in *Głos Polek*, January 2000.

[2] When Zielinski stepped down in 1987, she was succeeded by the vice president of the previous sixteen years, Helen Wojcik. When Wojcik retired in 1995, her successor was vice president Delphine Lytell. The tradition of vice presidential succession to the presidency had been unbroken going back to

Helen Zielinski was born in Pennsylvania and learned the Polish language as a child from her immigrant parents. Already active in the Alliance before 1939, she was elected financial secretary in PWA of A Group 81, the Daughters of Poland (*Córy Polski*) society after moving to Gary, Indiana, with her husband and young children. Later she was a leader in PWA of A Council 21. As a fraternal activist, Zielinski not only became known for her membership activities and work with children's choral and dance groups, she became a genuine celebrity in the organization. Possessed of a fine singing voice, Zielinski occasionally entertained her fellow members at their gatherings.[3]

Membership development was a major interest of Zielinski, something she shared with Łagodzinska and had learned from her Indiana mentors, Helena Sambor and Sofie Jerzyk. The latter two were leaders in sales within the Alliance in the 1940s and 1950s. Sambor herself had enjoyed an outstanding career in the national leadership, both as a national director and as a vice president; Jerzyk served as Indiana state president for many years.[4]

This commitment to membership development continued during Zielinski's tenure as vice president. In 1964 the PWA of A established a new and annual membership contest that culminated with the crowning of a May Queen or top salesperson on May 22; the Founders Day of the Alliance, a contest in which Zielinski was the first winner. The May Queen competition remains the most

---

1947; it would end only in 1999, as Director Virginia Sikora of Detroit won the presidency over Lytell.

[3] Zielinski in an interview with the authors credited Honorata Wołowska in urging that she strengthen her command of the Polish language, something she did with evidently good results. Zielinski also praised Łagodzinska for making her responsible for youth work when she became vice president. As Zielinski herself put it, although Łagodzinka never married, she was deeply interested in the recruitment of children into the Alliance and in promoting activities for them in the organization.

[4] Sambor's career in the PWA of A spanned more than thirty years, with her service as a national director (1924 to 1931 and 1951 to 1955) sandwiching eight years as vice president (1931 to 1939). She ran, unsuccessfully, for the presidency in 1947. Jerzyk headed District 3 (Indiana) from 1939 to 1955.

popular and well known of the Alliance's annual membership development activities.[5]

Elected to the vice presidency at the 1971 convention was Helen Wojcik of Chicago. Wojcik, whose mother Veronica Siwek, had for decades been a leader in the Alliance (in 1971 she retired as a national director after having served in that post since 1943), had been a member of Group 743, the Star of the Sea Society, from childhood. Her election as vice president came after a spirited contest with Director Charlotte Jagodzinska of Chicago. Jagodzinska continued to be active in the Alliance and went on to serve from 1975 to 1987 as president of District 1, which included the states of Illinois, Missouri, and Florida.

Elected at the same time to her first term as secretary general of the PWA of A was Julia Stroup of Chicago. Stroup succeeded Michalina Ferguson, a veteran leader in the organization who retired after a twelve-year tenure in the office. Reelected treasurer was Leokadia Blikowska, who had held this post since 1941. Blikowska continued to serve as treasurer until 1979, a record thirty-eight years after her initial appointment.[6]

Two memorable events helped inaugurate the new administration. The first, in September 1972, was a banquet celebrating Łagodzinska's contributions to the Alliance during her thirty-two years as president and vice president and her work on behalf of Polonia. More than eight hundred people honored her at the banquet, among them the leaders of other Polish American organizations and the Church.

At the start of 1973, the PWA of A began to celebrate its seventy-fifth anniversary in similarly stirring fashion. One of the highlights of what became a year-long observance of the Alliance's

---

[5] Zielinski also organized two new PWA of A groups: the Queen of Peace Society in Gary, Indiana; and the Poinciana Society in Fort Lauderdale, Florida.

[6] Blikowska lost her first run for treasurer in 1939 to Victoria Latwis by a 334 to 142 vote. Following the death of Latwis in 1941, Blikowska automatically became treasurer under the PWA of A by-laws. She then went on to be elected unanimously in her own right in 1943 and to win reelection after that eight more times.

diamond jubilee occurred at the shrine of the Virgin Mary in Doylestown, Pennsylvania, outside of Philadelphia. There at the basilica of the recently dedicated American Częstochowa, some twenty thousand people gathered; many were PWA of A members from around the country. From the time of its creation nearly twenty years before, the shrine had received continuing and substantial financial support from the Alliance.

The seventy-fifth anniversary culminated in November 1973 with a jubilee banquet attended by nearly one thousand members and guests of the PWA of A. During the run-up to this great event nearly four thousand new members were added to the ranks of the Alliance in connection with a special yearlong enrollment campaign. At the banquet itself, two hundred and fifty new insurance applications were presented to President Zielinski. In all, approximately four million dollars in new insurance had been purchased during the previous year.

Activism and an enthusiastic "can do" spirit were hallmarks of Helen Zielinski's presidency. Her energy showed in her extensive travels to visit the groups, councils, and state districts of the Alliance. On these occasions her encouraging words in promoting the organization's mission and its recruitment work had a galvanizing effect upon her audiences. In addition, the PWA of A continued to participate in symbolically important events such as the Polish Constitution Day parade in Chicago in early May and the Pulaski Day parade in New York in October. The advertising of the PWA of A and its products on Polish language radio programs was complemented by its sponsorship of the popular Bob Lewandowski Sunday television variety hour; this program reached thousands of viewers in the greater Chicago area and in the neighboring states of Indiana and Wisconsin. Zielinski's vivacity continued to show itself at PWA of A occasions; at one convention, for example, she and two colleagues, Helen Lis and Evelyn Lisek, gave a memorable Andrews Sisters-style performance for delegates who were awaiting the election returns for national officers.

THE PWA OF A COLLEGE SCHOLARSHIP PROGRAM

Beginning in the 1970s, the PWA of A greatly stepped up its sponsorship of college scholarships for young women and men holding insurance with the Alliance. The roots of the national PWA of A scholarship program went back to the 1950s. In the beginning, understandably, the sums of money that were distributed had been quite modest. In the four-year period from 1955 to 1959, fifty-seven young people received $10,572 in awards for an average of $203 each. Between 1959 and 1963, the amount was $12,185, with fifty-eight young women and seventeen young men receiving awards that averaged about $163.[7]

As originally devised, the scholarship program invited each of the fourteen PWA of A state districts to raise matching funds to supplement the amount that the national office had earmarked for the awards. These locally generated funds were then awarded to qualifying student members who resided in their districts. As a result, the amounts of the scholarships in the districts tended to vary, often substantially, depending on the number of scholarships distributed in any given year in a district and the amount of scholarship money that a particular district had raised. (For many years, some state districts and councils organized debutante balls as fundraisers. In some cases, the money these balls generated for scholarships accounted for as much as one-third of all the dollars the PWA of A awarded in a given year.)

At the Alliance's twenty-fourth convention in 1963, the delegates voted to increase substantially the amount of money set aside for scholarships. At the same time, they strongly supported continuing the policy of encouraging the state districts to generate matching funds for the program. The results were impressive. At the 1967 PWA of A convention, it was reported that $31,582 in awards had been distributed to 180 recipients over the previous four years. While the average amount of the awards remained about the same, approximately $175 each, the number of beneficiaries tripled.

Whereas the 1967 report reflected very favorably on the Alliance's commitment to the educational advancement of its young members, more significant was its leaders' recognition of the growing numbers of Polonia's young women and young men, who

---

[7] There were other opinions on how to assist student-members. One idea presented at the 1959 convention called upon the PWA of A to make zero interest college loans instead of scholarships, with the recipients expected to repay the debt in a reasonable amount of time after graduation. The proposal, however, was not adopted.

were going on to attain a college education. The trend continued in the years to come, as thousands of individuals of Polish origin went on to graduate from college, many of them continuing their academic and professional development after earning their diplomas. Their success was a fulfillment of the American dream of opportunity for all, a widely held belief within the Polish American community.

Between 1967 and 1971, 413 students received a total of $77,754 in awards. Leading the way in supplementing the national office funding policy in this period was District 8 of Massachusetts, which granted $22,045 to 82 students. Between 1971 and 1975, the scholarship program grew even larger, with 573 recipients awarded a total of $94,048. In 1979, a total of $102,310 was distributed; once again 573 students received awards in the previous four year period.

Between 1979 and 1983, 621 students were awarded $144,408 in scholarships. During the following four years, 918 students won a total of $159,308 in scholarships. In the sixteen years (1971 – 1987) in which Zielinski headed the Polish Women's Alliance of America, 2,865 young people were awarded $500,074 in scholarships.

The scholarship program clearly took off in this period. In the sixteen years between 1955 and 1971, 725 students had benefited from the program, to the tune of $122,093. Over the next sixteen years, each of these figures had quadrupled. Of course, there was yet another reason for the increase in the numbers of recipients and the amounts the Alliance distributed to them. This had to do with its success in recruiting youngsters into the organization from the 1950s onward. As these children had grown to college age, so also had the PWA of A's commitment to provide them with a substantial fraternal benefit.

Year after year since 1987, the Polish Women's Alliance of America scholarship program has continued to grow. During the eight-year presidency of Zielinski's successor, Helen Wojcik, the Alliance distributed $417,293 in scholarships to 1,495 recipients. By this time too, the PWA of A national office was committing $25,000 each year to the scholarship program and then matching the scholarship money sent to Chicago from the state districts.

During the four-year presidency of Wojcik's successor, Delphine Lytell, this record of service continued in the same direction.

To date, more than six thousand college scholarships have been awarded to students belonging to the Alliance. The combined amount of these grants exceeds $1.4 million.[8]

MEMBERSHIP DEVELOPMENT

For President Zielinski, her fellow national officers, and their successors, the promotion of membership remained a top priority after 1971. This was repeatedly emphasized at national conventions, annual meetings of state district presidents, in visits by national officers to district conventions, at council and group gatherings, and in the pages of the Alliance's official publication, *Głos Polek.* Members were urged to involve themselves in the sale of insurance and to attend insurance seminars sponsored by the Alliance. The PWA of A also encouraged their participation in state conventions of the National Fraternal Congress. More attractive and informative promotional materials were designed to describe the costs and benefits of PWA of A insurance products.

Under Zielinski's successor, Helen Wojcik, president of the Polish Women's Alliance of America from 1987 to 1995, membership development remained a top priority. President Wojcik conducted a large number of membership drives. Moreover, her dedication in this area went far beyond words and was more than matched by her actions.

Indeed, Wojcik was awarded the title of May Queen of the PWA of A for her achievement of top sales status in the organization in nineteen different years. Together with National Secretary General Maria Kubiak, Wojcik was cofounder of the Park Ridge Society, Group 819 of the PWA of A, at its national headquarters. This group currently includes more than two hundred adult members and some eighty juvenile members. It is one of the most active groups in the Alliance and regularly sponsors programs and speakers at its monthly meetings.

---

[8] Figures on scholarship awards are from the reports of the vice president of the Polish Women's Alliance of America, as published at the time of its quadrennial conventions.

President Wojcik also encouraged Irena Mickiewicz, one of the Alliance's longtime employees at its headquarters, to promote membership among Polish immigrants who were settling in Chicago from the 1970s and 1980s onward. Through Mickiewicz's efforts, a second new PWA of A group was established at the home office. This group included more than one hundred members in 2001. Its meetings focus on the promotion of the Polish cultural heritage.

Membership development, new sales plans, and the creation of an annuities program are achievements that marked Helen Wojcik's eight-year stewardship of the PWA of A. It was during her tenure that the Alliance began considering a direct billing plan for PWA of A groups that lacked a sufficient number of active officers to handle this critical responsibility. Wojcik's involvement as an officer in the workings of both the National and the Illinois Fraternal Congress organizations was also of much value to the Alliance. It was at these meetings that numerous useful ideas about the promotion of membership and fraternalism were discussed for future implementation.

All these efforts succeeded in bringing a steady stream of new members into the PWA of A. Still, as shown in the table below, the Alliance began to experience a gradual contraction from the mid-1960s onward – in its overall membership, in the size of its youth division, and in the number of its active local groups, many of which were subsequently merged to help keep them viable.

Membership In The Polish Women's Alliance Of America, 1967–1997[9]

	Total Members	Adults	Children	No. of Groups	No. of Wianki
1967	90,080	73,399	16,681	592	531
1971	86,351	71,034	15,317	559	496
1975	82,074	68,413	13,661	525	464
1979	77,387	65,140	12,247	479	420
1983	71,878	60,803	11,075	443	387
1987	66,711	56,790	9,921	412	367
1991	60,214	51,877	8,337	384	336
1994	58,032	49,293	8,739	356	309
1997	53,708	45,609	8,099	346	292

This downward trend has been a topic of considerable concern and numerous suggestions for improvement have been made at PWA of A conventions in recent years. These proposals have fallen into three general categories.[10]

One set of ideas focused on the ways in which the Alliance might improve its insurance and fraternal programs, thus making itself more attractive to new members. A second cluster of ideas dealt with professionalizing the fraternal's sales operations to make it more competitive in the Polish American community. A third approach suggested redefining, or at least repositioning, the Alliance to make its appeals more relevant to the interests and needs of potential insurance buyers, stressing the organization's

[9] Membership figures are from the quadrennial convention reports of the Secretary General of the Polish National Alliance. *Sprawozdania zarządu głównego i prezesek stanowych Związku Polek w Ameryce*, 1967, 1971, 1975, 1979, 1983, 1987, 1991, and 1995 (Reports of the members of the general administration and state presidents of the Polish Women's Alliance of America, 1967 to 1995).

[10] Proposals for dealing with membership decline are found in the minutes of the quadrennial conventions from 1971 onward. Most came from reports by particular committee at the conventions, namely those dealing with membership, education, and youth. *Protokóły sejmu Związku Polek w Ameryce*, 1971, 1975, 1979, 1983, 1987, 1991, and 1995 (Minutes of the conventions of the Polish Women's Alliance of America, 1971–1995).

American character as an insurance provider rather than its traditional ethnic ties.

Improving the Product: Proposals of this type have called for the development of new insurance products including those with higher dollar amounts of insurance. Expanding the range of fraternal benefits offered by the organization represented another side to this formula. Yet another proposal was to admit adult men as insured members.

Over the years, a number of these varied proposals have been enacted. By the 1990s the PWA of A was offering a number of permanent (or whole life) and term plans of insurance to meet the increasingly diverse needs and preferences of its members (who by then included men as well as women), whatever their ages and life situations. The amounts of insurance a member could purchase in any single policy had also increased considerably, to twenty-five thousand dollars.

In October 1984 and for the third time in its history, the PWA of A leadership had voted to issue a special dividend to all members. Once again, as in 1951 and 1968, members received this dividend in the form of added life insurance on their policies. This time, however, prospective members who joined as late as May 1, 1985, were also granted this special benefit, which was promoted as an inducement to join the Alliance. The fraternal also began offering an annuity plan aimed at helping members to save, on an income tax-deferred basis, toward their retirement. By the 1990s several annuities were available.

Other proposals to improve the Alliance's program, though well intended, were sometimes more problematic. Some aimed to generate new interest in the organization among young people in a variety of ways. Among the many suggestions in this vein were calls to create a permanent standing PWA of A youth committee in the home office, to encourage every group to organize an active youth circle (*wianek*) under its auspices, to establish a special youth-oriented page in *Głos Polek*, and to organize annual or biannual district youth conferences to complement the Alliance's quadrennial national youth conference. Some members argued that such conferences would be more successful if they were held on college campuses. Other ideas involved the promotion of a greater appreciation of the Polish language and culture and proposed organizing classes on these subjects at the council level, or subsidizing the programs of other educational groups for PWA of A members where they were available.

Such suggestions were not always well received. Indeed, at both the 1975 and the 1979 conventions, the chairwoman of the youth committee presented a resolution urging that the incoming general administration actually consider its recommendations, as this had not been the case, she argued, during the previous four years. More to the point, perhaps, were concerns as to whether such efforts to reach out to young people would bear much fruit.

A suggestion of a different and perhaps more practical nature called upon leaders of local PWA of A groups to improve the quality of their meetings so as to raise member interest and attendance. A related proposal called for the merging of small or inactive groups with more dynamic units so as to preserve the sense of the Alliance's mission at the grass-roots. By the 1970s, activists in the organization had become increasingly concerned over this matter.

Professionalization: Proposals for reform in this vein had the home office involved in working more systematically to identify and train insurance agents and financial secretaries to perform duties that were critical to the Alliance's future growth. The advocates of professionalization encouraged PWA of A local leaders to be more active in the National Fraternal Congress units in their states and to learn more about career opportunities in insurance sales.

But the task of professionalization and identifying candidates for the work was not one easily achieved, since insurance sales increasingly had to be pursued in the evenings and required substantial travel. In the past, membership recruitment had been less arduous. One joined the Alliance group in her neighborhood through the urgings of a friend or relative. The purchase of life insurance was understood to be a condition of membership in the organization, not an end in itself. One's desire for fellowship and active participation in the local group was at least as important a reason for joining as was one's ownership of an insurance policy.

Improving the business side of the Polish Women's Alliance of America's operations by professionalizing its sales efforts was, and remains, a sensible, even obligatory, objective, especially as the PWA of A moves into its second century of operation. Nonetheless, business was not the organization's sole original mission, nor was it responsible for the Alliance's subsequent expansion over the years. Rather, the PWA of A was recognized as a women's organization, one its members proudly embraced and directed. In a tangible way, its existence served notice to the larger Polonia that women counted as contributing and respected participants in the organized ethnic community.

Professionalizing the sales side of PWA of A faced another obstacle, one that the Alliance shared with other Polish American fraternal societies. This involved the aging of the Polish ethnic community, the depopulation of the old Polonia neighborhoods, the relocation and dispersal of large numbers of younger and more upwardly mobile third-and-fourth generation Polish Americans away from the central cities of the Northeast and Midwest to other parts of the country, and the difficulty in attracting substantial numbers of new members within the post-1970 Polish immigrant population.

Here a significant side issue confronting the PWA of A by the 1970s involved the location of its home office on Chicago's Near Northside "Polish triangle." There three major thoroughfares – Milwaukee Avenue, Division Street, and Ashland Avenue – intersected to form a busy hub of business, fraternal, cultural, and spiritual life. The triangle had served as a center of Polish ethnicity for more than seven decades and had even come to be called the capital of Polonia. This was no exaggeration. The district included not only the national headquarters of the Polish Women's Alliance of America but also those of the Polish National Alliance, its printing company, the Polish Roman Catholic Union of America, and the Polish American Congress. In addition, the triangle included the imposing Manufacturers' National Bank once run by John Smulski, and within easy walking distance were the massive Roman Catholic churches named in honor of Saint Stanislaus Kostka and the Holy Trinity.

Nostalgia notwithstanding, the delegates to the twenty-seventh convention in 1975 resolved to call on president Zielinski and her fellow officers to find a new location for the PWA of A home office. In June 1979, just prior to its twenty-eighth convention, an edifice located in the northwest Chicago suburban community of

Park Ridge was purchased at a cost of $2,050,000. The offices of the Alliance organization were soon moved to their new location. The new headquarters, at 205 South Northwest Highway, is a spacious and modern two-story structure that offers plenty of room for the fraternal for years to come. Dedicated on May 17, 1980, it immediately became, like its predecessor structures, a popular place of welcome to personages from Poland and Polonia, not to mention dignitaries from around the United States.[11]

Redefining the Organizational Mission: The original objectives of the PWA of A had stressed Polonia's need for an organization enabling women to play a more significant role in the ethnic community's patriotic work for Poland and providing them with welcome life insurance protection.[12] The emphasis from the start was thus one of promoting knowledge and appreciation of the Polish language and culture, both among the members of the organization and their children. The original and starkly serious PWA of A motto, *Czyn* (service), had succinctly set forth the aims of the Alliance. Another, somewhat later restatement of this idea, underscores the Alliance's special solidarity: *Ideał kobiety to siła narodu* (In the ideals of women are the strength of a nation).

Following Poland's restoration as an independent state in 1918, Alliance mission statements increasingly emphasized the need to foster patriotic sentiments towards the United States. Defending the good name of the Polish and Polish American people was also underscored. For example, on various occasions the organization's leadership went on record to complain about publications whose authors were seen to disparage the Polish heritage. A notable target was Chicago novelist Nelson Algren,

---

[11] Maria Loryś, "Nasze Domy" (Our headquarters), in Helen Zielinski, *Historia Związku Polek w Ameryce,* pp. 84 – 85.

[12] As the first historian of the Alliance put it: *"Od razu zostały określone jasno cele: ubezpieczenie na wypadek śmierci i pracy na niwie narodowej"* (from the start the aims were clear: insurance in case of death and patriotic work) Jadwiga Karłowicz, *Historia Związku Polek,* p. 28.

whose writings were considered especially demeaning in their depiction of Polish American life.[13]

Increased attention was also paid to stressing the value of the Polish religious heritage, something that was very important to the great majority of PWA of A members. As far back as the Alliance's sixteenth national convention in 1931, a resolution was approved to place a rendition of the picture of the Częstochowa Madonna on the obverse side of the Alliance's banner. The fraternal's motto was also changed at the same time to *Bóg i Ojczyzna* (God and country). In later years, the leadership of the Alliance proclaimed the "Virgin Mother of Częstochowa, Queen of the Polish Crown" as its patroness. This identification has continued to the present time, and from the 1950s onward, the PWA of A was heavily involved in providing financial support to the construction and maintenance of the Doylestown, Pennsylvania, shrine to the Częstochowa Madonna.

The religious dimension of the PWA of A self-image is apparent from even a cursory look at resolutions presented at its national conventions over the past quarter-century. Many of these have decried the decline of "Christian principles in American society" and the loss of respect for "family values." Such expressions demonstrate the existence of a strong conservative inclination among many PWA of A activists and their rejection of numerous aspects of the feminist agenda that began to be voiced in the 1960s.

A different trend, one that has surfaced over the past twenty-five years has been the complaint about the continued use of Polish in the organization's meetings and publications when only a minority of members is fluent in the language. The three official histories of the Alliance for example, are written in Polish and none has been translated into English. Similarly, *Głos Polek* continued to be published mainly in the Polish language into the 1980s, with only two to four of its pages appearing in English. The proceedings of the national conventions of the Alliance were also published in Polish until 1987, when for the first time the minutes of the

---

[13] Several of Algren's works were later made into feature-length movies; in these, most of the offensive ethnic characterizations that led to the PWA of A's complaints had been excised.

conclave and the quadrennial reports of the officers appeared in English.

These days, the great majority of PWA of A groups conducts their meetings and handles their business in English. And while the Polish language remains a significant and treasured aspect of the Alliance's heritage, its members and leaders have long become persuaded that the mission of the fraternal must be one of reaching out in the most effective manner to others. Significantly, on the occasion of the PWA of A centennial banquet in May 1998, the entire program was conducted in English; only the musical interludes involved the Polish language, e.g., in the singing of the Polish national anthems, "*Jeszcze Polska Nie Zginęła*" and "*Rota*," and the Alliance's own "*Marsz Związku Polek*" and in the presentations by the Lira Ensemble.

One effort to restate the purposes of the Polish Women's Alliance of America came at its thirty-second national convention in Chicago in September 1995. There a motion proposing a new mission statement was made by Jeanette Blasz of Group 440 in Chicago and seconded by Ann Davis of Group 214 in Pittsburgh. After some debate, a motion to decline the proposal was offered by Director Albina Świerzbińska of New Jersey and seconded by outgoing President Wojcik. Their concern was that the statement was imprecise and unclear, but their motion failed by a 162 – 70 vote. The proposal as approved by the convention read as follows:

The mission of the PWA of A is to meet the challenges of the 21st century. With the celebration of the 100th year anniversary in 1998, the PWA of A should affirm and continue the ideals and beliefs which our founders began. Not only women but all members of the family may become PWA of A members and enjoy its privileges and benefits.

It is necessary to encourage added participation and expansion, increase greater public awareness, develop further use by assessing information through educational programs and involvement with the global, social understanding, and be willing to adjust without compromising our principles.[14]

As mission statements go, this one fell short in several ways. First, it begged the question about the Alliance's objectives by assuming that everyone, including nonmembers, knew what they were. Second, it did not mention the character of the PWA of A as a fraternal insurance benefit society formed by women of Polish origin and heritage. Third, its goal of meeting unspecified 'challenges of the future" was a truism – in operating as viable social organizations, all groups must do this. In short the statement requires serious review and revision. Perhaps this will be done in the future.

THE POLISH WOMEN'S ALLIANCE AND THE POLISH AMERICAN CONGRESS

Under Helen Zielinski, Helen Wojcik, Delphine Lytell, and Virginia Sikora, the Polish Women's Alliance of America continued to play a leadership role in the life of the larger Polonia, in particular its political action federation, the Polish American Congress (PAC), and its charitable arm, the PAC Charitable Foundation. The Alliance's involvement in the PAC dated back to the birth of the congress in 1944 the last climactic year of World War II. Moreover, the Alliance's president at the time, Honorata Wołowska, had played a crucial role in the PAC's formation and early leadership activities. The PWA of A had continued its involvement with the PAC on all levels, local and national, under Wołowska's successor, Adela Łagodzinska.

Helen Zielinski, Helen Wojcik, Delphine Lytell, and Virginia Sikora in turn played constructive leadership roles in the Congress after 1971. Their involvement gave the Alliance many opportunities to display its members' dedication to fraternal, civic, and patriotic service. A few particularly important examples of this commitment may be mentioned here.

In 1979 PWA of A members were invited by their leaders to join in contributing to a fund drive then being conducted by the PAC Charitable Foundation. This drive's aim was to construct a

[14] *Minutes of the Thirty-second Convention of the Polish Women's Alliance of America, September 23 to 25, 1995* (Chicago, 1995) pp. 17 to 18.

hostel in Rome for Polish pilgrims visiting the "eternal city" to celebrate their faith with their fellow Pole, Pope John Paul II. The pope, formerly Karol Cardinal Wojtyła of Kraków, had been elected to the throne of St. Peter in October 1978. The hostel was a project close to the heart of the Holy Father because of his wish to ease the financial burdens Poland's Catholics faced in traveling to Rome from their economically troubled land. People of Polish heritage from around the world responded to the pope's invitation, and organizations like the PAC Charitable Foundation, which had been formed in 1971 with the support of the PWA of A, raised a considerable sum of money for the cause. (The charitable foundation continued the work of the *Rada Polonii Amerykańskiej* humanitarian federation. The *RPA,* which dated back to the mid-1930s and had been strongly supported by the PWA of A in its activities on behalf of Polish refugees during and immediately after the World War II. It was dissolved in 1971.)

Other benevolent efforts organized through the PAC and its charitable foundation came one after another in the 1980s and 1990s. All engaged the Polish Women's Alliance of America, its national leaders, state district units, councils, and groups. Every endeavor was given heavy publicity in the Alliance's official fraternal publication, *Głos Polek,* and in other ways too.

In the mid-1980s President Zielinski took a leadership role in promoting PAC support for the restoration of the Statue of Liberty. For more than a century the massive and enduring monument in New York Harbor had symbolized this country's welcome to the millions of immigrants who had entered the United States in search of better lives for themselves and their offspring. In all, $149,000 was collected in Polonia through the work of the PAC, its charitable foundation, and the Polish American fraternals, among them the PWA of A, whose members alone contributed one-third of the funds in the campaign. The project brought with it the full restoration of the monument to its original beauty under the leadership of a national citizens' committee chaired by Lee Iacocca, head of the Chrysler automobile corporation. On July 4, 1986, the statue was rededicated by President Ronald Reagan.

In 1989 Helen Wojcik, who had succeeded Zielinski as president in 1987 and was elected a PAC vice president the year after, was invited to chair another PAC charitable foundation fundraising effort. This one aimed to help create an immigration museum at Ellis Island less than a mile from the Statue of Liberty. Between 1890 and 1950, Ellis Island had been the port of entry for newcomers to America, among them several million from Poland. But by the 1980s its many buildings had fallen into neglect. The effort to restore the site as a museum recalling America's immigrant past required an even greater commitment of energy and financial commitment than the Statue of Liberty project. Nonetheless, Polonia under Wojcik's leadership proved equal to the task. At the time of the museum's formal dedication in September 1991, it was proudly announced that the PAC Charitable Foundation had raised $630,400 for the cause.[15]

At the 1995 PWA of A convention, President Wojcik presented a check in the amount of $115,000 to Adam Cardinal Maida, archbishop of Detroit, on behalf of another major fundraising project. This time the effort was in support of the building of the Pope John Paul II Cultural Center planned in Washington, D. C., near the Catholic University of America. The center was conceived as a permanent memorial to honor the Holy Father and his ideas and concerns. The check from the PWA of A was the very first to come from an American fraternal society.

In 1996 President Delphine Lytell, accompanied by Treasurer Olga Kaszewicz, traveled to Rome, where they participated in the founding organizational meeting that further committed Polonia to raising funds to establish the Pope John Paul II Cultural Center. The fund drive has proved to be one to which the members of the PWA of A, and indeed all of Polonia, have contributed generously. In October 2000, President Virginia Sikora announced that PWA of A members had contributed $150,000 to the cause. She further noted that the Alliance had pledged $250,000 in additional support over the next three years.

SERVING POLAND'S CAUSE: A CIVIC AND FRATERNAL ACTION

From the 1970s onward, the members and leadership of the Polish Women's Alliance of America within the Polish American

---

[15] Angela and Donald Pienkos, *The Polish Women's Alliance of America: Our Future is as Bright as Our Past Is Inspiring* (Chicago: Polish Women's Alliance of America, 1995), *passim*.

Congress and its charitable foundation focused once again on the Alliance's involvement in the causes of Poland's political freedom and its people's material betterment. The roots of this involvement went back to the Alliance's earliest days. But the efforts of Polonia and its member groups like the PWA of A were revitalized through a series of critical developments beginning in the late 1960s. These resulted, some twenty years later, in the collapse of the communist dictatorship in Poland itself and the birth of a new democratic political system. Even more significant, out of the Polish crisis came the end of communist rule throughout Eastern Europe and the Soviet Union in 1991. And with the U. S. S. R.'s disintegration came the close of the forty-year Cold War between the two superpowers that had locked the United States and the Soviet Russian Empire into an astronomically costly, always potentially deadly, rivalry of global proportions.[16]

From 1968 on, Poland's communist-ruled Soviet satellite regime was beset with a steadily worsening set of political and economic problems. In December 1970, the regime run by Władysław Gomułka since 1956 was removed in the aftermath of massive protests that were put down in bloody fashion by the military. Gomułka's successor, Edward Gierek, promised economic improvement and greater tolerance to criticism.

But by the mid-1970s, his regime too had lost what support it initially had, as the country's economy again plummeted sharply. The ascent of the archbishop of Kraków, Karol Cardinal Wojtyła, to the throne of St. Peter in October 1978 followed by the new pope's return visit to Poland in June 1979 generated both hope and a sense of empowerment among his people. Only a year later, in summer 1980, a new crisis resulting from Gierek's mismanagement of the worsening economy ultimately brought about the birth of the Solidarity trade union. With its formation a new chapter in Poland's modern history was written.

---

[16] On the extraordinary events in Poland from the election of Pope John Paul II through the victory of the Solidarity movement, see Timothy Garton Ash, *The Polish Revolution: Solidarity* (New York: Viking Press, 1985); and Raymond Taras, *Consolidating Democracy in Poland* (Boulder: Westview Press, 1995), pp. 71 – 111. See also Mark Brzezinski, *The Struggle for Constitutionalism in Poland* (London: Oxford University Press, 1998). The best work, among many, on the Holy Father is by George Weigel, *Witness to Hope: A Biography of John Paul II* (New York: Harper, 1999).

On August 31, 1980, the tense sit-down strike of the Lenin shipyards workers in Gdańsk was finally settled when the regime recognized, in an unprecedented action, the workers' right to their own officially recognized independent trade union association, *Solidarność.* Just a week later, Gierek was removed from office. But no cosmetic regime leadership change could reverse the rising tide of radical reform symbolized by what soon became a nationwide Solidarity union movement that within a few weeks included as many as ten million followers in a country of thirty-five million. Under its national chairman, thirty-seven-year-old Lech Wałęsa, a blacklisted electrician and union activist of peasant origin, Solidarity took a determined stance in holding to its newly won rights.[17]

But Solidarity's success in bringing about a transition from authoritarian communist party rule would not be swift or smooth. Indeed, on December 12, 1981, the Polish military, headed by General Wojciech Jaruželski, crushed the workers federation and arrested nearly all its leaders across the country. But the policies the general's martial law regime adopted over the next six and one-half years brought neither political order nor economic improvement. On the contrary, the situation steadily worsened and with it the danger of widespread violence. At last, in late 1988 the embattled regime agreed to serious talks with the leaders of the opposition as a way to deal, belatedly, with the national crisis.

The roundtable negotiations that convened in Warsaw on February 6, 1989, had consequences that were unimagined when they began. Made possible by the approval of the reform-minded Soviet leader Mikhail Gorbachev, the negotiations ended on April 5 with agreements providing for the full restoration of the Solidarity trade union, the right to publish its own uncensored national newspaper, and a commitment by the regime to hold new elections to the national parliament in June. These were the very proposals that Solidarity leaders had made to the regime in 1980 – 1981 to deal with the country's crisis at that time. Now, they were at last being accepted by Jaruželski and his allies.

---

[17] On the Gdańsk strike and its aftermath, see Katarzyna Madon-Mitzner, "*Dni Solidarności*" (Days of Solidarity), *Karta: Kwartalnik Historyczny* (Warsaw: Ministry of Culture and Art), 30, 2000, 4 – 103; and Antoni Dudek, *Solidarność: Twenty Years of History* (Warsaw: Polish Information Agency, 2000).

The parliamentary elections were themselves extraordinarily significant. First, a free and competitive national election was to be held for a new legislative body, the hundred-member Senate, a body whose actual role in decision making would be advisory in nature. More significantly, free elections were approved to fill 161 of the 460 seats in Poland's main law-making assembly, the *Sejm*. However, 299 seats were set aside for the candidates of the communist party (officially known as the Polish United Workers party) and its long subservient minor party adjuncts.

The brief, eight-week campaign ended on election day, June 4, 1989. The results were as amazing as the events of the previous four months. The candidates of the hastily created Solidarity-based "citizens committees" around the country won 99 of the 100 seats to the Senate (the remaining seat went to an independent candidate) and all 161 contested seats to the *Sejm*. In addition, and in the sharpest of rebukes to the regime, all but four of its 299 unopposed candidates were actually defeated for election when they failed to receive the required majority of the ballots cast in their districts. Following the debacle, the communist party leadership, after weeks of internal debate about its future strategy, at last took Gorbachev's advice and "entered the ranks of the parliamentary opposition." In September, the *Sejm* approved a Solidarity-led coalition cabinet headed by Prime Minister Tadeusz Mazowiecki, then a close associate of Wałęsa. For the first time since 1948, a democratic government was in power in Eastern Europe. Democratic political blocs soon replaced the communists in power in Hungary, East Germany, and Czechoslovakia. By mid-1990, only Albania remained under communist dictatorial rule. In August 1991 communism also came crashing down in Moscow and by December the U. S. S. R. had crumbled.

Throughout these heady, roller coaster-like years of hope, despair, and renewal, the members of the Polish Women's Alliance of America were no mere observers of the events. In Helen Zielinski, along with her successor, Helen Wojcik, the PWA of A was well represented in the top leadership of the Polish American Congress. Indeed, they were involved at every step the PAC took to influence the U. S. government in its approach to the lengthy Polish crisis.[18]

In August 1980, as the Solidarity trade union was forming during the workers' strike in Gdańsk, the leadership of the Polish American Congress issued its first formal memorandum to the Carter administration on the crisis. Declaring its full support for the Solidarity cause in the shipyards and for the "just demands" of the workers, the PACs executive committee urged the U. S. government to remain true to its stated foreign policy position of defending human rights in calling on the Soviet Union to refrain from intervening in Poland's internal affairs. Significantly, this PAC statement pushed for U.S. economic assistance to Poland conditioned upon the communist regime's reform of its corrupt system of central planning. President Carter, who was receiving continuing daily advice on the crisis from his national security adviser, Zbigniew Brzezinski, did take a tough position in opposing Soviet interference. Moreover, in September 1980, only days after the ending of the Gdansk strike, the U.S. government committed $670 million in credits to Poland in agriculture and technical assistance in response to Warsaw's constructive settlement of the strike.

Soon afterward, the PAC, in response to Lech Wałęsa's appeal to Polonia for much-needed emergency medical supplies to his troubled country, initiated a drive to purchase some $5.5 million in medicines for Poland. The drive, organized through the tax-exempt PAC Charitable Foundation, was successful. It quickly led to a series of other efforts directed by the charitable foundation in collecting a wide variety of consumer goods that were in short supply in Poland. Special drives raised funds for baby foods, shoes, goods for the elderly and for invalids, and clothing. By April 1983, the charitable foundation, working with the CARE agency and with the Catholic Church leadership in Poland, had provided aid valued at thirty-three million dollars.

On December 21, 1981, only nine days after the Polish regime's crackdown on Solidarity, three members of the PAC's top leadership visited President Reagan at the White House to present their views on the crisis. At this historic meeting, Reagan and Vice

---

[18] On the post 1980 events in Poland and the role of PWA of A leaders, see Donald Pienkos, *For Your Freedom, passim,* especially the documents section.

President George H. W. Bush spoke with PAC's President Aloysius Mazewski, Vice President Helen Zielinski, and Treasurer Joseph Drobot. They were joined by John Cardinal Krol, archbishop of Philadelphia, America's highest ranking Catholic churchman of Polish descent and an informal representative of the pope. The PAC memorandum called, among other things, for the immediate end of martial law, the release of all political prisoners confined by the regime, and the restoration of the Solidarity trade union to its previous independent status. These sensible ideas were incorporated into the Christmas message President Reagan delivered to the nation a few days later.

The December 20, 1981, memorandum objected to the proposed halt in U.S. government-sponsored food shipments to Poland, a policy that was nonetheless approved by the Reagan administration. The PAC view, one shared by Pope John Paul II and Solidarity, was that the perpetrator of the crisis was the Soviet regime. As a result, it was wrong to cause the innocent people of Poland to suffer from an economic embargo directed against the Polish government. However, the administration stubbornly held to its view on the issue. It was not until February 19, 1987, that the president, under pressure from the Holy Father, Wałęsa, the PAC, and their many friends across America, ended U. S. economic sanctions against Poland.

In October 1984 the Polish American Congress observed its fortieth anniversary at a banquet held in Chicago. More than six hundred guests attended the event, which featured recorded greetings from Pope John Paul II to Polonia and its chief political action organization. A notable symbolic moment involved the granting of special recognition to four of the founders of the Polish American Congress in 1944. These were Charles Rozmarek, president of the Polish National Alliance at the time and the first president of the PAC; John Olejniczak, president of the Polish Roman Catholic Union of America in 1944 and the PAC's first treasurer; Teofil Starzynski, president of the Polish Falcons of America in 1944; and Honorata Wołowska, president of the PWA of A in 1944 and the congress's first vice president.

No top-ranking Reagan administration representative attended the event, an indication of the emerging gap between

Polish Americans and the White House over the sanctions issue. (Earlier, in August 1984, Helen Zielinski had not attended a White House meeting at which more than one hundred leaders of the Polish American community gathered, ostensibly, to commemorate the fortieth anniversary of the Warsaw Uprising in the presence of President Reagan and a large number of leaders in his administration. Soon after this gathering, PAC President Mazewski announced his support of Reagan's reelection campaign.)

On September 25, 1985, the PAC protested General Jaruzelski's appearance at the fortieth anniversary ceremonies honoring the founding of the United Nations. Ironically, free Poland had not been represented at the UN's creation in San Francisco; sadly, it was the head of a military dictatorship that represented Poland forty years later. This time, President Zielinski lent her name and that of the Polish Women's Alliance of America to a statement paid for by the PAC and published in that day's edition of the *New York Times.* The half-page statement closed with a call for the communist regime to initiate a real dialog with the genuine representatives of the Polish people leading to a measure of reconciliation, to free all political prisoners, to desist from other acts of repression and intimidation, and to institute economic reforms to restore Poland's viability. Just four years later, all these aims would be realized.

In October 1987 Zielinski joined PAC president Mazewski and Treasurer Edward Dykla (newly elected as president of the Polish Roman Catholic Union of America) for a special visit to Rome. There the three fraternal leaders met privately with Pope John Paul II. The meeting was significant in underscoring their unity of views about Poland; it was yet another sign of the Holy Father's appreciation of Polonia's identification with his perspective on the situation in his homeland.

With the political and economic crisis in Poland starting to peak in the workers' demonstrations of May 1988, the PAC chose to put forth a series of memoranda addressed to the U.S. government. Each presented well-informed and practical perspectives on the situation and thereby demonstrated the PAC's grasp of the meaning of the events unfolding there. Thus, in its May 5, 1988, statement, the PAC executive committee (with Zielinski still a vice president; in November 1988 she would retire in favor of the new PWA of A President Helen Wojcik), denounced the "police terror and arrogance of the Polish communist dictatorship" and reaffirmed its "solidarity with the courageous and responsible stand of Polish workers and their leaders headed by Lech Wałęsa."

On the eighth anniversary of Solidarity's birth, the PAC executive committee, in an August 29, 1988 statement, once more reiterated its support for the movement, calling it "the inspirational and political force leading the Polish people in their struggle for national sovereignty and democratic freedoms." The statement went on to back the Polish regime's proposal to initiate talks with Solidarity and other democratic opposition movements as a possibly "significant opening leading towards national understanding."

In its October 3, 1988, statement in connection with the seemingly imminent start of the talks, the PAC executive committee, now temporarily headed by vice presidents Zielinski and Kazimierz Łukomski following president Mazewski's death in August, again spoke out strongly. After noting the breadth of Poland's crisis and the need for a genuine dialog to begin the process of national renewal, the committee pointedly emphasized that responsibility for the country's future rested squarely with the regime. The statement declared that "the road to national reconciliation is wide open. It is up to the government whether it will be pursued. The alternative is the disintegration of the country's national existence . . . . We expect that this time reasonableness and moderation will guide the government's position in the forthcoming negotiations. The future of the nation is at stake."

Soon after the talks concluded, the PAC expressed its satisfaction with the resulting agreements by issuing a statement on April 5, 1989, signed by the congress's new president Edward J. Moskal, its new vice president Helen Wojcik, and its three holdover executive officers, Vice President Łukomski, Treasurer Edward Dykla, and Secretary Bernard Rogalski. On June 8 in the wake of Solidarity's extraordinary parliamentary election victory, the executive committee issued another statement, this one notable for its solemn tone. One might have expected unbridled enthusiasm over the scope of Solidarity's triumph, but instead the PAC cautioned that "immense difficulties remain to be solved" before the democratic and economic reform-minded Solidarity movement could be expected to achieve its goals." The PAC executive committee issued a similarly nuanced statement following Tadeusz Mazowiecki's appointment as prime minister on August 23, 1989.

Such statements did not prevent the PAC from taking strong actions in support of the newly democratic Polish government following its installation in September 1989. In October Helen Wojcik was part of a twelve-member PAC delegation headed by President Moskal that traveled to Poland. There the group met with a host of top leaders in the new government and with the heads of the Roman Catholic Church. From these conversations they learned directly about the main problems facing the country and the ways Polonia and the United States might be of help. A few weeks later, the PAC gave Solidarity leader Wałęsa a hero's welcome when he traveled to Chicago as part of his week-long visit in this country. In March 1990, the PAC also hosted Prime Minister Mazowiecki during his visit to Chicago.

Throughout the 1980s and into the 1990s, the PAC charitable foundation continued to be especially active in gathering a wide assortment of medical supplies, food, clothing, educational materials, and agricultural equipment for Poland's people. These goods were distributed to those in greatest need by the Church. Between 1981 and 1990, goods valued at nearly $170 million and weighing more than ten-thousand tons had been shipped to Poland. By 1994 more than $200 million worth of aid had been delivered to the old homeland. This assistance made the PAC charitable foundation initiative the largest relief effort in the history of Polonia's humanitarian work for Poland. Its results surpassed even the great achievements of the *Rada Polonii* organization during World War II. Much of the success was a result of the generosity of the members of the Polish Women's Alliance of America.

The PWA of A's assistance to Poland's needy continued into the 1990s. In August 1992, a world congress of the Polonia sponsored by the newly established *Wspólnota Polska* (Polish community) society was held in Warsaw and Kraków. There, President Wojcik, Vice President Lytell and *Głos Polek* Editor Maria Loryś presented three large, modern vehicles specially built for transporting handicapped children to and from their homes and rehabilitation clinics in southern Poland. These vans had been purchased through donations made by PWA of A members in the months just preceding the congress, the first true world gathering of Polonia in history, one that brought together people of Polish origin from more than sixty countries, including the newly independent states of Lithuania, Ukraine, Belarus, Russia, and Kazakhstan, all of which had been part of the former Soviet Union.

President Wojcik and her fellow officers continued to play important roles in PAC work on Poland's behalf following the country's achievement of democratic self-government and independence. In 1990 the PWA of A supported successful PAC efforts to push for international recognition of Poland's western borders with the newly unified German federal republic. From 1993, the Alliance was involved in the campaign for Poland's entry into the North Atlantic Treaty Organization. In January 1994 President Wojcik took part in the critically significant discussions on NATO enlargement that took place in Milwaukee between leaders of the Polish American, Hungarian American, Czech American, and Slovak American communities and Vice President Albert Gore and other high-ranking representatives of the Clinton administration. These talks proved to be extremely important in shaping U. S. foreign policy in favor of NATO enlargement.[19]

On October 22, 1994, President Wojcik, once again in her capacity as vice president of the Polish American Congress, played a major leadership role in organizing and chairing an historic event, the fiftieth anniversary celebration of the founding of the PAC in the city where it had been created, Buffalo. More than one thousand guests attended the anniversary banquet and speeches were given by such luminaries as Poland's President, Lech Wałęsa, Prime Minister Waldemar Pawlak, U. N. Ambassador Madeleine Albright, New York Governor Mario Cuomo, and U. S. Senator Hank Brown of Colorado, one of the nation's foremost and most eloquent advocates of Poland's entry into NATO. The special anniversary

---

[19] Donald Pienkos, "Witness to History: Polish Americans and the Genesis of NATO Enlargement," *The Polish Review* 44, no. 3 (1999), 329 – 338; and Les Kuczynski, *Expansion of NATO: Role of the Polish American Congress* (Chicago: Alliance Printers and Publishers and Alliance Communications, 1999).

publication distributed at the event was put together by Wojcik and several of her PWA of A colleagues and fellow officers.[20]

The efforts to win U.S. support for Poland's entry into NATO did not lead to a quick or easy success; the leaders of the PAC were required to give a great amount of time and energy to the cause. At last, in July 1997 their efforts were rewarded; there, the sixteen member states of NATO met in Madrid and unanimously agreed to invite Poland, the Czech Republic, and Hungary into the alliance. On April 30, 1998, the members of the Senate of the United States approved the entry of these three countries into NATO by a vote of 80 to 19.

On March 12, 1999, the three countries were formally admitted into the Alliance at signing ceremonies held in Fulton, Missouri. There in 1946 Winston Churchill had delivered his famous "Iron Curtain" speech condemning both the division of Europe and Eastern Europe's submission to Soviet domination. Churchill's remarks ever after were identified as marking the beginning of the Cold War. In April 1999 the heads of the nineteen-member alliance met in Washington, D. C., to mark the fiftieth anniversary of NATO's founding. The events of that gathering were especially important for the PAC and Polonia, whose leaders organized a variety of ceremonies to celebrate Poland's entry into NATO and its recognition as one of the newest, and most committed, of this country's allies. Highlights of the celebrations, which were attended by a number of PWA of A leaders, including President Delphine Lytell and Honorary President Helen Wojcik, were gala gatherings held at the Polish embassy and the Capitol building. A banquet at the nearby Pentagon City Marriott Hotel drew over one-thousand jubilant guests.

The members of the Polish Women's Alliance of America felt a special pride in this historic achievement because it was an honorary member of the PWA of A, Senator Barbara Mikulski of Maryland, who had played an important role in the final vote and who was a ubiquitous, forceful, and proud presence at the

---

[20] Helen V. Wojcik, *Welcome to the Fiftieth Anniversary of the Polish American Congress, October 20 to 23, 1994* (Chicago: Alliance Printers and Publishers, 1994). See also, Donald Pienkos, *Polish American Congress: Half a Century of Service to Poland and Polonia* (Chicago: Alliance Printers and Publishers, 1994).

ceremonies in Washington, D. C., in 1999. The year before, on May 16, 1998, the senator had been the principal speaker at the one-hundredth anniversary dinner of the Polish Women's Alliance of America banquet that took place in the House of the White Eagle located in the northwest Chicago suburb of Niles.

There, before an audience of more than five hundred well wishers, Senator Mikulski eloquently praised Poland as America's new ally and then extolled the achievements of the Polish Women's Alliance of America, the organization to which both her mother and grandmother had belonged. As the Senator put it, "You have always believed in equality for women with men, you have practiced loyalty to both our Polish heritage and to America's best values, and you have been dedicated to your children. In your commitment to these central and core principles, you have shown that women do make a difference!"

Senator Mikulski then went on to add that:

Back a hundred years ago, this great women's organization had the   courage of its convictions in seeking to bring about the empowerment of women in American society. And this you have greatly helped in bringing about. What you did then was revolutionary. It should come as no surprise that the Polish Women's Alliance of America has gone on to be one of the most successful women's organizations in our country's history![21]

---

[21] From Senator Barbara Mikulski's speech to the Polish Women's Alliance of America at its centennial banquet, May 16, 1998.

THE POLISH WOMEN'S ALLIANCE OF AMERICA: OBJECTIVES, ORGANIZATIONAL STRUCTURE, ACTIVITIES

"Ziarnko do ziarnka, a będzie miarka." Grain to grain and there'll soon be a measure; in other words, by thrift and hard work, one will meet with success.

A traditional Polish proverb

In the year 2003 the Polish Women's Alliance of America ranked as the third largest Polish fraternal insurance benefit society in the United States. The Alliance was also the largest Polish American organization established by and for women of Polish heritage.[1]

The objectives of the PWA of A have been expressed in different words at different times over the past century. However, these statements of purpose have all contained a set of four core ideas that have defined its mission. These have included commitments:

—to foster a patriotic spirit toward the United States.

—to preserve knowledge of Polish history, literature, and language among the members of the fraternal so that they and succeeding generations maintain an appreciation of their heritage.

—to defend the honor, rights, and esteem for women of Polish origin and heritage and to promote a good opinion of women and their place in society. This belief has defined what might be called "PWA of A feminism," a philosophy rooted in the idea that women

---

[1] Three other Polish American women's fraternal insurance benefit societies have operated since the creation of the Polish Women's Alliance: the United Polish Women of America, the Association of Polish Women of the United States, and the Polish Women in America. The United Polish Women of America was founded in Chicago in 1912 and operated until 1985, when it was merged into the Polish National Alliance; at its peak it included about seven thousand members but by the 1980s had dropped to about one-third of that number. The Association of Polish Women of the United States was founded in Cleveland in 1913 and continues in existence, with about five thousand members. The United Polish Women of America, which was also founded in Chicago, dates back to 1920 and merged into the PNA in 1989. It then included about two thousand members.

merit respect for their contributions to the ethnic community and equal rights with men in working for its aims.

—to defend the good name of Poland and that of the people of Polish heritage in America. (From 1928 the PWA of A constitution went so far as to call the Alliance "the honor guard standing in defense of the Polish nation.")[2]

On the eve of World War I in 1914, women, as a result of the efforts of the PWA of A and its allies, were playing important roles in Polonia largely throughout their involvement in the Alliance and in other organizations, such as the PNA, the PRCUA, and the Polish Falcons, which by then were accepting women into their ranks. Women by this time were active in educational work with children, in cultural matters, in the charitable field, on behalf of the needy in the Polish community, and then, following the outbreak of the war, in their work for its victims in partitioned Poland.[3]

The Polish Women's Alliance of America was also a trailblazer in the insurance field. In 1900, only months after its formation as a national society, the PWA of A set up its own program of life insurance or as it was then called, burial insurance. To the surprise of some, it proved successful. PWA of A financial secretaries collected insurance premium payments efficiently, and the national office deposited them prudently. In turn, death benefits were paid promptly. As a result, the Alliance's reputation grew along with its membership and assets.

---

[2] Many early statements of the PWA of A mission emphasized the maintenance of the Polish language in America. For example, in the fraternal's constitution as revised in 1917, one of its top aims involved "the lifting of the cultural level of the Polish women through forming young people in the language, history, and literature of the fatherland."

[3] The constitution as revised in 1971 is especially specific here. Accordingly, the PWA of A took the responsibility of protecting the honor and rights of Polish womanhood and endeavoring to preserve esteem on their behalf. In addition, the Alliance committed itself to assisting women in acquiring a college education and encouraging their involvement in American political life. Every PWA of A constitution as revised from the Alliance's early years to the present time, have emphasized its commitment in Article 2 of the document, to the cause of Poland's independence.

The Alliance's business success enhanced its credibility as a patriotic society. This in turn led more women to commit themselves to its insurance program. By the end of the first decade of the twentieth century, the PWA of A had expanded far beyond its original base of operations. In the early days the Alliance was, for all practical purposes, a Chicago area society with fewer than one thousand members. In 1910 it counted more than eight thousand members in six states: Connecticut, Illinois, Michigan, Ohio, Pennsylvania, and Wisconsin. A year later the PWA of A would expand into the state of New York when several groups were formed there.[4]

THE PWA of A GROUP

From the start, the primary organizational unit of the Polish Women's Alliance of America has been the local group. Invariably a neighborhood or parish-connected society, the group was and remains an autonomous, self-governing body affiliated with the national PWA of A. Its members and the officers its members elect each year, have numerous responsibilities, most important of which is the recruitment of new members, an activity assisting the national body in carrying out its mission.

The PWA of A local groups meet usually on a regularly, monthly basis. Indeed, the frequency of group meetings may well have been important to the Alliance's growth at the grass-roots level.

Attendance and involvement in the local group enables PWA of A members to be better informed about the Alliance's aims and work. Through participation in the group's activities, members gain

---

[4] In 1915 more than thirty-five thousand women belonged to the Polish National Alliance, with a somewhat smaller number enrolled into the Polish Roman Catholic Union of America. PWA of A membership was then nearly fifteen thousand. Brożek, *Polish Americans 1854 – 1939*, pp. 217, 220, 224, and *passim*. These numbers suggest that as many as one adult woman out of eight in the then heavily Polish immigrant community belonged to one of these organizations. (The term Polonia, the community of individuals of Polish birth and ancestry living outside of Poland, is one that came into increased use in the 1920s. Prior to World War I, the more common name for the Polish community in America was *wychodźstwo*, the Polish emigration.)

the opportunity to learn parliamentary procedures and public speaking skills, become engaged in managing the group's business and administrative affairs, hold responsible elected office, and even represent the group at local, regional, and even national Polonia events. Such opportunities were especially important in the early years of the twentieth century; at that time there were almost no other opportunities for Polish women in America to become involved in democratically based organizations (aside from those provided by other Polonia organizations whose actions on behalf of women the PWA of A had itself influenced). For thousands of Polish women in America, the Polish Women's Alliance of America has been a veritable training school for participatory democracy.

Through their involvement in local groups women interested in becoming active in the PWA of A on the state and national level have gained valuable experience in campaigning for and winning the right to represent their fellow members as delegates to the Alliance's national convention, or *sejm*. At this event, delegates from around the country meet, debate, and decide the future policies of the organization, set its operating budget, and elect its national officers. As convention delegates, members also have the chance to travel to parts of the country they might not otherwise visit.

Members in the PWA of A group have similarly had opportunities to be involved in two other intermediate structures set up by the national leadership. One is the council, or *komisja*, an association of local groups. Its purpose is to coordinate the work of the local PWA of A groups in a particular town or section of a larger city in accord with the aims of the national organization. In the early years, progress in forming councils went slowly; however, in the 1920s and early 1930s, a substantial number of councils were established.

A second intermediary organization is the state division, which is set up, like its councils, to help maintain good relations and communications between the national headquarters in Chicago and its local groups around the country. The need for better coordination and supervision was particularly strong during the Alliance's first three decades, when the number of local groups rapidly mushroomed.

PWA of A Development by Decade, 1902 — 1931

Year	No. of Members	No. of Groups	Average Membership
1902	876	21	42
1912	10,930	143	76
1921	24,680	308	80
1931	65,321	657	99

The PWA of A group has traditionally been important for another reason. At its monthly meetings, members took the opportunity to pay their insurance premiums. This seemingly routine activity was nonetheless significant in linking participation in the Alliance with the commitment to insured membership in the fraternal.

In the more than century-long operation of the Polish Women's Alliance of America, 819 local groups have operated in the sixteen states (along with the District of Columbia) where the PWA of A is licensed to do business. As of 2003, these were California, Connecticut, Florida, Illinois, Indiana, Maryland, Massachusetts, Michigan, Minnesota, Missouri, Nebraska, New Jersey, Ohio, Pennsylvania, West Virginia, and Wisconsin. The number of active PWA of A groups has, of course, varied over the years — rising because of the formation of new local units, falling usually as a result of mergers.

The era of greatest group expansion came in the years between the Alliance's formation and the onset of the Depression of 1929. Over the past seventy-odd years, the number of groups has increased at a far slower pace, even as total membership continued to grow till the mid-1960s when it peaked at nearly one hundred thousand. Since then, both the total membership of the PWA of A and the number of its local groups have diminished. At the beginning of the twenty-first century, however, the typical PWA of A group included more than two hundred members, twice what it had been in the 1930s.

A serious problem facing the PWA of A since the 1970s has the decline in group activity, a development largely due to the relocation of many members away from the old, once heavily Polish immigrant neighborhoods in the central cities of America's Middle

West and Northeast where they had once been concentrated. The scattering of much of the Polish American population to outlying sections of the cities and the suburbs, and to other parts of the country because of retirement and job transfers, has made it much more difficult for the Alliance to maintain an active organizational life on the local level. A by-product of these changes has been the reluctance of older members to attend evening group meetings, especially when held far away from where they reside.

Then there is the general decline in interest and involvement in group organizational life among Americans, whatever their affiliations and ethnic backgrounds. This trend has many causes. It comes as a result of improvements in the comfort and quality of American homes over the past two generations, which has lessened the appeal of attending meetings of any sort after a hard day's work. The impact of television on the social habits of Americans is another factor. When one can be entertained and informed so readily in one's own home, it is more difficult to justify going out at night to meetings, especially when they require traveling fairly long distances. These factors have together greatly affected the traditional involvement of Americans in voluntary associations of all types.[5]

Nonetheless, much can be learned about the PWA of A by more closely examining its local groups. To do this, we have looked over several comprehensive sources of information about PWA of A groups, among them Jadwiga Karłowicz's history of the Alliance published in 1938 and President Helen Zielinski's overview of the fraternal.

In 1938, 640 PWA of A groups were active in fourteen states and the District of Columbia. In that year, the largest number of all PWA of A groups, 213, were in Illinois, with 176 of them in the city of Chicago. Ranked second in the number of groups was Pennsylvania with 153, followed by New York with 61 and Michigan with 57. Thus in its fortieth anniversary year, the Alliance remained concentrated on the local level in Chicago, with 28 percent of its member groups located in the city of its founding. Nearly half of all groups in the Alliance were in Illinois and

---

[5] Robert D. Putnam, *Bowling Alone: The Collapse and Revival of American Community* (New York: Simon and Schuster, 2000).

Pennsylvania; 76 percent of all PWA of A local units were in four of the fourteen states where it was licensed.

In 1981, slightly more than forty years later, the picture was somewhat different. In her study of the Alliance published that year, Zielinski provided information on 481 PWA of A groups. By then Pennsylvania had surpassed Illinois, 125 to 120, as the state having the largest number of groups. However, Pennsylvania and Illinois together still accounted for 51 percent of all groups in the Alliance. New York and Michigan again ranked third and fourth, with 39 and 38 groups, respectively. Together, these four states continued to account for 67 percent of all groups in the Alliance.

To provide a capsule view of the PWA of A groups over the years, the following lists identify every twenty-fifth PWA of A group based on the information from Zielinski's volume.

Selected PWA of A Groups

No.	Name	Location	Year Formed
1	Polish Women's Alliance Society	Chicago	1898
26	Love of Polish Women Society	Chicago	1902
51	God and Fatherland Society	Steubenville, OH	1905
76	Protectors of the Polish Crown Society	Cleveland	1907
101	Polish Women Worker's Society	Chicago	1910
126	Polish Women beyond the Wisła River Society	Chicago	1911
151	St. Rose Society	Milwaukee	1912
176	Star of Victory Society	Plymouth, PA	1913
201	Garland of Mary Society	South Bend	1914
226	St. Sophia Society	Detroit	1915
251	Rainbow Society	Chicago	1917
275	St. Jadwiga Society	Omaha	1918
301	St. Anne Society	Philadelphia	1920
326	Queen Wanda Society	Wilkes-Barre, PA	1921
351	St. Barbara Society	Simpson, PA	1922
376	Independence of Polish Women Society	Buffalo	1923
401	St. Elizabeth Society	Trenton, NJ	1924

426	Polish Women from Des Plaines Society	Lyons, IL	1924
451	God and Country Society	Dearborn, MI	1925
476	Star of Freedom Society	Salamanca, NY	1926
501	St. Anne Society	Conemaugh, PA	1927
525	Queen Jadwiga Society	Chicago	1927
551	Star of May Society	Chicago	1928
575	St. Teresa Society	Willimantic, CT	1930
601	Club Wanda Society	Irvington, NJ	1930
625	Ave Maria Society	Toledo	1931
651	Progress of Polish Women under the Protection of St. Teresa Society	Gowanda, NY	1931
676	Polish Women's Circle (later Polish Women's Voice) Society	Minersville, PA	1934
701	Emilia Napieralska Society	Binghamton, NY	1935
726	Our Lady of Częstochowa Society	South Boston	1936
751	Maria Skłodowska-Curie Society	Stevens Point, WI	1940
776	Our Lady of Perpetual Help Society	Adams, MA	1945
801	Ave Maria Society	Altoona, PA	1949

A review of these thirty-three groups and the date in which they were formed is illuminating. Four were established in the first decade of the PWA of A, between 1898 and 1908, while eight came into being between 1909 and 1918. Eleven were formed in the years between 1919 and 1928, a time of record prosperity and rapid PWA of A expansion. A drop-off occurred in the Depression-ridden years between 1929 and 1938, with seven groups formed in this period. The slump continued into the decade of 1939 to 1948, an era dominated by the events and priorities of World War II. Only one new group in the list was formed since 1948; in fact, only eighteen PWA of A groups in all have come into existence since 1949.

This slowdown indicates the Alliance reached a kind of saturation point in the forming of new groups sometime in the 1930s. In this respect the PWA of A experience runs parallel to those of the other major Polish American fraternal societies, the Polish National Alliance and the Polish Roman Catholic Union of

America, both of which underwent similar slowdowns at roughly the same time.

In addition, a look at the names adopted by these local groups offers a glimpse of their character and, perhaps, the values of their early activists at the time they were established. The largest number of groups (thirteen) took a religious patron, although the first of these, the St. Rose Society, was formed some fourteen years after the PWA of A's birth, in 1912. Eleven groups such as the Independence of Polish Women Society, formed in 1923, asserted their pride in the Alliance as a women's movement. Five emphasized a patriotic theme, such as the Protectors of the Polish Crown Society (1907). Three others sent out a mixed message in choosing a popular name, such as God and Country Society (two groups in the sample took this name, one in 1905, a second in 1925).

As the rate of new group formation slowed, the number of members in existing groups grew, as noted earlier. At its fortieth anniversary in 1938, the PWA of A counted two local groups having more than 400 members, eight groups with 300 to 400 members, and thirty-six groups with 200 to 300 members. Forty-three years later, in 1981, the organization included eleven groups with more than 400 members, twenty-two with 300 to 400 members, and seventeen others with 265 to 300 members.

Not only were there more "large" groups in the PWA of A in 1981 as compared to 1938, but these units also represented a greater share of the total national membership. In 1938, the fifty-one largest PWA of A groups together accounted for 12,911 members, or 20 percent of its entire adult membership. In 1981, the fifty largest PWA of A groups included 18,309 members, or 28 percent of the total. The two tables that follow list the largest PWA of A groups as of 1938 and 1981.

The Fifty-One Largest PWA Of A Groups In 1938

Rank	Name And Number	Year Formed	Location and District	Adult and Youth Members
1	Daughters of Poland under the Protection of Our Lady of Częstochowa (418)	1924	Hamtramck, MI(5)	552/53
2	Daughters of Poland (21)	1902	South Bend (3)	429/41
3	St. Joseph (65)	1906	South Bend (3)	348/40
4	Echo of Freedom (43)	1904	Cicero (1)	340/45
5	Mother of Sorrows (141)	1912	Holyoke, MA (8)	334/41
6	Mothers and Daughters under the Care of St. Teresa (602)	1930	Newark, NJ (10)	329/55
7	St. Catherine (469)	1925	Erie, PA (4)	313/50
8	St. Jadwiga (138)	1912	Chicago (1)	313/42
9	Our Mother of Consolation (132)	1912	E. Chicago, IN (3)	304/114
10	St. Anne (73)	1907	Chicago (1)	304/49
11	Unity of Polish Women (148)	1912	Philadelphia (10)	294/12
12	Mother of Perpetual Help (147)	1912	Hartford (9)	293/7
13	Queen Jadwiga (6)	1899	Chicago (1)	284/10
14	Our Mother of Częstochowa (214)	1915	Pittsburgh (2)	271/100
15	Daughters of Poland (81)	1908	Gary, IN (3)	264/40

16	Our Mother of Sorrows (300)	1920	Ambridge, PA (2)	263/73
17	Polish Women beyond the Wisła River (126)	1911	Chicago (1)	255/32
18	Star of Hope (111)	1911	S. Chicago (1)	249/20
19	Severyna Duchinska Society (18)	1901	Chicago (1)	247/20
20	Polish Women Citizens Club (589)	1929	Elizabeth, NJ	246/28
21	Unity and Harmony (31)	1903	Calumet City, IN (1)	245/37
22	Queen Jadwiga (213)	1915	Norwich, CT (9)	243/24
23	Unity of Polish Women (328)	1922	Scranton, PA (2)	240/99
24	Northern Star (104)	1910	Milwaukee (6)	231/9
25	St. Agnes (67)	1907	Bridgeport, CT (9)	230/15
26	St. Anne (309)	1920	Detroit (5)	228/60
27	Polish Crown (112)	1911	S. Chicago (1)	228/43
28	God and Country (335)	1922	South Bend (3)	224/42
29	St. Barbara (98)	1910	Chicago (1)	224/4
30	Polish Women in a Foreign Land (10)	1900	Chicago (1)	221/5
31	Queen Jadwiga (525)	1927	Chicago (1)	220/43
32	Love of Polish Women (25)	1902	Chicago (1)	220/12
33	St. Irene (61)	1905	Chicago (1)	218/33
34	St. Bronisława (224)	1916	Pittsburgh (2)	216/55
35	Queen Jadwiga (317)	1921	Chicopee, MA (8)	215/28

36	Our Mother of Częstochowa (45)	1904	Chicago (1)	215/4
37	Our Mother of Perpetual Help (122)	1911	Indiana Harbor, IN (3)	214/23
38	Palm of Victory (70)	1907	Chicago Heights (1)	213/50
39	Immaculate Conception (47)	1904	Chicago Heights (1)	213/13
40	St. Anne (57)	1905	Chicago Heights (1)	212/-
41	White Rose (42)	1904	Chicago Heights (1)	211/14
42	St. Jadwiga Circle (515)	1927	Erie, PA (4)	210/60
43	Polish Branches (380)	1923	Buffalo (4)	210/39
44	Star of Hope under the Protection of St. Jadwiga (77)	1908	Hammond, IN (3)	205/52
45	St. Veronica (84)	1909	Chicago (1)	203/50
46	Under St. Jadwiga's Protection (9)	1900	Hartford, CT (9)	202/7
47	Royal Crown of Poland (172)	1913	Kingston, PA (2)	197/17
48	Our Mother of Perpetual Help (128)	1911	Hammond, IN (3)	195/38
49	St. Vincent de Paul (170)	1913	Detroit (5)	192/32
50	Queen Jadwiga (72)	1907	Milwaukee (6)	190/23
51	Eliza Orzeszkowa (44)	1904	Chicago (1)	190/16

The Fifty Largest PWA Of A Groups in 1981

Rank	Name and Number	Year Formed	Location and District	Adult and Youth Members
1	Daughters of Poland under the Protection of Our Lady of Częstochowa (418)	1924	Hamtramck, MI (5)	821/107
2	Our Lady of Consolation (132)	1912	E. Chicago, IN (3)	620/230
3	St. Barbara (481)	1926	Detroit (5)	617/220
4	Mother of Perpetual Help (128)	1911	Hammond (3)	582/104
5	Mother of Sorrows (141)	1912	Holyoke (8)	562/112
6	Mother of Częstochowa (214)	1915	Pittsburgh (2)	502/103
7	St. Catherine (469)	1925	Erie (4)	496/101
8	Baltimore Society (568)	1929	Baltimore (12)	445101
9	Women of Good Work of St. Vincent de Paul (170)	1913	Detroit (5)	433/81
10	Star of Freedom of St. Jadwiga (77)	1908	Hammond, IN (3)	419/176
11	Women of Good Work of St. Anne (225)	1916	Hamtramck, MI (5)	424/106
12	Mother of Consolation (386)	1924	Detroit (5)	397/83

13	Queen Wanda (737)	1937	Bayonne, NJ (10)	397/70
14	Queen's Crown of Poland (675)	1934	Manayunk, PA (10)	390/140
15	Mother of the Rosary (422)	1924	Springfield, MA (8)	389/103
16	St. Bronisława (224)	1916	Pittsburgh (2)	383/87
17	Palm of Victory (70)	1907	Chicago Heights (1)	375/79
18	Crown of Poland (112)	1911	S. Chicago (1)	370/69
19	Active Women (440)	1925	Chicago (1)	36782
20	God and Country (451)	1925	Dearborn (5)	365/48
21	St. Anne (702)	1935	Baltimore (12)	354/66
22	Hope of Freedom (280)	1918	Hartford (9)	342/109
23	Mothers and Daughters of St. Teresa (602)	1930	Newark (10)	341/76
24	St. Anne (309)	1920	Detroit (5)	334/60
25	St. Teresa (480)	1926	Chicago (1)	333/88
26	God and Country (335)	1922	Chicago (1)	324/62
27	St. Anne (73)	1907	Chicago (1)	321/60
28	Mother of Częstochowa (591)	1929	Jersey City, (10)	321/40
29	St. Frances (728)	1937	Baltimore (12)	315/59
30	Queen Jadwiga (317)	1921	Chicopee MA (8)	314/64
31	Mother of the Scapular (439)	1925	Wyandotte, MI (5)	314/33
32	Maria Konopnicka (116)	1911	Milwaukee (6)	302/66

33	Wanda's Club (601)	1930	Irvington, NJ (10)	300/60
34	St. Jadwiga (408)	1924	E. Chicago, IN (3)	295/66
35	Poland Resurrected (305)	1920	South Bend (3)	294/54
36	St. Valeria (536)	1928	South Milwaukee (6)	290/94
37	Antonina Chrzanowska (137)	1912	Chicago (1)	290/42
38	St. Teresa of the Child Jesus (579)	1929	Omaha (11)	289/57
39	Progress Society (693)	1935	Chicago (1)	288/22
40	Queen Jadwiga (267)	1918	Du Pont, PA (14)	287/197
41	Maria Konopnicka (611)	1930	Bayonne, NJ(10)	284/72
42	Maria Skłodowska Curie (749)	1939	Hammond (93)	272/97
43	Holy Family (303)	1920	Pittsburgh (2)	270/92
44	St. Elizabeth (227)	1916	Detroit (5)	270/47
45	Polish Women's Voice (398)	1924	Shenandoah PA (14)	270/40
46	Crown of Poland (366)	1923	Gary (3)	269/60
47	Maria Skłodowska-Curie (211)	1915	Chicago (1)	268/63

48	St. Anne (665)	1932	Cleveland (7)	267/46
49	Society of Women (779)	1945	Linden, NJ (10)	265/99
50	Star of Hope (111)	1911	S. Chicago (1)	265/19

A look at the youth circles, or garlands, of the PWA of A (*wianki*) for the years 1938 and 1981 gives us still more information. In 1938, 31 of the Alliance's 51 largest groups reported that they had organized *wianki* having at least 25 members. Nineteen groups reported having circles but with fewer than 25 youngsters in them. One group was not listed as having its own youth circle.

Forty-three years later, 48 of the 50 largest PWA of A groups reported having *wianki* with at least 25 members. Twenty-five groups maintained youth circles with 75 or more members. Moreover, the *wianki* circles of the largest PWA of A groups in 1981 showed a combined membership of 3,484, an increase of 1,625 over the figures reported for the largest PWA of A groups in 1938.

Further findings can be derived from an examination of the two lists of the largest PWA of A groups. One involves the extent to which the two lists differ. Of the 51 largest groups in 1938, only 17 were still in this category in 1981. Putting things another way, 31 of the largest PWA of A groups in 1981 had not ranked among the top 50 in 1938 (two of these were formed after 1938.)

This finding says a lot about the voluntary nature of the PWA of A. Voluntary groups rise and fall based largely on the level of involvement by their cadres of activists. Furthermore, the tables above offer evidence of the impact of societal change in organizations like the PWA of A. Many of the neighborhoods that in 1938 were strongholds of Polish American ethnicity had diminished considerably as centers of Polonia 43 years later. Here again we see the effects of assimilation and the movement of younger members of the Polish ethnic population out of their old neighborhoods.

Also noteworthy is the slow reconfiguration of the PWA of A along geographical lines. In 1938, 21 of the 51 largest PWA of A groups were in the Chicago metropolitan area; in 1981 only ten of the largest groups were located there. In 1938 three groups were found in the greater Detroit area. In 1981 this figure had risen to nine.

In Indiana, nine large groups were identified in 1938; in 1981 this number was roughly unchanged, at eight. However, even here there was evidence of change; only four of the top groups at the time of the fortieth anniversary made the list in 1981.

Pennsylvania was found to be underrepresented among states having the largest number of large PWA of A groups in both counts, with six groups in each year. The reason for this is most PWA of A groups in that state have been located in smaller towns rather than in the big cities of Philadelphia and Pittsburgh.

THE PWA OF A COUNCILS AND DISTRICTS

Supplementing the Polish Women's Alliance of America's local groups as focal points of fraternal life and insurance activity have been the community-wide federations of PWA of A groups known as councils (*komisje*). These units were created to bring together representatives of the groups to help them achieve their objectives and to promote greater understanding and enthusiasm for the Alliance's mission. The councils also act as bridges between the local groups and the PWA of A home office and its national leadership. In addition, the councils offer erstwhile activists another arena to hone their leadership skills. Council gatherings also give PWA of A members the opportunity to become acquainted with visiting national leaders and other dignitaries as well.

The first PWA of A council was formed on March 22, 1911, in Milwaukee. That gathering brought together representatives from the five PWA of A groups in the city. Although its activities were productive, it was not until September 1919 that a second council was formed, in Pittsburgh, Pennsylvania. A third council was organized in 1920 in Detroit, Michigan. Over the next decade and with the encouragement of the national leadership headed by

President Emilia Napieralska, the idea of the PWA of A council at last took off.

In 1921 three councils were formed, in Wilkes-Barre, Pennsylvania, Buffalo, New York, and Holyoke, Massachusetts. In 1922 Cleveland became the home of the seventh PWA of A council, followed in 1923 by Hartford, Connecticut. In 1925 two councils (in Chicago and Dunkirk, New York) were set up, with South Bend, Indiana, establishing its own council in 1927. In 1928 Council 12 was called into being, in St. Louis.

On February 15, 1929, the very day following Chicago's infamous "St. Valentine's Day Massacre," a second PWA of A council was created in the "windy city." This was necessitated by the ballooning of Council 9, which by then included an incredible 165 local groups! Other Chicago-based councils soon followed, and by 1938 there were eight in existence.

In all, from 1929 to 1938 eighteen councils were set up. Besides those in Chicago, three were formed in Pennsylvania, two each in New York and Michigan and one each in Massachusetts, Ohio, New Jersey, and Nebraska. In the years since, seven more councils were created, for a total of 38 in the year 2000.

The delegates to the 1910 Milwaukee *sejm* also created a second intermediate coordinating and leadership institution that of the PWA of A state president. This individual was to be elected at the national convention and to represent the members of her district to the home office. Beginning in 1910, state presidents were elected in Ohio, Wisconsin, Indiana, and Michigan, with another state president elected to represent the combined area of Connecticut and Massachusetts. In 1912, a state president for western Pennsylvania was elected, together with ones for New York and Connecticut (by then separated from Massachusetts). In 1914, eastern Pennsylvania elected its first president, followed in 1916 by Indiana and in 1918 by Nebraska. Illinois, which was recognized as already having plenty of high level representation in the vicinity because of the presence of the national office in Chicago, did not elect its own first state president until 1924. In 1931 New Jersey chose its own PWA of A state president for the first time.

At the PWA of A's seventeenth convention in Chicago in 1935, the delegates reaffirmed the importance of the office of state president on the occasion of the twenty-fifth anniversary of its inception. Acting on a recommendation from its membership committee, the convention approved the creation of a new set of districts, each to be headed by a president elected by delegates gathered at regularly called conventions in each district (*obwód*, the plural form being *obwody*).

Initially there were eleven PWA of A districts: District 1, which included the states of Florida, Illinois, Missouri; District 2, which covered northeast and western Pennsylvania, except for Erie; District 3, Indiana; District 4, western New York together with Erie, Pennsylvania; District 5, Michigan along with the city of Toledo, Ohio; District 6, Wisconsin; District 7, Ohio (except for Toledo) along with West Virginia; District 8, Massachusetts; District 9, Connecticut; District 10, New Jersey, eastern Pennsylvania and Philadelphia; District 11, California and Nebraska.

In 1951 District 11 was reorganized, with Nebraska continuing as District 11 and California forming the new District 13. A new District 12 was established the same year, covering the state of Maryland and the District of Columbia. Pennsylvania (District 2) was divided into two districts, with the northeast and western parts of the state retaining the designation of District 2 and eastern Pennsylvania becoming District 14.[6]

---

[6] Brief histories of the districts can be found in the *Polish Women's of Alliance of America Centennial Celebration, May 16 – 17, 1998* (Chicago: Polish Women's Alliance of America, 1998), pp. 22 – 35. The names and in many case the photographs, of all PWA of A state and district presidents through 1980 is in Helen Zielinski's *Historia Związku Polek*, pp. 28 – 38. A complete list of state and district presidents is also found in the appendix of this book.

The women who have served in this important capacity merit special recognition for their years of dedicated work on behalf of the membership of the Alliance in their districts. Many gave decades of talented, generous effort to the mission of the organization, as can be seen from a review of the list in the appendix. Pelagia Wojtczak of Milwaukee, served for forty unbroken years as president of District 6

Several district presidents have played national roles in the Polish Women's Alliance of America, as officers or as candidates for positions in the general administration. Among the most notable of these women has been Honorata Wołowska, the longtime president of District 2, who was PWA of A president from 1935 to 1947; Secretary General Maria Porwit; Vice President Helena Sambor; and Maria Kryszak, editor of *Głos Polek*. Angelina Milaszewicz served as a national vice president of the PWA of A before her subsequent election as Illinois district president.

THE PWA of A'S INSURANCE PROGRAM: A REVIEW

The original insurance plan offered by the Polish Women's Alliance of America was a rudimentary form of coverage known as "assessment insurance." Upon her admission, a woman paid the Alliance an initiation fee. Afterward, she paid a constant sum of money (or assessment) over the remainder of her life in return for her burial insurance plan with the PWA of A. The amount of the death benefit initially ranged from one-hundred to five-hundred dollars.

A member was given a choice in paying her assessment on a monthly, quarterly, or yearly basis. But her total premium payment was the same regardless of her actual age at the time of her entry into the fraternal. Moreover, in its early days only women between the ages of seventeen and forty-five could purchase PWA of A insurance. This restriction was introduced because of the high mortality levels that then prevailed among women who were giving birth and the still relatively low life expectancy among adults. However, women above the age of forty-five were encouraged to join the Alliance as "social" or noninsured members.

On March 27, 1902, the Alliance learned of the death of Małgorzata Półchłopek, a member of Group 6, the Queen Jadwiga

(Wisconsin). She was followed by Rozalia Biedroń, state and then District president from 1927 to 1964, thirty-seven years in all. Maria Porwit's career is also especially noteworthy. State and then District 2 president from 1921 to 1939, Porwit then served twenty years as secretary general and another twelve years as District 14 president in Pennsylvania. In all, Porwit held a major office in the Alliance for fifty consecutive years.

Society, in Chicago. Półchłopek was the first PWA of A insured member to die. The formalities connected with the payment of the death benefit to her beneficiaries were handled promptly and properly, enhancing the Alliance's stature in the Polonia community.

But the PWA of A did not long rely on its program of assessment insurance. At the ninth convention in South Bend, Indiana, in 1912, the delegates approved a new insurance system, with progressive premium rates. Accordingly, younger women who joined the PWA of A paid lower insurance premiums than individuals who were older at the time of their admission. The idea of variable insurance premium rates was not entirely new — it had been debated for several years and had been rejected by a vote of 69 to 54 at the 1910 convention.

At its thirteenth convention in Chicago in 1921, the delegates raised insurance premiums for all contracts by four cents per month on every hundred dollars of coverage. This action, taken in the wake of the influenza epidemic following World War I, came in response to calls from state insurance departments urging the Alliance to collect higher premiums to be better meet serious obligations that might arise in the future. The move proved surprisingly uncontroversial. It added new funds that strengthened the Alliance's financial reserves. Perhaps even more significant, it resulted in no loss in members.

In 1922, the PWA of A general administration voted to enroll the Alliance into the National Fraternal Congress of America, the nationwide association of fraternal insurance benefit societies. Participation by the PWA of A in the NFCA, which continues to the present day, helps its leaders remain informed about the issues fraternals face in doing business and the changing types of insurance that become available.

NFCA membership helps the Alliance invest its reserves more efficiently and safely. It also keeps its officers informed of legal and political developments that affect the operations of nonprofit fraternals, especially the protection of their tax-exempt status. Many PWA of A members have been active in the conventions of the National Fraternal Congress over the years, at both the state and national levels.

In 1930 the PWA of A won Illinois department of insurance approval to offer a new type of life insurance product, one that complemented its traditional ordinary life plan. (Ordinary life insurance required its purchaser to pay premiums during her entire life in order to maintain her coverage.)

The new insurance offering was a twenty year payment certificate, one allowing a member to pay for the cost of her life insurance over the period of twenty years. This plan was approved at the 1935 PWA of A convention, along with another offering, a seven-year term insurance plan.

The term insurance product represented a significant change for the PWA of A. Unlike its permanent plans of insurance, the new term offering provided coverage for only seven years (the term the policy was to be in force). It was also less expensive than the fraternal's traditional whole-life or permanent plans since it did not include a savings feature.

In the years after, the PWA of A continued to add to its portfolio of insurance plans. The Alliance currently offers various permanent and term insurance options, each aimed at meeting its members' (and future members') varying needs and financial means. The fraternal has established several annuity plans helping members supplement their expected future retirement needs by setting up a safe and secure savings vehicle for themselves and their loved ones.

In the year 2003, the Polish Women's Alliance of America was offering the parents and grandparents of prospective juvenile members a variety of insurance plans. The purpose was to encourage adult members to enroll the next generation into the Alliance and thereby contribute toward their future, and that of the organization as well. Plans targeted toward young people included not only the Alliance's various whole life plans but also a single payment plan of life insurance, one that was very attractive because of its low cost to grandparents wishing to give their little ones something of lasting value. The PWA of A also sold a term plan of insurance for youngsters, one readily converted into a permanent plan of insurance as late as the insured person's twenty-third birthday. Another offering was an inexpensive accidental death plan of insurance.

As noted earlier, in the beginning the PWA of A offered insurance only to women between the ages of seventeen and forty-five. In 1917, one of these restrictions was lifted when the Alliance (and many other fraternals) won approval from the state insurance regulatory agencies to enroll girls under the age of seventeen as insured members. The PWA of A acted quickly to take advantage of this policy change. At first, the Alliance limited the amount of insurance that could be purchased on behalf of juveniles. Gradually these restrictions were lifted, as juveniles were made eligible to have as much coverage as adults.

This change benefited the Alliance in two ways. For one thing, it helped bring about a substantial increase in membership. But there was a second consequence of perhaps even greater significance. It involved the decision by the PWA of A to organize new programs for juvenile members, most of them on the local level and under the supervision of its groups. (In later years, youth programs would also be directed by the councils, state districts, and the national office.) The youth circles, *wianki,* operated under leaders chosen by the local groups. Soon they were engaged in organizing a variety of programs, among them ethnic dancing, singing, band practice, sports, and Polish language instruction. Some groups won recognition for the quality of their *wianki* activities; in later years the youth circles were brought together for jamborees at which their members could perform for one another and for larger audiences as well.

Over the years, the upper age limitations for insurance through the Alliance were also raised. Currently, any individual under eighty years of age may purchase one of the fraternal's life insurance products. The maximum amount of insurance available on any single policy purchased through the PWA of A has also been increased considerably. Whereas the typical policy in the early years past provided coverage of five hundred dollars; the current maximum amount of insurance is twenty-five thousand dollars.

In 1947, at the twentieth convention in Chicago, the delegates approved another expansion in membership eligibility. This time, young males under the age of seventeen were granted the right to be insured through the Alliance and to join its youth circles. In the 1980s, the Alliance extended insured membership privileges to adult men as well. (Thus far none has held elective office.) In addition the restrictions on membership to persons of Polish origin have been substantially liberalized. Today for all practical purposes anyone who wishes to join the Alliance may do so. The gradual transformation of the Polish Women's Alliance into a universal fraternal insurance benefit society is evident from a look at its current by-laws. Thus, Article 2, paragraph 2 of the PWA of A constitution defines eligibility for membership as follows: "Individuals, whether adult or juvenile, of Polish birth, descent, or conviction, may be eligible for membership in the Polish Women's Alliance of America."

An interesting sidelight to the story of PWA of A insurance involves the actions its officers have taken over the years to return surplus funds back to its members. This has occurred on three different occasions.

The first of these decisions followed a review of the Alliance's finances in 1951. At the request of President Adela Łagodzinska, the PWA of A's general administration approved a special dividend in the form of a grant of additional life insurance to all members at the time.

A similar action occurred in 1967 and followed on the general administration's request that its actuary, the firm of Stedry Hausen, do a review of its finances. A study was then conducted for the years between 1953 and 1967; it was then decided that the Alliance's solid financial position warranted the issuing of another special dividend. On the eve of its seventieth anniversary on May 21, 1968, the PWA of A declared the dividend of two-million dollars to all individuals who were members prior to January 1963. Once again this distribution took the form of additional insurance coverage to all eligible members.

In October 1984, the general administration, on the advice of the actuarial firm of Steiml and Associates, Inc., approved a third special dividend of two-million dollars to all members who belonged to the PWA of A between December 31, 1983, and May 1, 1985. Once again the dividend was distributed as a grant of additional life insurance. As a consequence of all these actions, PWA of A members saw their life insurance coverage increase by as much as 40 percent.

MEMBERSHIP DEVELOPMENT:

THE MAY QUEEN COMPETITION

In addition to the recruitment activities of PWA of A local groups and councils, important recruitment tools, a different type of Alliance activity has proved to be significant in helping boost membership over the past three and one-half decades. This activity is the annual May Queen membership drive.

The May Queen (*Królowa Majowa*) membership drive dates back to the presidency of Adela Łagodzinska. The May Queen competition recognizes women who in the previous year have led their council in bringing in new insurance applications. The awards are announced each May, around the time of the two most significant dates on the PWA of A calendar. These are May 22, the anniversary of the founding of the Alliance in 1898, and Mother's Day, the nationwide observance which from the beginning of the twentieth century has been celebrated on the second Sunday in May.

The May Queen competition has always received substantial publicity and has been a popular, often closely contested, event. Following the competition, photographs of each year's May Queens are published in *Głos Polek*. Under the current rules of the contest, the top sales person in a council is its May Queen. In addition, members who submit at least ten new insurance applications over the previous twelve months and who are runners-up to their council's May Queen are recognized as *świty*, members of the queen's court. *Świty* are also recognized for their work in *Głos Polek*.

GŁOS POLEK

A significant and enduring element in PWA of A life for more than ninety years has been its very own official fraternal publication, *Głos Polek*. The Alliance began publishing the newspaper, whose title translates as "The Voice of Polish Women," in 1902, and since 1910 the publication has continued without interruption.

Głos Polek keeps its readers informed about the aims, activities, and concerns of the Polish Women's Alliance of America. It has helped mobilize its members to volunteer their services on behalf of the organization's patriotic and benevolent causes. And it has served as a lifeline in linking the national organization with those members of the Alliance who cannot, for various reasons, participate in the meetings of their local group.

In 1902, the delegates to the third PWA of A convention voted to create their own monthly fraternal publication. The paper's first editor was Frank Wołowski, an associate editor of Chicago's *Dziennik Narodowy* (Polish national daily) paper, and husband of PWA of A, Secretary General, Łucja Wołowska. This attempt to establish its own publication, though well intentioned, was overly ambitious given the Alliance's very modest finances and membership at the time. Within a few months *Głos Polek* had to close up shop.

Over the next seven years, the Alliance relied on *Dziennik Narodowy* to publish a weekly page that featured news about its activities. PWA of A member Maria Iwanowska served as the page's editor until 1909; she was then succeeded by Jadwiga Michalska, another member of the Alliance. Michalska remained in charge until the eighth convention of the PWA of A in September 1910.

There the delegates approved the reestablishment of *Głos Polek,* this time as a weekly. Chicago banker and Polonia leader John Smulski agreed to have his publishing firm print the paper. Stefania Laudyn-Chrzanowska, an immigrant newcomer from Poland and a friend of former president Stefania Chmielinska, was appointed editor-in-chief of the restored publication. Its first issue appeared on November 3, 1910.

After the ninth PWA of A convention in 1912, Jadwiga Michalska returned to the post of editor-in-chief following a vote of the general administration. But she resigned only a few months later, in March 1913, to be replaced by Helena Setmajer. At the next convention, in 1914, delegates voted to return Laudyn-Chrzanowska to the editorship. The office of editor-in-chief would remain elective for the next fifty years, giving the woman holding the post a somewhat independent status in the Alliance.

Laudyn-Chrzanowska, a devotee of the PWA of A mission when she had resided in partitioned Poland, went on to serve four years as editor. Her work was marked by a deep-seated patriotism for the Polish cause, an especially timely stance given the outbreak of the World War I in 1914 and the homeland's restoration to independence in 1918. Laudyn-Chrzanowska was also a strong feminist and made the case for equal rights for women a regular feature in the newspaper.

But Laudyn-Chrzanowska was also a controversial editor who collided with several of her fellow officers. At the twelfth PWA of A convention in 1918 she was replaced by Zofia Jankiewicz. Shortly afterward, the former editor and her husband left the United States to settle permanently in newly independent Poland.

Jankiewicz stayed on as editor until March 1921, a few months before the thirteenth convention. In the interim, Dr. Maria Olgiert-Kaczorowska, the Alliance's veteran medical examiner, took the reins. Kaczorowska had first been elected medical examiner in 1906; after her brief stint with the newspaper, she continued as medical examiner until the late 1920s.

At the 1921 convention, the delegates elected Milwaukee's Maria Kryszak as editor. Kryszak had been active in the Alliance since the early 1900s and had first gained recognition when she succeeded in having the eighth convention held in her hometown. Already a member of the staff of Milwaukee's Polish language Catholic daily, *Nowiny Polskie,* when she was elected to head *Głos Polek*, Kryszak was also an activist in the city's politics. She would go on to be elected to seven two-year terms in the Wisconsin State Assembly.

Under Maria Kryszak's direction, *Głos Polek* emphasized reports on the activities of PWA of A local groups around the country and covered the business and organizational side of the fraternal more systematically. Information about Polish history and culture remained staples, along with stories that highlighted the aspirations of women in the steadily Americanizing Polish community.

Kryszak was active on the larger stage too. In 1934 she represented the Polish American press at the Second World Congress of Poles from Abroad held in Warsaw. Her trip, together with other visits made to Poland by PWA of A members, received substantial coverage in *Głos Polek*.

In 1939, Jadwiga Karłowicz, a published poet who only a year before had authored the first official history of the PWA of A on its fortieth anniversary, was elected editor to succeed the ailing Kryszak. Karłowicz's tenure proved to be even longer than her predecessor's and extended (with one four year interruption) to 1964, when she resigned from her post. At the twenty-first convention in 1951, Karłowicz made an unsuccessful run for the presidency against Adela Łagodzinska. Her campaign made her ineligible to seek reelection as editor and she was then replaced by Halina Paluszek. Prior to her own election, Paluszek had held several positions in the Chicago home office.

In 1955, a major change in the Alliance took place as the post of editor was made appointive. Karłowicz returned as editor, but this time with far less independence. When she resigned her post in 1964, she had been editor for twenty-one years.

In 1956, *Głos Polek,* after forty-five years as a weekly publication, began appearing twice monthly. For the next thirty-nine years the paper appeared on the first and third Thursday of each month, a schedule that ended in January 1995, when it became a monthly.

From its birth *Głos Polek* had been a Polish language newspaper; only infrequently were articles or announcements printed in English. However, in 1951 a significant change in policy occurred with the beginning of a section in the English language. This move was very tentative at first, with only about two of the paper's usual twelve pages of copy coming out in English. Melanie Sokołowska was made responsible for inaugurating this effort; soon after she was succeeded as head of the English section by Monica Sokołowska.

In 1971, following her retirement from the presidency, Adela Łagodzinska took over as editor of the English language section. She continued in this work until the late 1970s when she was succeeded by Maria Kubiak (later the Alliance's secretary general) and in the early 1980s by Delphine Lytell (vice president from 1987 to 1995 and president from 1995 to 1999). Mary Mirecki-Piergies followed Lytell as editor of the paper's English language section until 1999; she was succeeded by Gloria Waber, who also assumed the duties of directing the Alliance's public relations activities. Over the years after 1951, the English language section of *Głos Polek* was greatly expanded. Today, twelve or thirteen of the sixteen pages in each edition are printed in English, including the front page.

Following Jadwiga Karłowicz's resignation as the Polish language section editor of *Głos Polek* in January 1964, the Alliance was fortunate to secure the services of Maria Loryś to succeed her. Loryś would hold the post for the next thirty-one years. In the process, she would add her own special contribution to the newspaper's character and development.

Born in Poland, Loryś had taken part in her country's underground resistance to Nazi German domination in World War II. She even rose to officer's rank in the massive 350,000-member Home Army (*Armia Krajowa*). After the war, she participated in the underground's effort to oppose Poland's takeover by Soviet Russia. In 1946 she was obliged to leave Poland to avoid imminent arrest by communist authorities. In 1951 Loryś, her husband, and their two children arrived in America. Settling in Chicago, she was soon active in the city's Polish immigrant community.

Besides joining the Polish Women's Alliance of America, Loryś was active in several Polonia organizations, including the Polish Combatants' Association and the Polish American Congress.

With Loryś at the helm, *Głos Polek* provided a renewed focus on the PWA of A's historic concerns about Poland. At the same time, the publication gave regular and extensive coverage to the lengthening history of the Alliance. In addition, Loryś dedicated herself to writing the story of the PWA of A in book form, beginning where Karłowicz had left off in 1938 with her monograph, and published her work in 1980.

Loryś' book took the form of a second volume in the history of the Alliance and followed the chronological approach that Karłowicz had taken in her book. In this way Loryś brought the Alliance's story up to 1959. Like her predecessor's publication, the second volume devoted many pages to events at the national conventions of the PWA of A. Yet there were also some noticeable innovations in her work. For example, Loryś provided more extensive information about the membership and the fraternal's financial condition and included a good number profiles of PWA of A leaders. The work included a large number of photographs.

Loryś also assisted President Helen Zielinski in her authorship of a "third volume" of Alliance history, one that appeared in 1981. This significant book was distinguishable from its predecessor volumes in its emphasis on the main organizational aspects of PWA of A life and operations. The book thus included up-to-date material on the local groups, councils, and state divisions of the Alliance; it told the story of the fraternal's home offices, and traced the evolution of *Głos Polek*. This worthy, interesting, and well illustrated publication, like its two preceding volumes, appeared in the Polish language.

Following the PWA of A's 1995 convention, Loryś announced her retirement. She had served as editor of *Głos Polek* for thirty-one years, longer than any of her predecessors. She was followed by Grażyna Zajączkowska, also a native of Poland. Zajączkowska has worked to put out an interesting and informative Polish language section, in cooperation with the elected officers of the Alliance and the newspaper's English language editors. She, like Loryś, is active in the Polonia community organizations of Chicago.

In the year 2003, the monthly *Głos Polek* includes reports on the activities of the PWA of A national leadership and its state presidents and stories about the events that are organized by its local groups. General information about fraternalism and PWA of A insurance, annuities, and benefits is supplemented with data on sales and membership. Special coverage continues to be devoted to the annual May Queen competitions. A good deal of space is devoted to the Polish, Polish American, and PWA of A heritage, ethnic celebrations and foods, and famous Poles, particularly women.

A content analysis of the twenty-four issues of *Głos Polek* published in 1992 found that 308 stories on the PWA of A were included in the paper during that period. Of these, 28 came from the district units of the Alliance, 61 from the councils, and 217 from local groups. In all, 12 of the 14 PWA of A districts, 20 of its councils, and 99 of its local groups sent in at least one story or announcement during the year.

Other news pieces provided coverage of actions taken by the general administration to promote the work of the fraternal, news of membership drives, commemorations of the organization's anniversaries, coverage of the annual May Queen competition, and information about the larger Polonia community and Poland. Other features covered PWA of A insurance plans, its annual scholarship program, and the Alliance's charitable and benevolent work.[7]

WORK WITH YOUNG PEOPLE

Another area of PWA of A activity is its work on behalf of young people. The Alliance has been committed to nurturing an appreciation of Polish heritage among the young. From the Alliance's earliest years, its leaders dedicated themselves to calling on their fellow Polish women members and nonmembers alike, to use their authority as mothers to educate their children in the Polish language and to instill in them a consciousness and pride about Poland's history and culture. To help achieve this aim, the Alliance set up reading rooms and small libraries in the immigrant community and provided information about Polish culture in *Głos Polek*.

After it received permission in 1917 to enroll juveniles as insured members in the Alliance, the PWA of A organized a system of youth circles or "garlands" (*wianki*) to promote ethnic pride. Here the objective was to encourage every local group to set up its own *wianek* (singular for *wianki*), an aim that was eventually largely realized. In 1938, 459 of the PWA of A groups reported having circles and 272 of these units included at least ten children each.

In the early 1950s, more than 75 percent of the PWA of A groups had their own *wianki*; by the 1960s some 90 percent of all groups reported having their own youth circle. This level has been maintained to the present day.

---

[7] *Comparable studies were conducted for the years 1991 and 1993 and resulted in the same findings. A review of the contents of Głos Polek in 1996 after it had become a monthly edition brought similar results, although there* were obviously fewer articles in all.

Early *wianki* engaged their members in a variety of activities, depending on the interests and skills of their adult instructors. Beginning in the late 1930s a more pronounced effort to promote the training of youth circle leaders was begun by the national leadership. Here, the teaching of leaders about Polish music and dance was organized in a more systematic fashion. The home office also began sponsoring gatherings of *wianki* on the national level. In later years, these national *wianki* gatherings were supplemented by youth conferences held in state districts.

In the 1950s the Polish Women's Alliance of America began to develop another youth-oriented program of benefit to young members. This is the PWA of A's College Scholarship program.

Today the scholarship program is open to all male and female members of the Alliance who are enrolled in college as full-time students. The program has several distinctive features. All qualified applicants receive scholarship awards and are eligible for them throughout their years in school, regardless of financial need or academic standing. This means that the scholarship awards are not based on competition. Rather, they represent a fraternal benefit that is made available to all members who happen to be qualifying college students.

Another feature of the Polish Women's Alliance of America scholarship program involves the sources of the funds that are dispensed. Of course, the PWA of A is not unique among fraternals in offering scholarships. Usually, they fund these programs out of the annual operating budgets that are approved at their national conventions or at meetings of their executive boards. In the case of the Alliance, only part of the funds earmarked for scholarships is allocated in this fashion. Substantial amounts are also raised in the districts of the organization (usually through the debutante balls and other social events they sponsor). This money is then matched by the general administration of the PWA of A on a dollar for dollar basis. As a result, the amount distributed each year is far greater as is the level of organizational involvement in the program.

CIVIC, BENEVOLENT, AND PATRIOTIC SERVICE

As a not-for-profit fraternal insurance benefit society, the Polish Women's Alliance of America has devoted considerable time and energy to work on a variety of causes that serve the needs and interests of others, whether or not they belong to the Alliance. For its members, the PWA of A maintains a fraternal aid fund to assist needy individuals so they may continue to maintain their insurance protection. Assistance is also provided to members who have suffered particular misfortune because of extraordinary events like floods, fires, or earthquakes. Members of PWA of A groups have often shown great interest in organizing visits with members who happen to be ill or hospitalized, in nursing homes, or who have suffered the loss of a loved one. The groups continue to take seriously their responsibilities to send representatives to attend the wakes, funerals, and prayer services of deceased members.

The Alliance has given financial assistance to a wide variety of charitable agencies too. In the 1990s alone, these included the American Cancer Society, Christmas Seals, the Crusade of Mercy, Kiwanis, the Polish American Immigration and Relief Committee, Habitat for Humanity, Jubilee Ministries, several children's institutions located in Poland, and a number of homes for the aged, handicapped, and infirm in this country. The PWA of A as an organization, along with its members acting individually, have generously donated to the maintenance of the National Shrine of Our Lady of Częstochowa, located in Doylestown, Pennsylvania, outside of Philadelphia. The Alliance has supported the educational mission of the college, seminary, and high school that make up the Orchard Lake Schools near Detroit. The organization has also supported the establishment of the Pope John Paul II Cultural Center in Washington, D. C., located near the Catholic University of America.

Beginning in the early 1950s the Polish Women's Alliance of America provided financial support to the Catholic University of Lublin (*Katolicki Uniwersytet Lubelski,* or KUL) in eastern Poland. KUL was the one private institution of higher education that was permitted to operate in communist-ruled Poland; for that matter, it was the only private university allowed to exist in any of the countries under Soviet domination after World War II. The PWA of A and its members also contributed to the work of the *Rada Polonii Amerykańskiej* (Polish American Council) in the years during and after the World War II and have been very supportive of the Polish

American Congress Charitable Foundation since its creation in the early 1970s.

The Alliance has been active in a series of national fund drives directed by the Polish American Congress. This should come as no great surprise, since the president of the PWA of A has served in the leadership of the PAC since its inception and has been one of its vice presidents from the late 1940s up to the PAC election of 2000. In that year, the newly elected president of the PWA of A, Virginia Sikora, stepped aside and Treasurer Olga Kaszewicz was elected to the PAC post in her stead.

Over the past twenty years the many charitable and humanitarian drives organized under the auspices of the PAC and its charitable foundation have included work to help fund an international hostel for visiting pilgrims coming to Rome from Poland. This project was initiated soon after the election of Pope John Paul II in 1978. More recent efforts have involved successful drives to renovate the Statue of Liberty in New York and to establish an immigration museum at Ellis Island, the entry point for several million Polish immigrants between 1890 and 1951. Similarly, it was through the Alliance's generosity that three transport vans were shipped to Poland to enable handicapped children to get to and from their hospitals and rehabilitation clinics. These vans were donated by the PWA of A at ceremonies in August 1992 in Kraków, Poland. There, leaders of the Alliance, including President Helen Wojcik, took part in the world congress of Polonia held at the invitation of the newly established democratic government and its organization working with the Polish emigration, *Wspólnota Polska.*

This chapter is intended to supplement the preceding and chronologically based history of the Polish Women's Alliance of Alliance. In this review of the Alliance's institutional development and ideological mission, the aim has been to give readers a somewhat different appreciation of the PWA of A story. Despite the many dramatic changes that have occurred in the United States in the past century, the Polish Women's Alliance of America has remained committed to its historic aims. This is to the credit of its members and leaders, who over the past five generations have continued to devote themselves to its ideals.

One Hundred Years Later:
The Fifty Largest PWA of A Groups in 1998

Rank	Group Name/Number and Year Formed	Location and District	Adult and Youth Members
1	Our Lady of Consolation Society, Group 132 (1912)	E. Chicago, IN (3)	875/242
2	Queen Jadwiga Society, Group 267 (1918)	Du Pont, PA (9)	654/152
3	St. Theresa Society, Group 535 (1928)	Old Forge, PA (14)	578/48
4	Daughters of Poland Society, Group 418 (1924)	Hamtramck, MI (5)	546/52
5	Mother of Perpetual Help Society, Group 122 (1911)	E. Hammond, IN (3)	523/84
6	St. Bronisława Society, Group 224 (1916)	Pittsburgh (2)	501/102
7	Baltimore Society, Group 568 (1929)	Baltimore (12)	482/195
8	Mater Dolorosa Society Group 141 (1912)	Holyoke, MA (8)	479/86
9	St. Jadwiga Society, Group 37 (1904)	Whiting, IN (3)	474/93
10	St. Bernadette Society, Group 763 (1942)	Baltimore (12)	468/126
11	Our Lady of Częstochowa Society, Group 305 (1920) *	South Bend (3)	447/113
12	Active Polish Women Society, Group 440 (1925)	Chicago (1)	445/99
13	Maria Skłodowska-Curie Society, Group 211 (1915)	Chicago (1)	438/151
14	Głos Polek Society, Group 379 (1923)	Buffalo (4)	438/48
15	St. Theresa Society, Group 579 (1929)	Omaha(9)	436/348
16	Our Lady of the Rosary Society, Group 422 (1924)	Springfield, MA (8)	435/150
17	Palm of Victory Society,	Chicago	430/23

	Group 70 (1907)	Heights, IL (5)	
18	St. Barbara Society, Group 481 (1926)	Detroit (5)	407/47
19	Star of the Sea Society, Group 743 (1938)	Chicago (1)	377/89
20	St. Catherine Society, Group 469 (1925)	Erie (4)	375/53
21	St. Jadwiga Society, Group 77 (1908)+	Hammond, IN (3)	370/70
22	Our Lady of Częstochowa Society, Group 214 (1915)	Pittsburgh (2)	370/56
23	Queen of Peace Society, Group 815 (1964)	Gary, IN (3)	325/112
24	Crown of Poland Society, Group 112 (1911)#	Park Ridge, IL (1)	325/27
25	St. Theresa Society, Group 480 (1926)	Chicago (1)	321/58
26	Anna Chrzanowska Society, Group 137 (1912)	Chicago (1)	317/52
27	St. Anna Society, Group 225 (1916)	Hamtramck, MI (5)	316/16
28	Queen Jadwiga Society, Group 317 (1921)	Chicopee, MA (8)	310/35
29	St. Jadwiga Society, Group 561 (1929) **	Hamtramck, MI (5)	307/72
30	San Fernando Valley Society, Group 814 (1962)	Sherman Oaks (13)	305/208
31	Our Mother of Perpetual Help Society, Group 185 (1914)	Wallingford, CT (9)	304/99
32	Queen Jadwiga Society, Group 55 (1905)	Cleveland (7)	299/32
33	St. Ann's Society, Group 702 (1935)	Baltimore (12)	292/57
34	St. Theresa Society, Group 598 (1930)	Harrison, NJ (10)	286/115
35	Queen Wanda Society, Group 737 (1937)	Bayonne, NJ (10)	286/22
36	God and Country Society, Group 451 (1925)	Dearborn (5)	285/64
37	Immaculate Conception Society, Group 182 (1914)	Braddock, PA (2)	285/61

38	Our Mother of Perpetual Help Society, Group 306 (1920)	Natrona, PA (2)	281/22
39	Kraków Society, Group 341 (1922) ++	Pittsburgh (2)	274/26
40	Głos Polek Society, Group 530 (1927)	Nanticoke, PA (14)	270/51
41	Wreath of Mary Society Group 509 (1927)	Du Pont, PA (14)	267/119
42	Our Lady of Częstochowa Society, Group 591 (1929)	Jersey City (10)	263/22
43	St. Bronisława Society, Group 768 (1944) #	Milwaukee (6)	263/6
44	Crown of the Queen of Poland Society, Group 675 (1934)	Manayunk, PA (10)	260/13
45	Maria Skłodowska Curie Society Group 749 (1939)	Hammond (3),	258/52
46	St. Jadwiga Society, Group 275 (1923)	S. Omaha, NE (11)	258/32
47	St. Jadwiga Society, Group 408 (1924)	East Chicago (3)	255/74
48	St. Stanisław Kostka Society, Group 221 (1916)	Pittsburgh (2)	255/32
49	St. Anne Society, 73 (1907)	Chicago (1)	254/2
50	St. Sofia Society, Group 226 (1915)	Detroit (5)	251/79

*	Originally Poland Resurrected Society.
+	Originally the Star of Freedom Society.
**	Originally the Polish Women's Circle.
++	Originally the Kraków Women Society.
#	This group is currently on direct billing status; in other words, members pay their dues and insurance premiums directly to the home office of the Alliance and do not rely on a local financial secretary to perform this duty.

THE POLISH WOMEN'S ALLIANCE OF AMERICA: OUR FUTURE IS BRIGHT, OUR PAST INSPIRING

The history of the United States over the past century is replete with many momentous events and achievements. One involves the stories of the millions of immigrants from around the world who have entered, and continue to enter, into the mainstream of American life. This is an especially important saga for the more than two million immigrants from Poland who began settling here in the middle of the nineteenth century. Most arrived with little more than their dreams of a better life. Over the years they, their children, and their later descendants made those dreams a reality. In so doing, they have made a noteworthy contribution to American society.

A second story involves the expansion of opportunity for all Americans, a story that includes the many and sometimes extraordinary achievements of millions of women in their efforts to attain equal rights and standing with men in this country. The story of women in America is a work still in progress. But it is taking place everywhere, in our country's economy, in our cultural life, and in politics.

Both of these great stories are closely related to the history and development of the Polish Women's Alliance of America. Both deserve to be remembered too, for they tell much about what the PWA of A has stood for and what its members continue to stand for today.

Back in 1898 when the first Polish Women's Alliance of America society was formed in Chicago, women, whatever their national origins, possessed few citizen rights to compare with those enjoyed by their fathers, brothers, husbands, even their sons. Opportunities for women, in education, in the workplace, in the pursuit of professional careers, in the ownership of property, and in voting and holding public office did not exist at all or were greatly restricted.

As women of Polish origins, the founders of the Polish Women's Alliance of America had to overcome great obstacles to equality within their own ethnic community as well. While they enjoyed respect in the early Polonia for their skills and strengths as homemakers, mothers, and wage earners, the women belonging to the Polish immigrant community at the end of the nineteenth century were regarded at best as followers in the men-dominated secular and church organizations of the time. The world of the founders of the PWA of A was very different from the one we know today, more than a century later.

But the individuals who established the PWA of A, like those who joined them later, would not accept such restrictions. They were convinced that they possessed the intellectual, moral, and organizational ability to contribute to the immigrant community. Their aim was to win acceptance, as equal partners with men, in the causes that animated them. For in them pulsed the same aspirations for themselves and their families in their newly adopted country. And just like the men who led the organizations of early Polonia, the women who were becoming active in the burgeoning immigrant community often felt strongly about the freedom and well-being of the people of partitioned Poland.

The task of forging the Polish Women's Alliance of America was by no means smooth or easy, but once established, it would continue to grow in numbers, influence, and financial strength. The Alliance and its mission would also win the respect of the entire Polish American community. Further, the Alliance, through its members' concerns over the rights of women to full equality with men in the organizational life of Poland and their commitment to the education of children in their heritage, helped place these matters onto the agenda of every other Polonia organization.

Of great and historic significance was the wise decision of the Alliance's early leaders to base their operations on the foundation of fraternalism and the sale of insurance. In so doing, they were able to offer their targeted audience a set of practical, tangible reasons for becoming and remaining members of the PWA of A. These complemented the philosophically idealistic reasons that defined the movement's mission.

In both world wars, the fraternal beliefs of the members of the Polish Women's Alliance of America led them to expand their efforts on behalf of the people of Poland, both by organizing the gathering of clothing, foodstuffs, medical supplies, and educational materials for shipment to the victims of the conflicts and by working for Poland's political independence.

Through the generous work of thousands of its members and their friends, the PWA of A not only contributed greatly to these causes, it also invigorated the efforts of other organizations in Polonia, most notably the Polish Central Relief Committee in World War I and Polish American Council in World War II. These activities continued after the war, first through the Council and other civic and humanitarian agencies, and after 1980 through the Polish American Congress Charitable Foundation. All testified eloquently to the Alliance's fraternal solidarity with Polonia and the people of Poland.

Similarly, the Polish Women's Alliance of America has been active in supporting the cause of Polish independence and freedom. In World War I, the PWA of A was a leading participant in the Polish National Department, the first viable all-Polonia federation working for the Polish independence cause. During and after World War II, the Alliance again took a leadership role in the Polish American community's work for Poland through its participation in the Polish American Congress, formed in 1944. Whatever the specific cause embraced by the congress, whether it involved defense of Poland's post-war western borders, its support of the Polish Roman Catholic Church and the Polish Solidarity movement in the era of communist domination, or its efforts to promote the country's inclusion the NATO alliance in the post-communist 1990s, the Polish Women's Alliance of America was actively involved.

As a provider of life insurance (and, more recently, of annuities too), the Polish Women's Alliance of America has reached out to more than seven hundred thousand people and today includes nearly sixty thousand members all over the United States. The PWA of A offers its members secure and competitively priced insurance protection and a variety of other valuable fraternal benefits, including participation in local group activities, receipt of its monthly publication *Głos Polek,* and awards of college scholarships.

From the start the PWA of A operated out of its members' conviction that women, acting in concert, could achieve a host of objectives of genuine importance to the larger community to which they belonged. But the PWA of A commitment to equality was not one based on a demand for special rights or privileges. Rather, it was founded on a belief that equal rights included equal responsibility and respect, for men and women alike, in their joint service to the causes that inspired their participation in Polonia. This was and remains to this day the meaning of the PWA of A commitment to *równouprawnienie* (equality), a word as beautiful in its implications as it is hard for non-Polish speakers to say!

Because PWA of A members have always held to this definition of equality, they have been able to strive constantly to work with everyone with whom they have shared similar values. Further, the PWA of A commitment to *równouprawnienie* has allowed its members, generation after generation, to keep faith in the time-honored beliefs of the overwhelming majority of persons of Polish origin and ancestry in America, beliefs embodied in their religious traditions, commitment to the well-being and betterment of succeeding generations, patriotic loyalty to the United States, and dedication to maintaining the heritage of the Polish American community.

More than a century after its birth, the Polish Women's Alliance of America continues as a fraternal benefit society with deep roots in its rich Polish, Polish American, and American past. Today, as in the past, the PWA of A celebrates pride in its status as an organization founded by women and one that is dedicated to their ability to play leadership roles with men in American society. For more than one hundred years, the Alliance has remained true to its fraternal mission, a mission of service to and solidarity with the larger community.

The future of the Polish Women's Alliance of America can be equally bright, so long as its present and future members, regardless of their ages or individual backgrounds, continue to engage themselves in realizing its mission. Whether one's particular aims are purchasing life insurance protection, finding secure and productive forms of savings, or becoming actively involved in a fraternal society working on behalf of others, the Polish Women's Alliance of America serves a real purpose.

As the Polish Women's Alliance of America looks back on its centennial, one thing is clear. This is a movement whose members have remained faithful to the time-honored PWA of A principles embodied in words like God, service, country (*Bóg, Czyn, Ojczyzna*) and in the expression "In the ideals of women are the strength of a nation" (*Ideał kobiety to siła Narodu*). The Polish Women's Alliance of America and its record of service over the past century is proof positive of the contribution women have made in promoting the causes that have helped to make America, Polish America, and Poland better.

1848   The first Woman's Rights Convention in the United States is held in Seneca Falls, New York. Under the leadership of Lucretia Mott and Elizabeth Cady Stanton, the Convention drafts a Declaration of Sentiments modeled on the Declaration of Independence. It asserts the equality of women with men and contains twelve resolutions, one of which calls for the vote for women.

1873   In the case of *Bradwell v. Illinois*, the U. S. Supreme Court upholds the exclusion of women from the practice of law. In its decision, the "separate spheres" theory is put forward, in which the male spouse is defined as the breadwinner and the couple's public representative, while the woman's role dominates the family and the home. This theory becomes the basis for upholding many laws limiting women's rights and is the focus of much activism by women's groups and their allies in the decades afterward. It is only fully rejected in the 1970s by the Supreme Court.

1890   Formation of the National American Woman Suffrage Association (NAWSA) through the merger of the National Woman Suffrage Association led by Stanton and Susan B. Anthony and the American Woman Suffrage Association founded by Lucy Stone. Both were organized in 1869. The NWSA had formed as an all-women's movement with a commitment to equal rights, including a constitutional amendment granting women the right to vote. The AWSA included men and women and focused on winning the right to vote on a state- by-state basis.

1898   Beginnings of the Polish Women's Alliance of America in Chicago. Other women's fraternals formed in the same period to help meet the needs of the ever growing immigration (8.8 million entered this country between 1901 and 1910 alone) include the National Catholic Society of Foresters (formed in 1891) and the First Catholic Slovak Ladies Association (1892).

1920   Ratification of the Nineteenth Amendment to the U.S. Constitution stating that "the right of the citizens of the United States to vote shall not be denied or abridged by the United States on account of sex." The proposed amendment had been first introduced in Congress in 1878. Leading the effort is Carrie Chapman Catt, president of the NAWSA after 1915. After its success, the NAWSA is reorganized into the League of Women Voters.

1923   The American National Women's Party proposes an equal rights amendment to the Constitution. It languishes until 1972 when it is approved by Congress.

1935   The Social Security Act is approved. It includes several benefits for female workers and the female spouses of workers. Another element of the act is Aid to Families with Dependent Children (AFDC), a means-tested public assistance (or welfare) program providing cash benefits to children and their caretakers, usually women, when one or both parents are unable or unwilling to provide economic support. Over the years, this initially popular program became controversial and was abolished by Congress in 1996.

1961   John F. Kennedy establishes the President's Commission on the Status of Women. Its honorary chairwoman is Eleanor Roosevelt. The commission makes twenty-four recommendations in its influential 1963 report, *American Women,* the government's first statement focusing on women's concerns. These include equal pay for equal work, equal employment opportunities, paid maternity leave, and a litigation campaign based on the Fifth and Fourteenth amendments.

1964   A landmark U. S. Civil Rights Act is approved in Congress and signed by President Lyndon Johnson. Title VII of the act makes it illegal to discriminate against individuals in employment because of gender, race, color, religion, or national origin.

1968   President Johnson's Executive Order 11375 extends the principle of affirmative action to women and is strongly backed by the National Organization for Women, formed in 1966. The first executive order on the increasingly controversial issue of affirmative action was proclaimed in 1965 on behalf of racial and certain ethnic minorities.

1973   The U.S. Supreme Court grants the right to abortion in *Roe v. Wade*. In 1989, the Supreme Court partly reverses this controversial decision in *Webster v. Reproductive Health Services*.

1982   The controversial Equal Rights Amendment dies. Ratification of constitutional amendments required the approval of three-fourths of the states. The ERA won approval in 35 of the 38 states it needed.

1991   A new civil rights act reinforces the protections to women and minorities in the workplace that had first been guaranteed under the 1964 Civil Rights Act.

1993   Pope John Paul II issues an encyclical reaffirming the Roman Catholic Church's opposition to artificial birth control, divorce, abortion, and homosexuality. Earlier pronouncements by the pope had restated the Church's historic stands on these topics and matters such as the dignity of men and women, the nature and purpose of the family, the rights of all workers to a just wage, and feminism. These have been repeated in the *Catechism of the Catholic Church* and in John Paul II's best-selling book, *Crossing the Threshold of Hope*.

1998   The Polish Women's Alliance of America celebrates its centennial anniversary of service to Polonia to America, to Poland, and to the advancement of women.

PRESIDENTS OF THE POLISH WOMEN'S ALLIANCE OF AMERICA

Stefania Chmielinska, 1899 – 1900, 1900 – 1902, 1906 – 1910*

Genevieve Żołkowska, 1900

Anna Neumann, 1902 – 1906, 1910 – 1918

Emilia Napieralska, 1918 – 1935

Honorata Wołowska, 1935 – 1947*

Adela Łagodzinska, 1947 – 1971*

Helen Zielinski, 1971 – 1987*

Helen Wojcik, 1987 – 1995*

Delphine Lytell, 1995 – 1999

Virginia Sikora, from 1999

* Named honorary president of the Polish Women's Alliance of America following the completion of her tenure in office.

BIOGRAPHIES OF THE PRESIDENTS
OF THE POLISH WOMEN'S ALLIANCE OF AMERICA

STEFANIA CHMIELINSKA (1866 – 1939). President of the Polish Women's Alliance of America, 1899 – 1900, 1900 – 1902, 1906 – 1910. This modest immigrant woman is cherished as the "Mother" of the Polish Women's Alliance of America. A seamstress by trade, Chmielinska believed deeply in the cause of women's equality. She worked to form the first PWA of A group in Chicago in 1898 and in 1899 founded the national Polish Women's Alliance of America fraternal society. Despite the prejudice and difficulties that the fledging organization faced in its early years of existence, Chmielinska and her friends persevered; it was her privilege to live to see the Alliance grow into a mass movement and leadership force in the Polish American community. During her presidency, Stefania Chmielinska won approval from the state of Illinois of the Alliance's charter; initiated regular contacts with women leaders in Poland such as Maria Konopnicka; made the first attempt, in 1902, to create the PWA of A's own newspaper, *Głos Polek*; and established the fraternal's Educational Committee (*Komitet Oświaty*). In 1931 the PWA of A named her its first honorary president and proclaimed the organization's annual observance of May 22 as Founder's Day. Chmielinska was posthumously awarded the Gold Cross by the Polish government for her labors on behalf of its independence and the betterment of the immigration in America. (Maria Rokosz served as president of the Polish Women's Alliance of America society formed in May 1898 in Chicago; she continued in this position until November 1899, when Chmielinska was elected president at the founding meeting of the PWA of A by representatives of four women's groups. Genevieve Zołkowska was elected president at the first PWA of A *sejm* in June 1900; Chmielinska took her place at the end of that year. In both of these instances, Chmielinska was a member of the PWA of A leadership.)

ANNA NEUMANN (1860 – 1947). President of the Polish Women's Alliance of America, 1902 – 1906, 1910 – 1918. Born near Warsaw, Neumann came to Chicago with her parents as a youngster. Employed as a seamstress, she later was active in a cooperative whose members successfully sold the clothing they produced. Neumann joined the PWA of A in 1900 and was elected its president for the first time two years later. During her terms in office the Alliance tripled in size to twenty-one thousand members and increased its assets more than seven times, to $375,000. It was also during Anna Neumann's tenure that the Alliance opened its own permanent home offices in Chicago. Anna Neumann headed the Polish Women's Alliance of America during the dramatic years of World War I, a time in which the PWA of A played a leading role in every phase of patriotic work on behalf of the Polish independence cause. After leaving the presidency she became the fraternal's librarian and organized its museum. Anna Neumann was honored to receive Poland's Gold Cross of Service in recognition of her work for Poland's freedom. For her efforts on behalf of the Alliance she was named its second honorary president.

EMILIA NAPIERALSKA (1882 – 1943). President of the Polish Women's Alliance of America, 1918 – 1935. Emilia Napieralska joined the PWA of A 1901 and in 1910 was its elected secretary general. In 1918, she was elected president of the Alliance, thereby becoming the first American-born woman to hold this office. An effective and dynamic speaker in the Polish and English languages, she won acclaim throughout Polonia in 1915 for her World War I statement on behalf of Poland's freedom at the International Women's Peace Conference that was held in the Netherlands. As president of the PWA of A Emilia Napieralska led the successful effort to have Chicago's Crawford Avenue renamed Pulaski Road. In 1928 she headed an extended PWA of A tour, or pilgrimage, of the newly independent Poland, the first of many the Alliance would sponsor over the years. Napieralska's dynamism and leadership skills made her the pride of the Polish American community of her day and the personification of the best qualities that Americans of Polish descent brought to Polonia and its causes. When Napieralska left office following the 1935 PWA of A *sejm*, the organization included sixty-thousand members and reported assets of $4.5 million. In 1939 she was named an honorary president of the Polish Women's Alliance of America.

HONORATA WOŁOWSKA (1875 – 1967). President of the Polish Women's Alliance of America, 1935 – 1947. Born in Poland, Honorata Wołowska was an activist in the PWA of A beginning in 1900 and worked on its behalf in Pennsylvania and throughout the eastern part of the United States. During World War I and after she was also a national vice president of the Polish Falcons Alliance and promoted the enlistment of men into the Polish army that later fought on the Allied side during the conflict. Elected president of the Alliance in 1935, Wołowska's tenure was closely connected with the PWA of A's humanitarian and political efforts on behalf of the Polish people during World War II. The Alliance was thus also a key participant in the work of the Polish American Council (*Rada Polonii Amerykańskiej*). In 1944, the Alliance became a founder of the Polish American Congress (*Kongres Polonii Amerykańskiej*) political action federation which worked for Poland's postwar freedom and independence. At the congress's first national convention in Buffalo, Wołowska was elected its national vice president. Following her retirement from the presidency of the PWA of A, she was named its honorary president. She remained engaged in the life of the fraternal for many years afterward.

ADELA ŁAGODZINSKA (1896 – 1990). President of the Polish Women's Alliance of America, 1947 – 1971. Born in Chicago, Adela Łagodzinska learned the Polish language as an adult. Joining the PWA of A in 1919, she was elected its vice president in 1939 and succeeded to the presidency at the 1947 *sejm* following Honorata Wołowska's retirement. Łagodzinska's twenty-four-year tenure proved to be the longest in the fraternal's history. Her administration was marked by a notable increase in membership and financial strength and by a number of successful initiatives aimed at attracting the younger generation into the life of the Alliance. Within the Polish American community, Łagodzinska was both a vice-president in the Polish American Congress and a national secretary of the *Rada Polonii Amerykańskiej* humanitarian federation. On several occasions she traveled to Poland to gauge the country's actual situation and needs; in 1958 the PWA of A followed her recommendation and began making substantial contributions to the Catholic University of Lublin and other worthy Polish causes. Following her retirement, Łagodzinska, as honorary president of the Alliance, edited the English-language section of the PWA of A publication, *Głos Polek*. She was also active in the work of a number of cultural organizations, among them the Polish American Historical Association, whose aims included the sharing of knowledge of the Polish experience in America.

HELEN ZIELINSKI. President of the Polish Women's Alliance of America, 1971 – 1987. Born in Indiana, Helen Zielinski was elected president of the PWA of A in 1971 after having served for twelve years as the organization's vice president under Łagodzinska. As head of the PWA of A, Zielinski focused on developing youth programs and on promoting membership. Zielinski had been the first May Queen, a title going to the top salesperson in the Alliance in a given year. During her presidency the PWA of A in 1979 moved its national headquarters to a new building in the Chicago suburb of Park Ridge, Illinois. Helen Zielinski was active as a vice president of the Polish American Congress and focused her energies on a series of humanitarian and cultural causes of importance to *Polonia*. These included her involvement in national fundraising campaigns to build a Polish pilgrims' hostel in Rome following the election of Pope John Paul II, to restore the Statue of Liberty in New York Harbor, and to preserve the American shrine of Our Lady of Częstochowa in Doylestown, Pennsylvania. Helen Zielinski is the author of the third volume of the Polish-language history of the PWA of A. In 1981 Zielinski took part in a White House meeting of PAC leaders with the President Ronald Reagan over the crisis in Poland. In 1987 she represented the PWA of A and the PAC at a meeting with Pope John Paul II in Rome. Upon her retirement, Zielinski was named an honorary president of the Polish Women's Alliance of America.

HELEN WOJCIK. President of the Polish Women's Alliance of America, 1987 – 1995. Chicago's Wojcik was elected president after having served for sixteen years as the vice president of the PWA of A. Under her leadership, the Alliance expanded the computerization of its insurance operations, promoted the development of new insurance and investment products, and initiated the systematic training of sales personnel in the organization. As a vice president of the Polish American Congress, Wojcik led the national fund drive establish the Ellis Island Immigration Museum in New York Harbor. In October 1989 she took part in the crucial PAC initiative to underscore its support for Poland's new Solidarity-led government by joining the delegation of *Polonia* leaders who traveled to Warsaw to speak with the country's highest political and religious leaders. As PWA of A president she led a fund drive to purchase three medical transport vans for handicapped children in Poland; these vans were given to Polish medical authorities in 1992. In 1994 Helen Wojcik chaired the fiftieth anniversary celebration of the founding of the Polish American Congress in Buffalo. This historic event was attended by a number of top Polish and American leaders, including President Lech Wałęsa and Ambassador Madeleine Allbright. Upon her retirement, Helen Wojcik was named an honorary president of the Polish Women's Alliance of America. In 2001, the Polish government and *Wspólnota Polska* honored Wojcik and her predecessor, Helen Zielinski, for their years of dedicated service to the cause of Poland and its people.

DELPHINE LYTELL. President of the Polish Women's Alliance of America, 1995 – 1999. Born in South Bend, Indiana, in 1944, Delphine Mackowski Lytell earned a degree in English literature at St. Mary's College in Indiana. She then taught at the high school level and was a librarian in Indiana and Illinois. Active in *wianki* as a youth (her mother, Eleonor Mackowski, ws a PWA of A District 3 president), Lytell in 1984 was named editor of the English-language section of *Głos Polek* and was elected vice president of the PWA of A in 1987. She won reelection to this office in 1991 and in 1995 was elected president at the Alliance's thirty-second *sejm*. In summer 1992, Delphine Lytell joined President Wojcik and *Głos Polek's* Editor Maria Loryś to represent the Alliance at the world congress of *Polonia* held in Warsaw and Kraków. There, the PWA of A donated three medical transport vans the fraternal's members had purchased to help meet the needs of handicapped children. In June 1996 President Lytell and Treasurer Olga Kaszewicz represented the PWA of A in a Vatican meeting with Pope John Paul II; this meeting brought together the leaders of a number of American societies that were raising funds to support the creation of the Pope John Paul II Cultural Center being planned in Washington, D. C. In 1999 Lytell was narrowly defeated in her reelection effort at the thirty-third PWA of A *sejm* by National Director Virginia Sikora of Michigan.

The elective office of state president was created at the eighth convention of the Polish Women's Alliance of America in 1910 to advance the work of the Alliance in various regions of the country Elected by delegates in each district, the office of state president became an important link between the national leadership and the local groups of the PWA of A In 1935 the delegates to the seventeenth PWA of A convention voted to set up a new system of territorial districts, with state presidents becoming the elected heads of these units The boundaries of each district, called *obwód* in Polish (plural form *obwody*) were redrawn at that time At first there were eleven districts. In 1951 three new districts were established to create units that were more contiguous in character, for a total of fourteen districts. District presidents meet annually with the national officers of the PWA of A to review the operations and activities of the fraternal.

State Presidents, 1910 – 1935

Ohio
Dr. Frances Konrad-Filipiak, 1910 – 1917
Helena Jabłońska, 1918 – 1920, 1928 – 1931
Casimira Makowska, 1921 – 1927
Helena Jarzynska, 1931 – 1939

Wisconsin
Stanisława Petrykowska, 1910 – 1917
Maria Kryszak, 1918 – 1921+
Marta Rożewicz, 1921 – 1924
Barbara Kluczynska, 1924 – 1943

Connecticut and Massachusetts
Albina Budaj, 1910 – 1913

Connecticut
Constance Gulczynska, 1914 – 1917
Agnieszka Wałczynska, 1918 – 1921
Agnieszka Hajdasz, 1921 – 1924
Frances Owsiak, 1924 – 1939

Massachusetts
Stefania Grabowska, 1914 – 1920

Dr. Julia Bauman, 1921 – 1935

Indiana
Stanisława Wawrzon, 1910 – 1915
Antonina Hon, 1916 – 1935

Michigan
Frances Szymańska, 1910 – 1915
Maria Skwierczynska, 1916 – 1917
Jadwiga Gibasiewicz, 1918 – 1943

Western Pennsylvania
Wanda Ruminska, 1912 – 1913
Maria Hipnerowska, 1914 – 1915
Honorata Wołowska, 1916 – 1935+

Eastern Pennsylvania
Maria Szakalun, 1914 – 1920
Maria Porwit, 1921 – 1939+

New York
Berta Dorasiewicz, 1912 – 1917
Marta Mazorowska, 1918 – 1921
Stanisława Eisporn, 1921 – 1927
Rozalia Biedroń, 1927 – 1964

Nebraska
Maria Sempek, 1918 – 1927
Anna Tutro, 1927 – 1943

Illinois
Łucja Wołowska, 1924 – 1927+
Anna Klarkowska, 1927 – 1935+

West Virginia
Józefa Kosiba, 1927 (then merged with Ohio)

Maryland, New Jersey, and the District of Columbia
Maria Daneska, 1931 – 1945

With the redrawing of district borders at its seventeenth convention in 1935, the district presidents of the PWA of A have been as follows:

District I: Illinois, Florida, and Missouri
Angelina Milasiewicz, 1935 – 1943+
Amelia Szlak, 1943 – 1951; 1959 – 1975
Albina Szudarska, 1951 – 1959
Charlotte Jagodzinska, 1975 – 1987+
Dorothy Polus, from 1987

District II: Pennsylvania until 1951, then northeast and parts of western Pennsylvania
Maria Porwit, 1935 – 1939*+
Florence Knapp, 1939 – 1974
Jean Zakrzewski, 1974 – 1995
Margaret Golofski, 1995 – 1999
Marie Jasenak, from 1999

District III: Indiana
Bronisława Brecław, 1935 – 1939
Sophie Jerzyk, 1939 – 1955
Helena Sambor, 1955 – 1959+
Joanna Zotkiewicz, 1959 – 1979
Helena Lis, 1979 – 1983
Eleonor Mackowski, 1983 – 1988
Evelyn Lisek, from 1988

District IV: Western New York and Erie, Pennsylvania
Rozalia Biedroń, 1927 – 1964+
Irene Cwiklinska, 1964 – 1979
Jean Pilch, 1979 – 1995
Christine Wozniak, from 1995

District V: Michigan and Toledo, Ohio
Jadwiga Gibasiewicz, 1918 – 1943
Janina Rzeczkowska, 1943 – 1959
Aniela Jonik, 1959 – 1971
Bronisława Ślubowska, 1971 – 1983
Helen Wojdynski, 1983 – 1991

Irene Kay, from 1991

District VI: Wisconsin
Barbara Kluczynska, 1924 – 1943
Pelagia Wojtczak, 1943 – 1983
Harriet Burns, 1983 – 1987
Angelina Jagodzinska, 1987 – 1990
Sue Mikolajczyk, from1990

District VII: West Virginia and Ohio, except for Toledo
Helena Jarzynska, 1931 – 1939
Monica Pawlowski, 1939 – 1943; 1947 – 1963
Elizabeth Schwarten, 1943 – 1947
Janina Twardzik, 1963 – 1971
Eleonore Tomkalski, 1971 – 1995
Mercedes Spotts, 1995 – 2000
Eugenia Stolarczyk, from 2000

District VIII: Massachusetts
Tekla Starzyk, 1935 – 1943
Anna Januszewska, 1943 – 1967
Amelia Bednarz, 1967 – 1991
Jane Bielski, 1991 – 1999
Sylvia Morytko, from 1999

District IX: Connecticut
Frances Owsiak, 1924 – 1939
Stanisława Stecewicz, 1939 – 1947
Helena Robakiewicz, 1947 – 1965
Julia Leniart, 1965 – 1987*
Sophie Marshall, from 1987

District X: New Jersey, eastern New York State, and Philadelphia
Maria Daneska, 1931 – 1945
Adela Jaskiewicz, 1945 – 1963
Helena Loboda, 1963 – 1967
Leah Laskowska, 1967 – 1975
Genevieve Orłowska, 1975 – 1983
Anna Woitkowska, 1983 – 1991
Marion Listwan, from 1991

District XI: California and Nebraska until 1951 and then only Nebraska

Anna Tutro, 1927 – 1943
Katarzyna Tomaszkiewicz, 1943 – 1945
Victoria Ciurej, 1943 – 1951
Catherine Kosiba, 1951 – 1970
Sophie Robak, 1970 – 1987
Stella Ciurej, 1987 – 1993
Mary Kaczmarek, from 1994

District XII: Maryland and the District of Columbia, established in 1951
Martha Welzant, 1951 – 1979
Victoria Lukaszewska, 1979 – 1991
Regina Lennon, from 1991

District XIII: California, established in 1951
Wanda Dettling, 1951 – 1967
Florence Mika, 1967 – 1980
Florence Swait, from 1981

District XIV: Eastern Pennsylvania, established in 1951:
Anna Paruch, 1951 – 1955
Marie Lesniak, 1955 – 1959
Maria Porwit, 1959 – 1971+*
Rozalia Afeldt, 1971 – 1973
Blanche Petrus, 1973 – 1979*
Klementine Mashinski, 1979 – 1991*
Felicia Perlick, from 1991

+Presidents who continued in their offices after the reorganization of state divisions in 1935.

*Presidents who were elected to national office in the Polish Women's Alliance of America.

Frank Wołowski, Editor, 1902 – 1903. Wołowski, the husband of Łucja Wołowska, an early officer of the Polish Women's Alliance, was simultaneously an editor with Chicago's *Dziennik Narodowy* (Polish national daily newspaper). Working with him was Leon Nowak, an activist in Chicago's Polish community. While the initial effort to establish *Głos Połek* failed after ten months for financial reasons, *Dziennik Narodowy* continued to print a special page for the PWA of A on a regular basis under the editorships of Maria Iwanowska (between 1903 and 1909) and Jadwiga Michalska (from 1909 to 1910).

Stefania Laudyn-Chrzanowska, Editor, 1910 – 1912, 1914 – 1918. The first editor of the restored weekly *Głos Polek* was established by the PWA of A at its eighth *sejm*. The first issue of the publication appeared on November 3, 1910, and continued as a weekly until 1956, when it became a biweekly newspaper. In 1994 *Głos Polek* became a monthly.

Jadwiga Michalska, Editor, 1912 – 1913. Named editor after the ninth PWA of A *sejm.* Michalska was replaced in March 1913 by Helena Setmajer. At the tenth PWA of A *sejm* in 1914, Laudyn-Chrzanowska was elected editor and served in this capacity until 1918.

Zofia Jankiewicz , Editor, 1918 – 1921. Elected editor at the twelfth PWA of A *sejm.* Jankiewicz resigned in 1921 and was replaced by Dr. Maria Ołgiert-Kaczorowska.

Maria Kryszak, Editor, 1921 – 1939. A native of Milwaukee and later a member of the Wisconsin state legislature, Kryszak was elected editor at the thirteenth PWA of A *sejm.*

Jadwiga Karłowicz, Editor, 1939 – 1951, 1955-1964. Karłowicz authored the first history of the PWA of A, a work that appeared in 1938.

Halina Paluszek, Editor, 1951-1955. Elected editor at the twenty-first PWA of A *sejm* when Karłowicz unsuccessfully sought the presidency. In 1955 Karłowicz returned to the editorship.

Maria Loryś, Editor, 1964-1995. Appointed to replace Karłowicz after her resignation, Loryś continued on as editor until her retirement following the thirty-second convention. Taking over for Loryś was Grażyna Zajączkowska, a native of Poland, as editor of the Polish language section of the newspaper in January 1996.

Beginning in 1951, the Polish language *Głos Polek* began including an English language section on a regular basis for the benefit of its burgeoning American-born readership. Editors of the English language section have been Melanie Sokołowska, Monica Sokolowski, Adela Łagodzinska, Delphine Lytell, and Maria Kubiak. Mary Mirecki-Piergies was responsible for the ever growing English section from 1987 to 1999. At the end of 1999 she was succeeded by Gloria Jean Waber, who was also appointed to serve as director of public relations for the fraternal.

The office of medical examiner was elective until a change in the PWA of A Constitution in 1965 made the post subject to appointment by the general administration. The following individuals have served as medical examiner:

Dr. Maria Dowiatt-Sass, 1901 – 1906

Dr. Maria Olgiert-Kaczorowska, 1906 – 1931

Dr. Felicia Cienciara, 1931 – 1939, 1943 – 1956

Dr. Frances Kapuścinska, 1939 – 1943

Dr. Melania Polniaszek, 1956 – 1959

Dr. Józefa Narolewska, 1959 – 1971

Dr. Maria Wieczorek, from 1971

Helena Fleming-Czachorska, 1914 – 1935

Barbara Fisher, 1935 – 1947

Stefania Błaszczenska-Cieślewicz, 1947 – 1971

Genevieve Zaczek, 1971 – 1979

Alice Borzym, 1979 – 1991

Judith Pietrucha, from 1991

First Convention: June 12, 1900, Pulaski Hall, Chicago.   24 delegates representing 264 members in attendance.

Officers elected at the convention:

President: Genevieve Zołkowska

Vice President: Stefania Chmielinska

Secretary General: Łucja Wołowska

Treasurer: Maria Rokosz

Directors: Elżbieta Tokarska, Maria Kaczorowska, Maria Wleklinska-Wejna,   Władysława   Krentz, Bronisława Wawrzynska

Second Convention: June 15, 1901, Pulaski Hall, Chicago. Delegates from 16 groups in attendance. Membership: 506, Treasury: $360.04

Officers elected at the convention:

President: Stefania Chmielinska

Vice President: Anna Neumann

Secretary General: Antonina Fabiańska

Treasurer: Aniela Tomaszewska

Directors: Bronisława Wawrzynska, Maria Łabucka, Julia Smoczynska, Teofila Śniegocka, Augusta Kula

Third Convention: June 17 to 19, 1902, Holy Trinity Church Hall, Chicago. Delegates from 21 groups in attendance. Membership: 876, Treasury: $1,746.63

Officers elected at the convention:

President: Anna Neumann, by unanimous vote

Vice Presidents: Bronisława Ostrowska, W. Świniarska, and P. Susala were elected.

Secretary General: Antonina Fabiańska, by majority vote

Treasurer: Aniela Tomaszewska, by unanimous vote

Directors: Teofila Śniegocka, Julia Smoczynska, Maria Łabucka, Bronisława Wawrzynska, Stanisława Szeszycka

Fourth Convention: June 22 to 24, 1903, Holy Trinity Church Hall, Chicago.   Delegates from 28 groups in attendance. Membership: 1,400, Treasury: $4,000

Officers elected at the convention:

President: Anna Neumann   by unanimous vote

Vice President:	Stanisława Szeszycka	48 votes – elected
	Bronisława Ostrowska	18 votes
	A. Augustynowicz	14 votes
	Maria Łabucka	9 votes

| Secretary General: | Antonina Fabiańska | 48 votes – elected |
| | Łucja Wołowska | 42 votes |

| Treasurer: | Leokadia Kadów | 51 votes – elected |
| | Aniela Tomaszewska | 40 votes |

Directors: Bronisława Wawrzynska, Maria Łabucka, Teofila Śniegocka, Augusta Kula

Fifth Convention: June 27-29, 1904, Walsh Hall, Chicago. Delegates from 41 groups in attendance. Membership and treasury data were not available.

Officers elected at the convention:

President: Anna Neumann   by unanimous vote

| Vice President: | Stanisława Szeszycka | 38 votes – elected |
| | Stefania Chmielinska | 37 votes |

Secretary General:	Antonina Fabiańska	by unanimous vote
Treasurer:	Leokadia Kadów	by unanimous vote
Directors:	Aniela Tomaszewska, W. Świniarska, N. N. Fijałkowska, A. Zaremba, Antonina Mussor.	

Sixth Convention: June 25 to 30, 1906, Pulaski Hall, Chicago. 125 delegates in attendance. Membership: 4,302 in 64 groups. Treasury: $15,084.97.

Officers elected at the convention:

President:	Stefania Chmielinska	81 votes – elected*
Vice President:	Jadwiga Pawelkiewicz	94 votes – elected
	Frances Rytlewska	25 votes
Secretary General:	Łucja Wołowska	104 votes – elected
Treasurer:	Leokadia Kadów	114 votes – elected
Directors:	J. Gronkiewicz, Maria Perłowska, Anastasia Nowak, Maria Wleklinska-Wejna, Bronisława Wawrzynska.	

*President Neumann refused to run for reelection after having been nominated.

Seventh Convention: September 13 to 18, 1908, St. Stanislaus Church Hall, Cleveland.   Membership: 5,952 in 79 groups. Treasury: $33,181.76

Officers elected at the convention:

President:	Stefania Chmielinska	67 votes – elected
	Anna Neumann	46 votes
Vice President:	Jadwiga Pawelkiewicz	79 votes – elected
	Aniela Tomaszewska	20 votes
	Eleonora Łagocka	15 votes
Secretary General:	Łucja Wołowska	94 votes – elected

	Zofia Jankiewicz	20 votes
Treasurer:	Leokadia Kadów	105 votes – elected
Directors:	Teofila Śniegocka, Stanisława Szeszycka, J. Gronkiewicz, Maria Perłowska, Maria Baranowska.	

Eighth Convention: September 19 to 24, 1910, Kościuszko Armory Hall, Milwaukee. Membership: 7,681 in 103 groups. Treasury: $52,849.49.

Officers elected at the convention:

President:	Anna Neumann	71 votes – elected
	Stefania Chmielinska	58 votes
Vice President:	Maria Wleklinska-Wejna	96 votes – elected
	Aniela Tomaszewska	32 votes
Secretary General:	Emilia Napieralska	by unanimous vote
Treasurer:	Leokadia Kadów	by unanimous vote
Directors:	Teofila Śniegocka, Stanisława Szeszycka, Maria Piotrowicz, Maria Szóstakowicz, Maria Kuflewska.	

Ninth Convention: August 26 to 30, 1912, at St. Hedwig's Church Hall in South Bend, Indiana. Membership of 10,930 in 143 groups. Treasury: $99,313.71.

Officers elected at the convention:

President:	Anna Neumann	103 votes – elected
	Stefania Chmielinska	79 votes
Vice President:	Jadwiga Pawelkiewicz	76 votes – elected
	Maria Wleklinska-Wejna+	69 votes
	Maria Rokosz	36 votes
Secretary General:	Emilia Napieralska	148 votes – elected
	Bronisława Wawrzynska	31 votes

| Treasurer: | Leokadia Kadów | 104 votes – elected |
| | Łucja Wołowska | 81 votes |

| Directors: | Stanisława Szeszycka, Joanna Andrzejewska, Tekla Karge, Józefa Specjal, Karolina Sowinska. | |

Tenth Convention: September 21 to 26, 1914, at the Polish Women's Alliance Headquarters in Chicago. Membership: 14,448 in 190 groups. Treasury: $166,699.04.

Officers elected at the convention:

| President: | Anna Neumann | by unanimous vote |

Vice President:	Angelina Milasiewicz	98 votes – elected
	Stefania Chmielinska	96 votes
	Stanisława Szeszycka	42 votes

| Secretary General: | Emilia Napieralska | 164 votes – elected |
| | Joanna Andrzejewska | 78 votes |

| Treasurer: | Łucja Wołowska | 163 votes – elected |
| | Leokadia Kadów | 78 votes |

| Directors: | Maria Wleklinska-Wejna, Maria Kuflewska, Józefa Specjal, Karolina Sowinska, Zofia Sypniewska. | |

Eleventh Convention: September 25 to 30, 1916, Dom Polski, Buffalo. Membership: 17,558 in 227 groups. Treasury: $254,407.35.

Officers elected at the convention:

| President | Anna Neumann | by unanimous vote |

| Vice President: | Stefania Chmielinska | 110 votes – elected |
| | Angelina Milasiewicz | 92 votes |

| Secretary General: | Emilia Napieralska | by unanimous vote |

| Treasurer: | Łucja Wołowska | by unanimous vote |

| Directors: | Maria Kuflewska, Tekla Karge, Helena Szymańska, Stefania Raczkowska, Rozalia Petlak. |

Twelfth Convention: September 23 to 28, 1918, Dom Polski, Detroit. Membership: 21,109 in 272 groups. Treasury: $374,894.69.

Officers elected at the convention:

President:	Emilia Napieralska	154 votes – elected
	Leokadia Kadów	35 votes
Vice President:	Stefania Chmielinska	107 votes – elected
	Angelina Milasiewicz	86 votes
Secretary General:	Joanna Andrzejewska	140 votes – elected
	Maria Kryszak	52 votes
Treasurer:	Łucja Wołowska	by unanimous vote
Directors:	Antonina Mussor, Tekla Karge, Józefa Specjal, Stefania Raczkowska, Valeria Chojnacka.

Thirteenth Convention: August 22 to 27, 1921, Polish Women's Alliance headquarters, Chicago. Membership: 24,680 (including 1,422 children) in 308 groups. Treasury: $584,205.87.

Officers elected at the convention:

President:	Emilia Napieralska	181 votes – elected
	Leokadia Kadów	84 votes
Vice President:	Angelina Milasiewicz	134 votes – elected
	Anna Klarkowska	131 votes
Secretary General:	Victoria Latwis	142 votes – elected
	Valeria Boguszewska	124 votes
Treasurer:	Joanna Andrzejewska	219 votes – elected
	Joanna Wiśniewska	35 votes

Directors: Rozalia Petlak, Valeria Chojnacka, Mieczysława Dorańska, Felicjanna Truszczynska, Antonina Gawarecka.

Fourteenth Convention: August 18 to 23, 1924, Irem Temple, Wilkes-Barre, Pennsylvania. Membership: 31,787 (including 3,522 children) in 387 groups. Assets: $1,107,761.60.

Officers elected at the convention:

President:	Emilia Napieralska	by unanimous vote
Vice President:	Angelina Milasiewicz	165 votes – elected
	Antonina Gawarecka	122 votes
Secretary General:	Victoria Latwis	181 votes – elected
	Maria Porwit	116 votes
Treasurer:	Joanna Andrzejewska	240 votes
	Clara Serwatkiewicz	55 votes

Directors: Rozalia Petlak, Valeria Chojnacka, Felicjanna Truszczynska, Helena Sambor, Agnieszka Lenard.

Fifteenth Convention: August 21 to 27, 1927, Polish Women's Alliance headquarters, Chicago. Membership: 43,249 (including 6,708 children) in 479 groups. Assets: $1,808,424.26.

Officers elected at the convention:

President:	Emilia Napieralska	289 votes – elected
	Anna Klarkowska	44 votes
Vice President:	Angelina Milasiewicz	172 votes – elected
	Antonina Gawarecka	85 votes
	Maria Rączka	50 votes
	Julia Preyss	27 votes
Secretary General:	Victoria Latwis	220 votes – elected
	Maria Porwit	121 votes
	Bronisława Wawrzynska	8 votes

| Treasurer: | Joanna Andrejewska | 284 votes – elected |
| | Tekla Karge | 56 votes |

Directors: Valeria Chojnacka, Felicjanna Truszczynska, Helena Sambor, Agnieszka Lenard, Clara Rybak.

Sixteenth Convention: September 20 to 26, 1931, Hotel Willard, Washington, D.C. Delegates from 657 groups in attendance. Membership: 65,321 (including 12,604 children) in 657 groups. Assets: $3,090,206.45.

Officers elected at the convention:

President:	Emilia Napieralska	by unanimous vote
Vice President:	Helena Sambor	217 votes –elected
	Honorata Wołowska	196 votes
Secretary General:	Victoria Latwis	340 votes – elected
	Maria Porwit	77 votes
Treasurer:	Joanna Andrzejewska	by unanimous vote
Directors:	Antonina Mussor, Rozalia Petlak, Antonina Gawarecka, Agnieszka Lenard, Salomea Jachimowska	

Seventeenth Convention: September 23 to 28, 1935, Polish Women's Alliance headquarters, Chicago. Membership: 60,666 (including 7,786 children) in 631 groups. Assets: $4,531,139.51.

Officers elected at the convention:

President:	Honorata Wołowska	222 votes – elected
	Clara Swieczkowska	175 votes
Vice President:	Helena Sambor	by unanimous vote
Secretary General:	Joanna Andrzejewska	by unanimous vote
Treasurer:	Victoria Latwis	272 votes – elected
	Maria Porwit	163 votes

Directors: Rozalia Petlak, Antonina Gawarecka, Salomea Jachimowska, Gertrude Potocka Uznańska, Maria Łopacinska.

Eighteenth Convention: September 24 to 30, 1939, Niagara Falls, New York. 471 delegates in attendance. Membership: 64,818 (including 7,343 children) in 646 groups. Assets: $5,434,905.94 as of June 30, 1939.

Officers elected at the convention:

President:	Honorata Wołowska	by unanimous vote
Vice President:	Adela Łagodzinska	by unanimous vote
Secretary General:	Maria Porwit Valeria Boguszewska	260 votes – elected 216 votes
Treasurer:	Victoria Latwis Leokadia Blikowska+	334 votes – elected 142 votes
Directors:	Gertrude Potocka Uznańska, Albina Damsz, Bronisława Wolnik, Bronisława Jakubowska.	

Nineteenth Convention: September 26 to October 2, 1943, Belleview-Stratford Hotel, Philadelphia. Membership: 64,887 (including 6,271 children) in 657 groups. Assets: $7,462,592.10.

Officers elected at the convention:

President:	Honorata Wołowska	by unanimous vote
Vice President:	Adela Łagodzinska	by unanimous vote
Secretary General:	Maria Porwit	by unanimous vote
Treasurer:	Leokadia Blikowska	by unanimous vote
Directors:	Bronisława Jakubowska, Constance Rybinska, Veronica Siwek, Helena Sala, Bronisława Karczewska.	

Twentieth Convention: September 28 to October 4, 1947, Congress Hotel, Chicago.   526 delegates in attendance. Membership: 67,899 (including 6,424 children) in 666 groups. Assets: $9,914,581.84.

Officers elected at the convention:

President:	Adela Łagodzinska	387 votes – elected
	Helena Sambor	168 votes
	Clara Swieczkowska	84 votes
Vice President:	Bronisława Karczewska	361 votes – elected
	Maria Łopacinska	85 votes
	Gertrude Potocka Uznańska	71 votes
Secretary General:	Maria Porwit	by unanimous vote
Treasurer:	Leokadia Blikowska	443 votes – elected
	Antonina Gawarecka	74 votes
Directors:	Barbara Fisher, Bronisława Jakubowska, Veronica Siwek, Michalina Ferguson, Helena Boratyn	

Twenty-first Convention: September 22 to 28, 1951, William Penn Hotel, Pittsburgh. 552 delegates in attendance. Membership: 79,690 (including 10,258 children) in 667 groups. Assets: $12,656,838.73.

Officers elected at the convention:

President:	Adela Łagodzinska	387 votes – elected
	Jadwiga Karłowicz	156 votes
Vice President:	Bronisława Karczewska	369 votes – elected
	Gertrude Potocka-Uznańska	167 votes
Secretary General:	Maria Porwit	377 votes – elected
	Amelia Szlak	167 votes
Treasurer:	Leokadia Blikowska	by unanimous vote

| Directors: | Helena Sambor, Barbara Fisher, Veronica Siwek, Helena Sala, Michalina Ferguson |

Twenty-second Convention: September 25 to 30, 1955, Statler Hotel, Detroit. 515 delegates in attendance. Membership: 86,667 (including 14,337 children) in 661 groups.   Assets: $15,690,851.43.

Officers elected at the convention:

President:	Adela Łagodzinska	468 votes – elected
Vice President:	Barbara Fisher	261 votes – elected
	Helen Sala	243 votes
Secretary General:	Maria Porwit	369 votes – elected
	Michalina Ferguson	138 votes
Treasurer:	Leokadia Blikowska	399 votes – elected
	Amelia Szlak	108 votes
Directors:	Gertrude Potocka Uznanska, Veronica Siwek, Charlotte Jagodzinska, Maria Hojda, Stefania Piech.	

Twenty-third Convention: September 26 to October 2, 1959, Lord Baltimore Hotel, Baltimore. 468 delegates from 346 groups in attendance. Membership: 90,302 (including 16,699 children) in 643 groups. Assets: $19,835,094.22.

Officers elected at the convention:

President:	Adela Łagodzinska	279 votes – elected
	Bronisława Karczewska	110 votes
	Hełlena Klimaszewska	75 votes
Vice President:	Helen Zielinski	240 votes – elected
	Maria Porwit	219 votes
Secretary General:	Michalina Ferguson	264 votes - elected
	Józefa Czarnecka	145 votes
	Jadwiga Karłowicz	55 votes

| Treasurer: | Leokadia Blikowska | 340 votes – elected |
| | Halina Paluszek | 122 votes |

| Directors: | Veronica Siwek, Charlotte Jagodzinska, Stefania Piech, Anna Zych, Rozalia Baczynska. |

Twenty-fourth Convention: September 22 to 28, 1963, Chicago.   480 delegates from 364 groups in attendance. Membership: 91,101 (including 17,489 children) in 620 groups. Assets: $23,664,666.

Officers elected at the convention:

| President: | Adela Łagodzinska | 338 votes – elected |
| | Bronisława Karczewska | 137 votes |

| Vice President: | Helen Zielinski | 462 votes – elected |

| Secretary General: | Michalina Ferguson | 383 votes – elected |
| | Albina Szudarska | 90 votes |

Treasurer:	Leokadia Blikowska	312 votes – elected
	Halina Paluszek	89 votes
	Rozalia Baczynska	72 votes

| Directors: | Veronica Siwek, Charlotte Jagodzinska, Maria Hojda, Stefania Piech, Anna Zych. |

Twenty-fifth Convention: September 24 to 29, 1967, Cleveland. 442 delegates from 317 groups in attendance.   Membership: 90,080 (including 16,681 children) in 592 groups.   Assets: $26,736,254.

Officers elected at the convention:

| President: | Adela Łagodzinska | 343 votes – elected |
| | Wanda Dettling | 96 votes |

| Vice President: | Helen Zielinski | 421 votes – elected |

| Secretary General: | Michalina Ferguson | 420 votes – elected |

| Treasurer: | Leokadia Blikowska | 425 votes – elected |

Directors:	Veronica Siwek, Charlotte Jagodzinska, Maria Hojda, Stefania Piech, Anna Zych.

Twenty-sixth Convention: September 25 to 30, 1971, Hartford. 385 delegates from 280 groups in attendance. Membership: 86,351 (including 15,317 children) in 559 groups. Assets: $28,683,657.

Officers elected at the convention:

President:	Helen Zielinski	303 votes – elected
	Genevieve Zaczek	79 votes
Vice President:	Helen Wojcik	220 votes – elected
	Charlotte Jagodzinska	158 votes
Secretary General:	Julia Stroup	198 votes – elected
	Theodosia Sosnowska	127 votes
	Albina Szudarska	51 votes
Treasurer:	Leokadia Blikowska	315 votes – elected
Directors:	Maria Hojda, Stefania Piech, Monica Sokolowski, Helena Podborny, Irene Hossa	

Twenty-seventh Convention: September 27 to October 1, 1975, Pittsburgh. 350 delegates from 247 groups in attendance. Membership: 82,074 (including 13,661 children) in 525 groups. Assets: $30,707,809.

Officers elected at the convention:

President:	Helen Zielinski	314 votes – elected
Vice President:	Helen Wojcik	284 votes – elected
Secretary General:	Julia Stroup	324 votes – elected
Treasurer:	Leokadia Blikowska	208 votes – elected
	Helen Sokolowska	34 votes
Directors:	Michalina Ferguson, Monica Sokołowski, Helena Podborny, Irene Hossa, Albina Świerzbińska	

Twenty-eighth Convention: September 22 to 28, 1979, Hyatt Regency Hotel, Dearborn. 274 delegates from 189 groups in attendance. Membership: 77,387 (including 12,247 children) in 479 groups. Assets: $32,776,104.

Officers elected at the convention:

President:	Helen Zielinski	247 votes – elected
Vice President:	Helen Wojcik	253 votes – elected
Secretary General:	Julia Stroup	256 votes – elected
Treasurer:	Monica Sokolowska	176 votes – elected
	Louise German	96 votes

Directors: Michalina Ferguson, Irene Hossa, Albina Świerzbińska, Olga Kaszewicz, Bronisława Petrus

Twenty-ninth Convention: August 27 to September 1, 1983, Marriott Hotel, Chicago.   280 delegates from 200 groups in attendance. Membership: 71,878 (including 11,075 children) in 443 groups. Assets: $34,118, 128.

Officers elected at the convention:

President	Helen Zielinski	184 votes – elected
	Eleonor Tomkalski	96 votes
Vice President:	Helen Wojcik	246 votes – elected
Secretary General:	Julia Stroup	233 votes – elected
Treasurer:	Monica Sokolowski	246 votes – elected

Directors: Irene Hossa, Albina Świerzbińska, Olga Kaszewicz, Virginia Sikora, Łucyna Migała.

Thirtieth Convention: August 22 to 27, 1987, Holiday Inn, Merrillville, Indiana. 279 delegates from 180 groups in attendance. Membership: 66,711 (including 9,921 children) in 412 groups. Assets: $36,414,404.

Officers elected at the convention:

President:	Helen Wojcik	246 votes – elected
Vice President:	Delphine Lytell	161 votes – elected
	Łucyna Migała	114 votes
Secretary General:	Maria Kubiak	139 votes – elected
	Antoinette Trela	137 votes
Treasurer:	Monica Sokolowska	251 votes – elected
Directors:	Irene Hossa, Ałbina Świerzbińska, Olga Kaszewicz, Virginia Sikora, Julia Leniart.	

Thirty-first Convention: September 14 to 19, 1991, Hilton Waterfront Hotel, Buffalo. 277 delegates from 175 groups in attendance. Membership: 60,214 (including 8,337 children) in 384 groups. Assets: $39,454,161.

Officers elected at the convention:

President:	Helen Wojcik	265 votes – elected
Vice President:	Delphine Lytell	262 votes – elected
Secretary General:	Maria Kubiak	200 votes – elected
	Antoinette Trela	73 votes
Treasurer:	Olga Kaszewicz	251 votes – elected
Directors:	Albina Świerzbińska, Virginia Sikora, Clementine Mashinski, Regina Klebek-Solms, Lillian Pesdan.	

Thirty-second Convention: September 23 to 27, 1995 O'Hare Marriott Hotel, Chicago. 299 delegates from 136 groups in attendance. Membership: 58,032 (including 8,739 children) in 356 groups as of December 31, 1994. Assets: $43,916,146

Officers elected at the convention:

President: Delphine Lytell   153 votes – elected[++]
                    Łucyna Migała   132 votes

Vice President: Elizabeth Kubacki   213 votes – elected

Secretary General: Maria Kubiak   259 votes – elected

Treasurer: Olga Kaszewicz   271 votes – elected

Directors: Albina   Świerzbińska,   Virginia   Sikora,
                    Clementine Mashinski, Regina Klebek-Solms,
                    Julie Benton

Thirty-third Convention: August 14 to 18, 1999, Holiday Inn,
Secaucus, New Jersey. 233 delegates in attendance. Membership
and assets not specified.

Officers elected at the convention:

President: Virginia Sikora   120 votes elected[+++]
                    Delphine Lytell   116 votes

Vice President   Sharon Zago   117 votes elected[++++]
                    Elizabeth Kubacki   115 votes

Secretary General: Grażyna Migała   133 votes elected
                    Marie Owoc   106 votes

Treasurer   Olga Kaszewicz   235 votes elected

Directors: Julie   Benton,   Marsha   Russo,   Carmen
                    Czerwinski, Helen Simmons, Antoinette Trela
                    Vander Noot

[+]According to the PWA of A constitution and by-laws, a vacancy in
the national leadership caused by the death or resignation of an
elected officer is filled by appointing the defeated candidate for the
same office who received the greatest number of votes at the
previous convention. The individuals so identified automatically

replaced the winning candidate after her death during her term in office.

[++]1995 result was from the second or run-off ballot in which the top two candidates competed for the presidency. On the first ballot Lytell received 135 votes, Migała 133, and Sharon Zago 16 votes. No candidate received a majority, thereby requiring the run-off.

[+++]This 1999 decision came on the second ballot. On the first ballot, there was a tie for the presidency, with each candidate receiving 120 votes.

[++++]This 1999 decision came on the third ballot. On the first and second ballot, three candidates competed for the office of vice president with no one receiving the required majority. The three candidates were Zago, Kubacki, and Irena Mickiewicz. On the third ballot, Mickiewicz dropped out and Zago was elected by two votes.

Note: At the 1931 convention the *Pittsburczanin* publishing company won by a 208 to 207 vote over the *Dziennik Zjednoczenia* the right to print *Głos Polek*. Following the closing of the *Pittsburczanin* in 1975, the Detroit-based *Dziennik Polski* won the rights to print the paper until it too went out of business in 1985. *Głos Polek* has since been composed at the PWA of A headquarters and printed in Indiana.

March of the Polish Women's Alliance of America at its Centennial in 1998

"Niech Nasz Związek Polek Żyje"

Niech nasz Związek Polek żyje z Bogiem się rozwija,

Siostra każda, ducha krzepi, nigdy nie zabija!

Razem więc razem, dobrą wolą świećmy,

Zgodę i szlachetność, społeczeństwu nieśmy. (bis)

U nas każdej, droga nam jest organizacja własna,

A przed nami przyszłość siostry, wielka jest i jasna.

Czuwajcie Siostrzyce, czuwajcie strażnice

Pierwszy u nas Związek Polek w Ameryce. (bis)

The March of the Polish Women's Alliance goes back to the early 1930s. It is sung to the Polish national anthem, "Jeszcze Polska nie Zginęła." Below is the English language version of the March provided by past director Albina Świerzbińska in December 2001. These are the words currently used by the PWA of A.

Our Alliance, may it prosper, may God always bless us!
Good will ever let us foster, let no one deny us!

Refrain:

So then, together, let us help each other,
Mary of the Bright Mount pray for us, Our Mother.

March of the Polish Women's Alliance of America
Its Fiftieth Anniversary in 1948

"Marsz — w Sercach Naszych"

W sercach naszych tkwi niespożyta siła

Miłość ofiarna goreje w nich jak stos.

Choć droga trudna, twarda i zawiła.

Związkowi Polek! Związkowi Polek!

Jasny Stwarzamy los!

Związkowi Polek! Związkowi Polek!

Jasny Stwarzamy los!

Poprzez wszystkie stany, miasta,

Niechaj rośnie, niechaj wzrasta!

Niechaj Polskie ma oblicze

Związek Polek, Związek Polek,

Związek Polek w Ameryce!

Związek Polek! Związek Polek w Ameryce!

The words to this March, titled "In Our Hearts," may be freely translated as follows:

In our hearts beats an extraordinary power, a generous love burns with great intensity. Though the road may be long, hard, and even confusing, the destiny we forge for our Polish Women's Alliance will be a bright one! Through all the states and towns, may our Polish Women's Alliance grow and flourish and may our Polishness show itself to all!

Primary Sources

Constitutions and By-Laws of the Polish Women's Alliance of America, adopted and amended in 1917, 1928, 1931, 1939, 1947, 1951, 1959, 1971, 1979, 1991.

First Convention of the Polish Civilian War Relief Unit for Immediate Aid through the American Red Cross: September 22, 1940. Chicago: Alliance Printers, 1940.

Głos Polek (The Voice of Polish Women), the official publication of the Polish Women's Alliance of America, 1903, 1910 to the present.

Księga pamiątkowa sejmu szesnastego Związku Polek w Ameryce, Washington, D. C. (Souvenir album of the sixteenth convention of the Polish Women's Alliance of America in Washington, D. C. Chicago: Polish Women's Alliance of America, 1931).

National Yet Neighborly: The Polish Women's Alliance of America, brochure, (Chicago: Polish Women's Alliance of America, 1995).

Osinski, Henry J. *Report on Organization and Operation of Mission in Poland, December 1945 – January 1947.* Chicago: American Relief for Poland, 1947. Mimeographed.

"Our 90th Anniversary: How and Why the Polish Women's Alliance of America was Formed." Manuscript in the office of *Głos Polek*, 1988.

Pamiętnik diamentowego jubileuszu Związku Polek w Ameryce, 1898 – 1973 (Diamond jubilee souvenir book of the Polish Women's Alliance of America, 1898 – 1973. Chicago: Polish Women's Alliance of America, 1973).

Pamiętnik na cześć Panny A. E. Napieralskiej w dowód jej piętnastoletniej pracy na stanowisku urzędniczki Związku Polek w Ameryce, 1910 – 1925 (Souvenir book in honor of Emilia Napieralska in connection with her fifteen years of work as an officer of the Polish Women's Alliance of America, 1910 – 1925. (Chicago: Polish Women's Alliance of America, 1925).

Pamiętnik jubileuszowy 25-cioletnej rocznicy Towarzystwa Córy Polskiej pod Opieką Matki Boskiej Częstochowskiej, 1902 – 1927. (Souvenir book on the occasion of the 25th anniversary of the Society of the Daughters of Poland under the Care of the Blessed Mother of Częstochowa, 1902 – 1927).

Pamiętnik poświęcenia Domu w czasie 35-ej rocznicy 30-go Kwietnia, 1933 (Memorial album covering the dedication of the home office at the time of its 35th anniversary. Chicago: Polish Women's Alliance of America, April 30, 1933).

Pamiętnik XIV sejmu Związku Polek w Wilkes-Barre, Pennsylvania, 1898 – 1924 (Souvenir book from the fourteenth national convention of the Polish Women's Alliance of America in Wilkes-Barre, Pennsylvania, 1898 – 1924. Chicago: Polish Women's Alliance of America, 1924).

Pamiętnik sejmu XV-go Związku Polek w Ameryce odbytego w Chicago, Illinois 21 – 27-go Sierpnia, 1927 (Souvenir book from the fifteenth national convention of the Polish Women's Alliance of America, August 21 – 27, 1927 in Chicago). Chicago: Polish Women's Alliance of America, 1927.

Pamiętnik sejmu XX-go i złotego jubileuszego Związku Polek w Ameryce. (Souvenir album from the twentieth convention and the golden anniversary of the Polish Women's Alliance of America. Chicago: Polish Women's Alliance of America, 1947).

Pamiętnik 30-letniej rocznicy założenia Związku Polek w Ameryce i rozwinięcia sztandaru organizacyjnego w dniu 4-go listopada 1928 w Chicago, Illinois (Souvenir book from the thirtieth anniversary of the founding of the Polish Women's Alliance of America and the displaying of the banner of the organization in Chicago. Chicago: Polish Women's Alliance of America, 1928).

Pienkos, Angela and Donald. *The Polish Women's Alliance of America: Our Future Is as Bright as Our Past Is Inspiring.* Chicago: Polish Women's Alliance of America, 1995. Brochure.

Polish American Congress in Press Clippings, vol. 1, 1944 – 1948; vol. 2, 1948 – 1952; vol. 3, 1952 – 1954. Chicago: Alliance Printers and Publishers.

Polish Women's Alliance of America Centennial Celebration, May 16 – 17, 1998. Chicago: Polish Women's Alliance of America, 1998.

Program zjazdu Polonii i Polaków z zagranicy, prezydium zjazdu, komisje, i spis delegatów. Kraków, 19 – 23 Sierpnia, 1992 (Organizational program of the Congress of *Polonia* and Poles from Abroad, leadership of the congress, committees, and list of delegates, August 19 – 23, 1992, in Kraków, Poland.

Protokół z obrad konferencji Polskich organizacyj bratniej pomocy, duchowieńststwa i prasy Polskiej, Chicago, 4-go Marca, 1944 roku. (Minutes of the meeting of the conference of Polish fraternals, clergy, and Polish language press, Chicago, March 4, 1944).

Protokół z plenarnego posiedzenia komitetu wykonawczego Kongresu Polonii Amerykańskiej, 22-go Marca, 1944 roku. (Minutes of the plenary meeting of the executive committee of the Polish American Congress on March 22, 1944).

Protokoły sejmu Związku Polek w Ameryce (Minutes of the national conventions of the Polish Women's Alliance of America for the years 1916, 1918, 1921, 1927, 1931, 1935, 1939, 1943, 1947, 1951, 1955, 1959, 1963,1967, 1971, 1975, 1979, 1983, 1987, 1991, 1995. In Polish until 1983, thereafter in English. Chicago: Polish Women's Alliance of America).

Pycior, Helena. "Marie Curie in America and *Polonia,*" unpublished presentation to recipients of the Polish American Scholarship Awards at the University of Wisconsin, Milwaukee, May 1986.

Statistics of Fraternal Benefit Societies. Indianapolis: National Fraternal Congress of America, annual publication.

Sprawozdania zarządu głównego i prezesek stanowych Związku Polek w Ameryce. (Convention reports of the members of the general administration and the state presidents of the Polish Women's Alliance of America, 1916, 1918, 1921, 1927, 1931, 1935, 1939, 1943, 1947, 1951, 1955, 1959, 1963, 1967, 1971, 1975, 1983, 1987, 1991, 1995. In Polish until 1979, thereafter increasingly or fully in English. Chicago: Polish Women's Alliance of America).

Światowy Związek Polaków z Zagranicy: *II Zjazd Polaków z Zagranicy, 6 – 9 Sierpnia roku 1934* (Second Congress of World Union of Poles from Abroad, Warsaw, 1935).

Swietlik, Francis. *The Polish Displaced Persons.* Chicago: American Relief for Poland, 1946.

"Testimonial Banquet for Honorary President Helen V. Wojcik, Chicago, December 9, 1995."

Works Projects Administration of the United States of America: *Polish Language Publications Translations Project in Chicago, 1937.*

Związek Polek w Ameryce, 1898 – 1923: Pamiętnik Jubileuszowy (Polish Women's Alliance of America, 1898 – 1923: A jubilee album. Chicago: Polish Women's Alliance of America, 1923).

Związek Polek w Ameryce: Pamiętnik Sejmu Siedemnastego ZPwA, 22-28-go Września, 1935 roku, Chicago, Illinois (The Polish Women's Alliance of America: Souvenir book from the seventeenth national convention of the PWA of A, September 22 – 28, 1935 in Chicago. Chicago: Polish Women's Alliance of America, 1935).

Secondary Sources: Monographs: Jane Addams, Emily G. Balch, and Alice Hamilton: *Women at the Hague: The International Congress of Women and Its Results.* New York: Macmillan, 1915.

Ash, Timothy Garton. *The Polish Revolution – Solidarity.* New York: Viking Books, 1985.

Olive Banks. *Faces of Feminism: A Study of Feminism as a Social Movement.* New York: St. Martin's Press, 1981.

Bilek, Romuald. *Jak powstał Kongres Polonii Amerykańskiej* (How the Polish American Congress arose). Chicago: Privately published, 1984.

Bolek, Francis, ed. *Who's Who in Polish America: A Biographical Dictionary of Polish-American Leaders and Distinguished Poles Resident in America.* 3d ed., New York: Harbinger House, 1943.

Boles, Janet K. and Diane Long Hoeveler. *Historical Dictionary of Feminism.* (Lanham, MD.: Scarecrow Press, 1996).

Bourne, Peter G. *Jimmy Carter: A Comprehensive Biography from Plains to Post Presidency.* New York: Scribners, 1997.

Browne, J. F. *Surge to Freedom: The Fall of Communist Rule in Eastern Europe.* Durham, NC: Duke University Press, 1991).

Brożek, Andrzej. *Polish Americans 1854 – 1939.* Warsaw: Interpress Publishers, 1985. Originally published in the Polish language in 1977 under the title *Polonia Amerykańska, 1854 – 1939.*

Brzezinski, Zbigniew. *Power and Principle: Memoirs of the National Security Adviser, 1977 – 1981.* New York: Farrar, Straus, Geroux, 1983.

Buczek, Roman. *Stanisław Mikołajczyk* vol. 2., Toronto: Century Publishing Company, 1996.

Bukowczyk, John J. *And My Children Did Not Know Me: A History of the Polish Americans.* Bloomington, Indiana, University Press, 1987.

Bukowczyk, John J., ed. *Polish Americans and Their History: Community, Culture and Politics.* Pittsburgh: University of Pittsburgh Press, 1996.

Cott, Nancy F. *The Grounding Of American Feminism.* New Haven: Yale University Press, 1987.

Curie, Eve. *Madame Curie, A Biography.* Garden City, NY: Doubleday, Doran and Company, 1937.

Dallek, Robert. *Franklin D. Roosevelt and American Foreign Policy, 1932 – 1945.* New York: Oxford University Press, 1979.

Davies, Norman. *God's Playground: A History of Poland,* 2 vol. New York: Columbia University Press, 1982.

Deckard, Barbara Sinclair. *The Women's Movement: Political, Socioeconomic, and Psychological Issues.* New York: Harper and Row, 1983.

Doder, Dusko and Louise Branson. *Gorbachev: Heretic in the Kremlin.* New York: Viking, 1990.

Dziewanowski, M. K. *Poland In The Twentieth Century.* New York: Columbia University Press, 1977.

Fuchs, Lawrence H. *The American Kaleidoscope: Race, Ethnicity, and the Civic Culture.* Hanover and London: Wesleyan University Press, 1990.

Gates, Robert M. *From the Shadows: The Ultimate Insider's Story of Five Presidents and How They Won the Cold War* (New York: Simon and Schuster, 1996).

Gati, Charles. *The Bloc that Failed: Soviet – East European Relations in Transition.* Bloomington, Indiana: Indiana University Press, 1990.

Garlinski, Józef. *Poland In The Second World War.* London: Macmillan, 1985.

Goldman, Marshall. *What Went Wrong With Perestroika?* 2d ed. New York: W. W. Norton, 1993.

Greenspan, Karen. *The Timetable of Women's History.* New York: Simon and Schuster, 1994.

Haiman, Mieczysław. *Zjednoczenie Polskie Rzymsko-Katolickie w Ameryce, 1873 – 1948* (A history of the Polish Roman Catholic Union of America, 1873 – 1948). Chicago: Polish Roman Catholic Union of America, 1948.

Haiman, Mieczysław and Roman Dybowski. *Za naszą i waszą wolność: żołnierzowi polskiemu walczącemu o honor i wolność Ojczyzny w hołdzie* (For our freedom and yours: In honor of the Polish soldier fighting for the honor and freedom of the Polish Fatherland). New York: Polish Information Center, 1941.

Halecki, Oskar. *A History of Poland.* New York: Dorset Press, 1992. Additional updated material by Anthony Polonsky and Thaddeus V. Gromada.

Jaworski, Rudolf and Bianka Pietrow-Enker, ed. *Women in Polish Society.* Boulder: East European Monographs, 1992.

Kabczynska, Krystyna, et al., ed. *Korespondencja Polska Marii Skłodowskiej Curie: 1881 – 1934* (The Polish Correspondence of Maria Skłodowska-Curie, 1881 – 1934. Warsaw: *Instytut Historii Nauki* P.A.N., 1994).

Karłowicz, Jadwiga. *Historia Związku Polek w Ameryce: przyczynki do poznanią duszy wychodźstwa Polskiego w Stanach Zjednoczonych Ameryki Północnej* (A history of the Polish Women's Alliance of America: Contributions to a knowledge of the spirit of the Polish immigration in the United States of North America). Chicago: Polish Women's Alliance of America, 1938.

Kieniewicz, Stefan. *The Emancipation of the Polish Peasantry* Chicago: University of Chicago Press, 1969.

Kowalski, Włodzimierz T. *Walka dyplomatyczna o miejsce Polski w Europie, 1939 – 1945* (The diplomatic struggle for Poland's place in Europe, 1939 – 1945). 2d ed. Warsaw: Ksiazka i Wiedza, 1967.

Kruszka, Wacław. *A History of the Poles in America to 1908*, part one. Edited by James S. Pula. Washington, D. C.: Catholic University of America Press, 1993.

Kuczynski, Les. *Expansion of NATO: Role of the Polish American Congress.* Chicago: Alliance Printers and Publishers and Alliance Communications, 1999.

Kukiel, Marian. *Dzieje Polski porozbiorowe, 1795 – 1921 (*A history of partitioned Poland, 1795 – 1921. 2d ed., London: B. Swiderski, 1963).

Kuron, Jacek, and Jacek Żakowski. *PRL dla początkujacych* (The Polish People's Republic for Beginners. Wrocław: Wydawnictwo Dolnośląskie, 1995).

Lopata, Helena Z. *Polish Americans,* 2d rev. ed., New Brunswick, NJ: Transaction Publishers 1994.

Loryś, Maria. *Historia Związku Polek w Ameryce* (A history of the Polish Women's Alliance of America. Chicago: Polish Women's Alliance of America, 1980).

Lukas, Richard. *The Strange Allies: The United States and Poland, 1941 to 1945.* Knoxville: University of Tennessee Press, 1978.

Lukas, Richard. *Bitter Legacy: Polish-American Relations in the Wake of World War II.* Lexington: University of Kentucky Press, 1982.

Malia, Martin. *The Soviet Tragedy: A History of Socialism in Russia, 1917 to 1991.* New York: The Free Press, 1994.

Miłosz, Czesław. *The History of Polish Literature* (Toronto: Collier-Macmillian, 1969).

Novak, Michael. *The Rise of the Unmeltable Ethnics* (New York: Macmillan, 1971).

Olszewski, Adam: *Historia Związku Narodowego Połskiego.* (A History of the Polish National Alliance), 5 vol. Chicago: Alliance Printers and Publishers, 1968.

Orłowski, Józef: *Helena Paderewska w pracy narodowej i społecznej, 1914 to 1929* (Helena Paderewska's patriotic and social work for Poland, 1914 – 1929). Chicago: Privately published, 1929.

Osada, Stanisław: *Historia Związku Narodowego Polskiego* (A history of the Polish National Alliance). Chicago: Alliance Printers and Publishers, 1905, 1957.

Pacyga, Dominic A.: *Polish Immigrants and Industrial Chicago: Workers on the South Side, 1880 to 1922.* Columbus: Ohio State University Press, 1991.

Pease, Neal: "This Troublesome Question: The United States and the 'Polish Pogroms' of 1918 to 1919," paper delivered at the annual meeting of the Polish American Historical Association, Chicago, January 10, 2000.

Piątkowski, Romuald, comp. and ed. *Pamiętnik I wzniesienia odsłonięcią pomników Tadeusza Kościuszki i Kazimierza Pułaskiego tudzież połączonego z tą uroczystością pierwszego Kongresu narodowego Polskiego w Washingtonie, D.C.* (Memorial on the occasion of the unveiling and dedication of the monuments to Kościuszki and Pułaski in connection with the First Polish national Congress in Washington, D. C.). Chicago: Polish National Alliance, 1911.

Pienkos, Angela T. *A Brief History of Polanki, Polish Women's Cultural Club of Milwaukee, 1953 – 1973.* Milwaukee: *Polanki* and Franklin Press, 1973.

Pienkos, Angela T. *Federation Life Insurance of America, 1913 to 1976.* Milwaukee: Haertlein Printers, 1976.

Pienkos, Donald E. *PNA: A Centennial History of the Polish National Alliance of the United States of North America.* New York and Boulder: Columbia University Press and East European Monographs, 1984.

Pienkos, Donald E. *One Hundred Years Young: A History of the Polish Falcons of America, 1887 – 1987.* New York and Boulder: Columbia University Press and East European Monographs, 1987.

Pienkos, Donald E. *For Your Freedom through Ours: Polish American Efforts on Poland's Behalf, 1863 – 1991.* New York and Boulder: Columbia University Press and East European Monographs, 1991.

Pietrzyk, Leslie. *Pears on a Willow Tree.* New York: Bard Publishers, 1998.

Porwit, Maria. *50 – Letnia rocznica Związku Polek w Ameryce* (On the occasion of the fiftieth anniversary of the Polish Women's Alliance of America). Chicago: Polish Women's Alliance of America, 1947.

Puacz, Edward. *Polonia w U. S. A.: Dziś i jutro* (Polonia in the U. S. A.: today and tomorrow). Chicago: Polonia Book Store and Publishers, 1976.

Pula, James S. *Polish Americans: An Ethnic Community.* New York: Twayne Publishers, 1995.

Rachwald, Arthur. *In Search of Poland: The Superpowers' Responsibility to Solidarity, 1980 – 1989.* Stanford: Hoover Institution, 1990.

Rada koordinacjyna Polonii wolnego świata, 1978 – 1992 (A history of the Coordinating Council of the World Polonia, 1878 – 1992). Toronto, 1992.

Radio Free Europe Research: *The Pope in Poland.* Munich, 1979.

Radzik, Tadeusz. *Polonia Amerykańska wobec Polski, 1918 – 1939* (American Polonia and Poland, 1918 – 1939). Lublin: Wydawnictwo Polonia, 1990.

Renkiewicz, Frank, comp. and ed.. *The Poles In America, 1608 to 1972. A Chronology and Fact Book.* Dobbs Ferry, New York: Oceana Publications, Inc., 1973.

Rothschild, Joseph. *Return to Diversity: A Political History Of East Central Europe Since World War II. 2nd ed.* New York: Oxford University Press, 1993.

Schmidt, Alvin J. *Fraternal Organizations.* Westport, CT: Greenwood Press, 1980.

Sheer, Lynn. *Failure Is Impossible: Susan B. Anthony in Her Own Words.* New York: Time-Life Books, 1995.

Szulc, Tad. *Pope John Paul II: A Biography.* New York: Scribner Publishers, 1995.

Stpiczynski, Tadeusz. *Polacy w Świecie* (The Poles around the World). Warsaw: Main Statistical Office, 1992.

Taras, Raymond. *Consolidating Democracy in Poland.* Boulder: Westview Publishers, 1995.

Thomas, William and Florian Znaniecki, *The Polish Peasant in Europe and America*, 2 vol., New York: Dover Publications, 1958.

Tomczak, Anthony C., ed. *Poles in America: Their Contribution to A Century of Progress.* Chicago: Polish Day Association in Cooperation with A Century of Progress International Exposition, 1933.

Topolski, Jerzy. *Historia Polska od czasów nájdawniejszych do 1990 roku.* (A History of Poland from the Earliest Times to the Year 1990. Warsaw and Kraków: *Oficyna Wydawnicza Polczek*, 1992).

Uminski, Sigmund H. *The Polish Pioneers in Virginia.* New York: Polish Publications Society of America, 1974.

Wachtl, Karol. *Polonia w Ameryce: dzieje i dorobek* (American Polonia: Its history and legacy). Philadelphia: Privately published, 1944.

Waldo, Arthur L. *Sokolstwo przednia straż narodu:* (The Falcons' movement, vanguard of the Polish Nation). 5 vol. Pittsburgh: Polish Falcons of America, 1953 – 1987.

Waldo, Arthur L. *Teofila Samolinska: Matka Związku Narodowego Polskiego w Ameryce* (Teofila Sąmolinska: Mother of the Polish National Alliance in America). Chicago: Edward Rozanski, 1980.

Walter, Jerzy, comp., *Czyn zbrojny wychodźstwa Polskiego w Ameryce: zbiór dokumentów i materiałów historycznych* (The military service of the Polish immigration in America: A collection of documents and historical materials). New York: Polish Army Veterans Association, 1957.

Wandycz, Piotr. *The Lands of Partitioned Poland, 1795 to 1918.* Seattle: University of Washington Press, 1974.

Wandycz, Piotr. *The United States and Poland.* Cambridge: Harvard University Press, 1980.

Weigel, George. *Witness to Hope: A Biography of John Paul II.* New York: Harper, 1999.

Wieczerzak, Joseph. *A Polish Chapter in Civil War America: The Effects of the January Insurrection on American Public Opinion.* New York: Twayne Publishers, 1967.

Wytrwal, Joseph A. *Behold! The Polish Americans.* Detroit: Endurance Press, 1977.

Zamoyski, Adam. *Paderewski.* New York: Athenaeum Press, 1982.

Zamoyski, Adam: *The Polish Way: A Thousand-Year History of the Poles and Their Culture.* New York: Franklin Watts, 1988.

Zglenicki, Leon, ed., *Poles of Chicago, 1837 – 1937.* Chicago: Polish Pageant, Inc., 1937.

Zielinski, Helen. *Historia Związku Polek w Ameryce: Sprawy Organizacyjne, 1898 – 1979.* (A history of the Polish Women's Alliance of America: Organizational matters, 1898 – 1979). Chicago: Polish Women's Alliance of America, 1981.

Secondary Sources: Articles and Papers

Anker, Laura. "Women, Work and Family: Polish, Italian and East European Immigrants in Industrial Connecticut, 1890 – 1940", *Polish American Studies* 45, no. 2 (1988): 23 – 50.

Bernstein, Carl. "The Holy Alliance," *Time*, February 24, 1992, pp. 28 – 35.

Białasiewicz, Wojciech, et al. "Jak powstał Kongres Polonii Amerykańskiej?" (How did the Polish American Congress arise?) Special Issue of *Dziennik Związkowy.* Chicago: October 21 – 23, 1994.

Blejwas, Stanislaus. "Old and New Polonias: Tensions within an Ethnic Community" *Polish American Studies* 38, no. 2 (1981): 55 – 83.

Białasiewicz, Wojciech et al. "Krok po kroku do NATO: Działalność Kongresu Polonii Amerykańskiej na rzecz wprowadzenia Polski do Paktu Północnoatlantyckiego, 1989 – 1999" (Step by step to NATO: The involvement of the Polish American Congress in Bringing Poland into the North Atlantic Pact, 1989 – 1999). Special two weekend issues of *Dziennik Związkowy.* Chicago: March 12 – 14, 19 to 21, 1999.

Blobaum, Robert E.   "The 'Woman Question' in *Fin-de-Siecle* Poland," paper presented at the 58th annual meeting of the Polish Institute of Arts and Sciences of America in Kraków, Poland, June 17, 2000.

Bukowczyk, John.   "Harness for Posterity the Values of a Nation: Fifty Years of the Polish American Historical Association and Polish American Studies", *Polish American Studies*, 50 no. 2 (1993): 5 – 104.

Erdmans, Mary Patrice.   "Immigrants and Ethnics: Conflict and Identity in Polish Chicago", *The Sociological Quarterly* 36, no. 1 (1995): 175 – 195.

Erdmans, Mary Patrice. "Polonia in the New Century: We Will Not Fade Away", *Polish American Studies* 57, no. (2000): 5 – 24.

Galush, William. "Purity and Power: Chicago Polonia Feminists, 1880 – 1914", *Polish American Studies,* 47, no. 1 (1990): 5 – 24.

Greene, Victor R.   "Pre-World War I Emigration to the United States: Motives and Statistics", The Polish Review, 6, no. 3 (1961): 45 – 68.

Januszewski, David. "The Case for the Polish Exile Government in the American Press, 1939 to 1945", *Polish American Studies,* 43, no. 1 (1986): 57 to 97.

Kantowicz, Edward R. "Polish Chicago: Survival through Solidarity" In *Ethnic Chicago,* rev. and exppanded ed. Edited by Melvin Halli and Peter Jones, pp. 214 – 238. Grand Rapids, MI: William B. Erdmans Publishers, 1984.

Karłowicz, Jadwiga. Foreword to Maria Konopnicka: *Zbiór nowel i obrazków* (Collected short stories and drawings).   Pittsburgh: Polish Women's Alliance of America, 1945.

Kesting, Robert W. "American Support of Polish Refugees and Their Santa Rosa Camp", *Polish American Studies,* 48, no. 1 (1991): 78 – 90.

Kruszewski, Z. A. "The Polish American Congress, East – West Issues, and the Formulation of American Foreign Policy" in *Ethnic*

Groups and U. S. Foreign Policy, edited by M. E. Ahrari. New York: Greenwood Press, 1986.

Kryszak, Mary O. "Polish Women's Alliance: Reminiscences," In *Poles of Chicago, 1838 – 1939,* edited by Leon Zglenicki, pp. 154 – 159. Chicago: Polish Pageant, Inc., 1939.

Larsh, William: "W. Averill Harriman and the Polish Question, December 1943 to August 1944," *East European Politics and Societies,* 7, no. 3 (1993): 513 – 554.

Lopata, Helena Z. "Polish Immigration to the United States of America: Problem of Estimation and Parameters" *The Polish Review* 21, no. 4 (1976): 85-108.

Lopata, Helena Z. "Polish American Families" In *Ethnic Families in America: Patterns and Variations,* edited by Charles H. Mindel and Robert W. Habenstein. New York: Elsevier, 1981.

Lopata, Helena Z. "Intergenerational Relations in Polonia," In *The Polish Presence in Canada and America,* edited by Frank Renkiewicz pp. 271 – 284. Toronto: The Multicultural Society of Ontario, 1982.

"Maria Loryś. Biography" in *Twenty-Third Annual Heritage Dinner and Dance,* October 26, 1991, p. 9. Chicago: Illinois Division of the Polish American Congress, 1991.

Parot, Joseph J. "The 'Serdeczna Matka' of the Sweatshops: Marital and Family Crises of Immigrant Working Class Women in Late Nineteenth Century Chicago," In *The Polish Presence in Canada and America,* edited by Frank Renkiewicz, pp. 155 –182. Toronto: The Multicultural Society of Ontario, 1982.

Pienkos, Donald E. "Pillars of American and Polish American Life: Sketches of Polonia's Four Leading Fraternals" (The Polish Roman Catholic Union of America, the Polish National Alliance, the Polish Falcons of America, and the Polish Women's Alliance of America) In *Twenty-Third Annual Heritage Dinner and Dance* October 26, 1991, pp. 12 – 14. Chicago: Illinois Division of the Polish American Congress, 1991.

Pienkos, Donald E. "Polish Americans and Poland: A Review of the Record," *Fiedorczyk Lecture in Polish American Studies*, Central Connecticut State University, April 25, 1993.

Pienkos, Donald E. "America, Poland and the Polish American Community: Defining and Preserving Polish Ethnicity in the United States," In *The Polish Diaspora: Selected Essays from the Fiftieth Anniversary International Congress of the Polish Institute of Arts and Sciences of America*, edited by James S. Pula and M. B. Biskupski, vol. 2, pp. 85 – 98, Boulder: East European Monographs, 1993.

Pienkos, Donald E. *Polish American Congress: Half a Century of Service to Poland and Polonia.* Chicago: Alliance Printers and Publishers, 1994.

Pienkos, Donald E. "Poland, the Issue of NATO Expansion and the Polish American Congress," *The Polish Review,* 40, no. 2 (1995): 181 to 195.

Pienkos, Donald E. "Witness to History: Polish Americans and the Genesis of NATO Enlargement," *The Polish Review,* 44, no. 3 (1999): 329 – 338.

Pinkowski, Edward. "The Great Influx of Polish Immigrants and the Industries They Entered," In *Poles in America: Bicentennial Essays,* edited by Frank Mocha, pp. 303 – 370. Stevens Point, WI: Worzalla Publishing Company, 1978.

Pycior, Helena. "Reaping the Benefits of Collaboration While Avoiding Its Pitfalls: Marie Curie's Rise to Scientific Prominence," *Social Studies of Science,* 23 (1993): 301 – 323.

Radzialowski (Radzilowski), Thaddeus. "Let Us Join Hands: The Polish Women's Alliance," In *Immigrant Women*, edited by Maxine Schwartz Seller, 2nd rev. ed., pp. 190 – 196. Albany: State University of New York Press, 1994. Originally published in the *Review Journal of Philosophy and Social Science,* 2 (1977): 183 – 203.

Radzilowski, Thaddeus C. "Reinventing the Center: Polish Immigrant Women in the New World," In *Something of My Very Own to Say: American Women Writers of Polish Descent* edited by

Thomas S. Gladsky and Rita Holmes Gladsky, pp. 11 – 23. Boulder: East European Monographs, 1998. This work includes a biography and selection from the writings of Stefania Laudyn-Chrzanowska (1872 – 1942), the first woman editor-in-chief of *Głos Polek*.

Renkiewicz, Frank. "An Economy of Self-Help: Fraternal Capitalism and the Evolution of Polish America," In *Studies in Ethnicity: The East European Experience in America*, edited by Donald Pienkos, Philip Shashko, and Charles Ward, pp. 71 – 91. Boulder: East European Monographs, 1980.

Szymczak, Robert: "An Act of Devotion: The Polish Gray Samaritans and the American Relief Effort in Poland, 1919 – 1921," *Polish American Studies*, 43, no. 1 (1986): 13 – 36.

Wieczerzak, Joseph. "Pre and Proto-Ethnics: Poles in the United States before the Immigration after Bread," *The Polish Review*, 21, no. 3 (1976): 7 – 38.

Winid, Bogusław: "Dreams of Trans-Atlantic Brotherhood: Warsaw and the Polish-American Community, 1919 – 1939," reprinted in the English language monthly supplement of *Gwiazda Polarna* (The Polar Star, Stevens Point, WI, February, April, June, August, and September 1997). Originally published as "Sentiment versus Reality: Polish Diplomacy and the Polish American Community, 1919 – 1939," In *Perspectives in Polish History: Occasional Papers in Polish and Polish American Studies*, edited by Stanislaus A. Blejwas. Polish Studies Program, Central Connecticut State University, no. 1 (1996).

Walter Zachariasiewicz: "The Organizational Structure of Polonia," In *Poles of America: Bicentennial Essays*, edited by Frank Mocha, pp. 627 – 670. Stevens Point, WI: Worzalla Publishers, 1978.

Zubrzycki, Jerzy: "Emigration from Poland in the 19th and 20th Centuries," *Population Studies*: *A Journal of Demography*, 6 (1952 – 1953): 248 – 272.

Other Sources:

Mazewski, Aloysius A. *Welcome to the Fortieth Anniversary of the Polish American Congress, May 15, 1984, in Chicago, Illinois.* Chicago: Alliance Printers and Publishers, 1984.

Wojcik, Helen V. *Welcome to the Fiftieth Anniversary of the Polish American Congress, October 20 – 23, 1994,* Chicago: Alliance Printers and Publishers, 1994.

Presentations on the Polish Women's Alliance of America on its centennial delivered at the fifty-sixth annual meeting of the Polish Institute of Arts and Sciences of America at Georgetown University, June 13, 1998: Albina Świerżbinska, "Growing Up in the Polish Women's   Alliance";   Myra   Lenard,   "Remembering   Adela Łagodzinska: Polonia Leader and President of the Polish Women's Alliance of America, 1947 – 1971"; Theodore Zawistowski, "The Polish Women's Alliance in Northeastern Pennsylvania;" Donald E. Pienkos, "The Polish Women's Alliance on Poland's Behalf, 1905 – 1998."

The Emblem of the Polish Women's Alliance of America

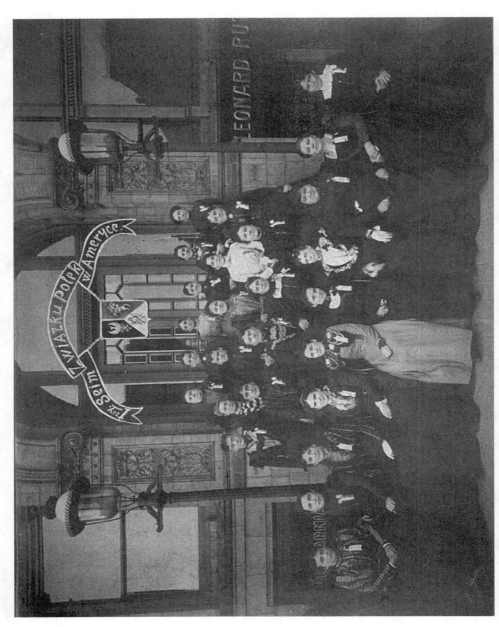

Delegates to the first national convention of the Polish Women's Alliance, June 6, 1900, Chicago, Illinois

Stefania Laudyn-Chrzanowska, first editor of *Glos Polek*

PWA of A members gather at Milwaukee, Wisconsin's Kosciuszko monument to help mark the Alliance's 25th anniversary, October 27, 1923. National President Emilia Napieralska stands between the two costumed children.

President Napieralska (left) leads the first PWA of A pilgrimage to the newly independent Poland (1928)

One of the hundreds of PWA of A children's circles, or Garlands (*Wianki*) formed after 1918. This is Philadelphia's "White Rose" Garland, organized by Group 301, the St. Ann's Society. The photo is from 1928.

DOM ZWIĄZKU POLEK W AMERYCE, CHICAGO, ILLINOIS, 1933

**The PWA of A national headquarters in Chicago,
greatly expanded and renovated, 1933.**

**The Polish Women's Alliance national headquarters in Park Ridge, Illinois,
the home of the PWA of A since 1979.**

The portrait of Nobel laureate and honorary PWA of A member Maria Sklodowska Curie is unveiled in 1940 at the PWA of A Library in Chicago. From the left: PWA of A Vice President Adela Lagodzinska, daughter and biographer Eve Curie, under the portrait next to the French Consul, and PWA of A President Honorata Wolowska, second from right.

PWA of A World War II humanitarian activity at the home office.
From left: Halina Paluszek, Bronislawa Karczewska, Maria Lopacinska, Anna Zlotowska.

One of the two B-25 bombers named in honor of the PWA of A by the United States War Department in recognition of the support of Alliance members on behalf of victory in World War II.

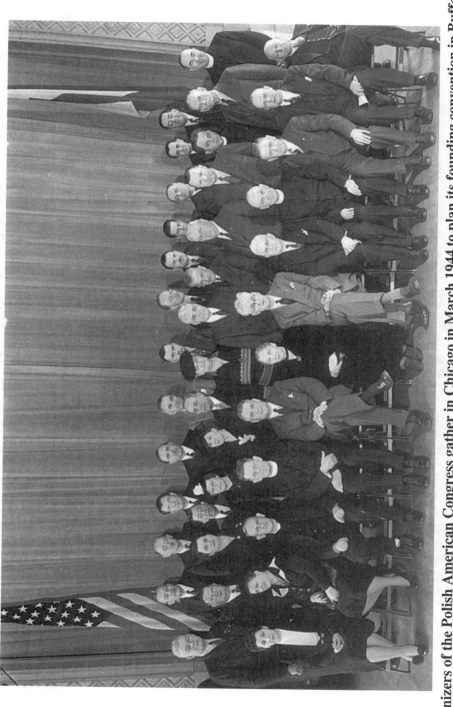

Organizers of the Polish American Congress gather in Chicago in March 1944 to plan its founding convention in Buffalo, New York. PWA of A President Honorata Wolowska is seated front row center. To her right is Charles Rozmarek, President of the Polish National Alliance. To her left is John Olejniczak, President of the Polish Roman Catholic Union of America. At the right is Dr. Teofil Starzynski, President of the Polish Falcons of America.

The national leadership of the Polish Women's Alliance of America on the eve of its fiftieth anniversary in 1948. From left front row: Treasurer Leokadia Blikowska, Vice President Adela Lagodzinska, President Honorata Wolowska, Secretary General Maria Porwit, Director Helena Sala; standing: Director Bronislawa Jakubowska, Medical Examiner Felicia Cienciara, Director Veronica Siwek, *Glos Potek* Editor Jadwiga Karlowicz, Director Bronislawa Karczewska, Counsel Barbara Fisher, Director Constance Rybinska.

PWA of A pilgrimage to Poland, 1957, Jasna Gora Monastery, Czestochowa: seated at the left is President Lagodzinska. Next to her is Cardinal Stefan Wyszynski, Archbishop of Warsaw and Gniezno and Primate of Poland.

President Adela Lagodzinska and Vice President Helen Zielinski at a 1960s PWA of A youth conference.

December 21, 1981: President Helen Zielinski is part of the PAC delegation at the White House with President Ronald Reagan and Vice President George H.W. Bush. They meet following the communist regime's repression of the Polish Solidarity movement. From her left are: PRCUA President Joseph Drobot, PNA and PAC President Aloysius Mazewski, and Cardinal John Krol of Philadelphia.

The PWA of A leadership, 1985. Seated from left: Treasurer Monica Sokolowski, Vice President Helen Wojcik, President Helen Zielinski, Secretary General Julia Stroup. Standing from left: Directors Irene Hossa, Lucyna Migala, Virginia Sikora, Olga Kaszewicz, and Albina Mazewski.

November 1987: Pope John Paul II meets with PAC leaders in the Vatican. From left: PAC Treasurer and PRCUA President Edward Dykla, PAC Vice President and former PWA of A President Helena Zielinski, and PAC/PNA President Aloysius Mazewski.

United States Senator Barbara Mikulski, the newest honorary member of the Polish Women's Alliance of America in 1998. Congratulating her are President Helen Wojcik, Treasurer Monica Sokolowski (left) and Maryland State PWA of A President Victoria Lukaszewski.

October 1989: PWA of A President and PAC Vice President Helen Wojcik is part of the PAC delegation that visits Poland to support the new Solidarity-led government. From left, Bishop Czeslaw Domin, former U.S. Congressman Roman Pucinski, Eugene Rosypal of the PAC Charitable Foundation, PRCUA President Edward Dykla, Michigan PAC President Paul Odrobina, PNA Treasurer Casimir Musielak, PAC/PNA President Edward Moskal, PNA Controller Alex Przypkowski, and PAC Director Myra Lenard. Photographed at the Jasna Gora monastery.

Glos Polek **Editor Maria Lorys presents Kazimierz Dziewanowski, Poland's Ambassador with copies of the three volume history of the Polish Women's Alliance of America.**

President Delphine Lytell (left), with Secretary General Maria Kubiak, Treasurer Olga Kaszewicz, and Msgr. Stanley Milewski, preparing to celebrate the 100th anniversary Mass honoring the members of the PWA of A through the years.

PWA of A participants at annual manifestation at the American Czestochowa shrine in Doylestown, Pennsylvania.

The national leadership of the Polish Women's Alliance of America entering its second century and new millennium of service.

At the 100th Anniversary Banquet: Lucyna Migala leads a youth contingent of the Lyra Ensemble in song.

Chicago auxiliary Bishops Alfred Abramowicz (left) and Thaddeus Jakubowski, with *Wianki* members and the PWA of A standard just prior to Mass.

**Virginia Sikora,
current president of the PWA of A**